Inclusive Leadership

A volume in
Contemporary Perspectives on Supervision and Instructional Leadership
Sheryl Cowart Moss, *Series Editor*

Contemporary Perspectives on Supervision and Instructional Leadership

Sheryl Cowart Moss, *Series Editor*

Advancing Supervision in Clinically Based Teacher Education: Advances, Opportunities, and Explorations (2022)
   Rebecca West Burns, Laura Baecher, and Jennifer K. McCorvey

Inclusive Leadership

From Theory to Practice

edited by

Sheryl Cowart Moss
Georgia State University

Rolandria Justice Emenuga
Justice Consulting Group

INFORMATION AGE PUBLISHING, INC.
Charlotte, NC • www.infoagepub.com

Library of Congress Cataloging-in-Publication Data

A CIP record for this book is available from the Library of Congress
http://www.loc.gov

ISBN: 979-8-88730-668-1 (Paperback)
979-8-88730-669-8 (Hardcover)
979-8-88730-670-4 (E-Book)

This book series is endorsed by the Council of Professors of Instructional Supervision

Copyright © 2024 Information Age Publishing Inc.

All rights reserved. No part of this publication may be reproduced, stored in a retrieval system, or transmitted, in any form or by any means, electronic, mechanical, photocopying, microfilming, recording or otherwise, without written permission from the publisher.

Printed in the United States of America

CONTENTS

Foreword ix
David DeMatthews

Introduction xiii
Sheryl Cowart Moss and Rolandria Justice Emenuga

SECTION I

EXAMINING THE INFLUENCES OF RESEARCH IN DISABILITY SERVICES, SOCIAL JUSTICE LEADERSHIP CULTURAL PROFICIENCY, AND PROGRAM DESIGN

1 Beyond "Hang in There": A Qualitative Examination of How Inclusive Principals Support Beginning Special Education Teachers 3
   Erica D. McCray, Margaret L. Kamman, Maya Israel, Alexandria N. Harvey, and Emily Crews

2 "And Only Connect!": Inclusive Leadership in a New Zealand Context 23
   Sylvia Robertson

3 Principal Influence on Success for Students With Disabilities: An Exploration of Educator Perceptions of Inclusive Leadership .. 43
   Zak Dominello, Vanessa Giddings, and Amie Cieminski

4 Inclusive Teacher Educator Leadership: Situating Reflective Practice Within Theory, Partnerships, and Equity in an Undergraduate Dual Licensure Educational Preparation Program 63
William Hunter, Wesam Salem, Keishana Barnes, Logan Caldwell, and Jennifer Bubrig

5 Navigating the In-Between: Defining the Third Space for Educational Leadership Programs 81
James A. Zoll, Sheri Hardee, and Catherine Rosa

SECTION II

PRACTICAL APPLICATIONS: INCLUSIVE LEADERSHIP IN ACTION

6 Practicing Inclusive Leadership by Nurturing and Developing Teacher Leaders 101
Marla McGhee

7 Disrupting the Status Quo: A Call for True Equity in Special Education 121
Toni Barton

8 Equity Labs—Can They Increase Teacher and Leader Effectiveness? 139
Georgia Evans

9 Actions of Equitable, Socially Just, Culturally Responsive, and Inclusive Educational Leaders 159
Amie B. Cieminski and Kristine J. Melloy

SECTION III

NARRATIVES—PERSONAL PERSPECTIVES ON THE FIELD

10 Exploring Inclusive Leadership Through Tonglen: A Contemplative Framework for Supervision 181
Steve Haberlin and Ian Mette

11 Building a Stronger Leader Preparation Model: Inclusive Practice Grounded in Research and Experience 199
Karen Caldwell Bryant, Jami Royal Berry, Robin Christian, Niles Davis, Michele Dugan, Brian Keefer, Kristen McRae, and Summer Tuggle Smith

12 Inclusive Leaders Building Bridges to Learning 217
Heather P. Williams and Jennifer L. Snow

13 Rafael's Story: A Portrait of a Latinx School Leader in Georgia ... 237
Taylor Barton

Conclusion 253
Sheryl Cowart Moss and Rolandria Justice Emenuga

About the Contributors 255

FOREWORD

Much ink has been spilled writing about inclusion and the challenges of serving struggling learners, unengaged learners, and students with disabilities in general education classrooms within neighborhood schools. In the United States, most research on inclusion focuses on students with disabilities identified under the Individuals with Disabilities Education Act (IDEA). Researchers have investigated approaches and interventions to support struggling students and students with disabilities as well as school-wide systems like multi-tiered systems of support (MTSS) that strengthen instructional quality and provide actionable data for teachers. Despite these promising practices, many students continue to struggle in schools and longstanding inequities persist. For example, racial disproportionality in special education identification and exclusionary discipline persists (Cruz et al., 2021) as do significant disparities in achievement and other outcomes between students with disabilities and their peers (Gilmour et al., 2019). We also know that evidenced-based practices and systems are often not well-implemented and that many educators receive limited training in their pre-service preparation (Gersten et al., 2017). Moreover, many so-called "best-practices" are not culturally appropriate and do not provide teachers with the tools and mindsets to capitalize on the cultural and linguistic capital of their students. Budget shortfalls, teacher turnover, district bureaucracy, and other organizational constraints can also limit a school's ability to provide the highest-quality inclusive education, especially in states, regions, and locales that maintain inadequate and inequitable systems of school finance.

Inclusive leaders working within schools are uniquely positioned to create and sustain inclusion even when constraints and roadblocks exist. In this book, the editors and contributors examine inclusive leadership and its power to significantly impact how struggling learners and students with disabilities are served. Much of the work focuses on principals, who are uniquely positioned to lead their schools away from segregation and toward inclusive and culturally sustaining practices. However, inclusive leadership—the leadership that supports creating and sustaining high-quality inclusive schools for each student—is not prescriptive and does not consist of a checklist of practices. Schools are too complex for such prescriptions as are the educators, families, and students they serve. Rather, inclusive leadership must be viewed both as a theory rooted in principles of social justice and as an organizational theory that helps to shed light on the complexity of equity-oriented change. Inclusive leadership, however, cannot just be viewed as a set of principles and theory but instead also must include a set of mindsets and practices that can be applied by leaders as they work to support inclusion in their unique contexts.

From start to finish, the editors and contributors of this book acknowledge the complex work of inclusive leadership and bring a framework, research, stories, and new ideas to readers interested in better understanding the topic. The book's focus on inclusive leadership is not narrowly focused just on principals, but rather each chapter recognizes the many critical elements to inclusive schools that include principals, but also general and special education teachers, students, and families. To be clear, teachers and students can be inclusive leaders who can play critical roles in promoting inclusion. Relatedly, the book acknowledges the importance of high-quality principal preparation as well as the potential power of district and university partnerships that can help build capacity for inclusive leadership. While the book reviews a broad array of inclusive leadership literature, several chapters focus primarily on practical applications and the lived experiences of leaders as well as their mindsets, strategies, and practices. Inclusive leadership, especially in places where inclusion requires a significant shift, is intensive and even exhausting work. This recognition is made especially clear in one chapter focused specifically on how principals can support novice special education teachers. The book captures the emotions and stress of inclusive leadership as well as offering insight into how to work and lead productively through challenging times.

The editors and contributors to this book have made an important contribution to the field of educational leadership and to practitioners seeking to create and sustain inclusive schools. The emphasis on inclusive leadership sits closely with me as a former school leader, central office administrator in special education, and as a faculty member teaching in principal and superintendent preparation programs. The work of creating and sustaining inclusive schools is critically important and aligned with other important social justice issues confronting schools today (DeMatthews et al., 2021). I am in solidarity with the editors and contributors in this book because I have seen firsthand the power of inclusive leadership and the way a school's commitment to inclusion can transform pedagogy and practice, but more importantly the lives of students. I have witnessed the positive impact of inclusive leadership for students with disabilities and their peers in my own school as an administrator and as a researcher in schools across the country. I have also seen and researched the complexity of inclusive leadership, the stress and demands of engaging in such efforts, and the physical and emotional toll it can take on a principal and on all school personnel (DeMatthews, 2018). This book offers a holistic and full account of inclusive leadership, which helps move the field forward.

Inclusive Leadership: From Theory to Practice is a critical resource for the field and one that has a potential to influence the next generation of education researchers and practitioners interested in creating more inclusive schools. Importantly, the book offers important insights for readers with diverse interests as well as a well-honed framework for applying inclusive leadership in diverse contexts. I hope you find the well-developed content as insightful as I did and that you commit to creating more inclusive schools for all students, especially students with disabilities.

—**David DeMatthews**
The University of Texas at Austin

REFERENCES

Cruz, R. A., Kulkarni, S. S., & Firestone, A. R. (2021). A QuantCrit analysis of context, discipline, special education, and disproportionality. *AERA Open, 7*, 23328584211041354.

DeMatthews, D. E. (2018). Urban principal narratives on including black boys with emotional disabilities. *Journal of School Leadership, 28*(3), 401–430.

DeMatthews, D. E., Serafini, A., & Watson, T. N. (2021). Leading inclusive schools: Principal perceptions, practices, and challenges to meaningful change. *Educational Administration Quarterly, 57*(1), 3–48.

Gersten, R., Jayanthi, M., & Dimino, J. (2017). Too much, too soon? Unanswered questions from national response to intervention evaluation. *Exceptional Children, 83*(3), 244–254.

Gilmour, A. F., Fuchs, D., & Wehby, J. H. (2019). Are students with disabilities accessing the curriculum? A meta-analysis of the reading achievement gap between students with and without disabilities. *Exceptional Children, 85*(3), 329–346.

INTRODUCTION

Imagine with us for a moment. Let's step into the shoes of a newly hired principal. Let's call her Ms. Hope. She has all of the excitement and trepidation that comes with taking on leadership in a new school. As one of her first tasks, Ms. Hope must choose an entrance for a new building. This sounds simple enough, but faculty, students, and parents have strong opinions. There is funding for either stairs or a ramp, not for both, but Ms. Hope does have the power to choose. She can build the stairs, a more conventional and traditional approach. Several powerful stakeholders want to preserve the aesthetics of the entrance and strongly oppose buildng a ramp first. Choosing to build a ramp first would allow more people to have access right away. Those who could use the stairs can still use the ramp. Those who could not use the stairs are not hindered. What should she do?

In another example, let's say Ms. Hope also faces changing demographics in her new school. Students who do not fit the cultural or learning profiles the school has typically enrolled are arriving in significant numbers. Some teachers are complaining that their students are not capable of handling the assignments they typically give. The new students and their families don't seem to respond to the teachers' communication in the ways they expect. Teachers are frustrated. Families are not engaged. Ms. Hope has a choice here, too. Many choices. What should she do?

An inclusive leader would choose to build the ramp while working to understand the perspectives and gain the support of opposing stakeholders. An inclusive leader would also choose to learn about the new students and their families. An inclusive leader would seek out the cultural capital

Inclusive Leadership, pages xiii–xxii
Copyright © 2024 by Information Age Publishing
www.infoagepub.com
All rights of reproduction in any form reserved.

these new families bring and use it to equip her faculty and staff to welcome and support them. An inclusive leader would build a literal bridge with the ramp and a metaphorical bridge with targeted family outreach and staff development. For an inclusive leader, such decisions are just part of a worldview that looks for opportunities to remove barriers and encourage involvement. Doesn't that sound inspiring? In these simple examples, the answers seem easy enough, but authentic inclusive leadership is also quite complex.

In reality, as anyone who has been in leadership knows, there are problems that present themselves, and there are the underlying causes and dynamics. Underlying causes may be veiled, but they have a strong impact on organizational culture and climate. They are quite often the real problems. Dynamics are the forces that determine what people are willing to say and do, what they will notice, and what they will ignore. These influences reside in the borderlands between what we say we do and what we really do. This is where lip service and authenticity do battle.

For school leaders, problems do not appear one at a time. McDaniel and Gruenert (2018) estimated that principals make an average of 300 decisions each day. That is a staggering figure. In any school, there are human and political dynamics that can be quite emotional. Structures and processes can invite or exclude. Symbols can take on unintended meaning; they can unite or divide (Bolman & Deal, 2021). Removing barriers and inviting others into organizations can throw symbols and processes, often the "sacred cows" in organizations, into disarray. This kind of leadership can upset power structures. Leaders frequently hear, "but we have always done it this way!" in response to these sorts of changes. Removing barriers can trigger strong emotions and resistance (Bolman & Deal, 2021).

Change manifests in unique ways in educational settings, and it is not unusual to find schools where hegemony is the norm (Evans, 2001). Teachers with long tenure, schools with high turnover rates, schools where many faculty and staff members were former students, suburban schools with rapidly changing demographics, urban schools with high transiency rates...all these circumstances require organizations to process change in ways that are unique to educational settings. As noted in Berry, Cowart Moss, and Gore (2018), this work requires hypervigilant attitudes, intentional actions, and discernment of contexts. It is exhilarating and exhausting. As De Matthews and colleagues caution, burnout is a real concern for inclusive leaders (2021).

A HISTORICAL PERSPECTIVE

We would like to think we have improved educational climates and processes from the days of Frederick Taylor's Scientific Management Theory (1919). Although Taylor was a mechanical engineer, his theory was embraced in schools. In Taylor's model, students are not seen as individuals. Processes are strictly detailed, and variances are discouraged. Several years later, John Dewey saw things differently, and he caused fear in many quarters when he proposed teaching to student interests. Then, he incurred the wrath of both traditionalists and progressives when he dared to suggest that neither were correct. Dewey posited that the real challenges in education were deeper than the "-ists and -ives" and jargon of the day. Dewey suggested that leading in schools is different, and much more difficult, than managing in well-worn paths (1938).

Schools are often impacted by what happens outside the organization, for which the leader has no control . We can flash forward from Taylor and Dewey to the frights of the space race between the United States and the Soviet Union in the 1950's, and the subsequent publication of *A Nation at Risk* (Gardener, et al, 1983), where we see a quick return to strict structural norms. In 1964, the *Civil Rights Act* was hailed as a new era of equal opportunity and inclusiveness, although schools like those in South Carolina's corridor of shame, and many others, would beg to differ. Let's flash forward again to 1975 and the passage of PL-94-142, the *Education for all Handicapped Children Act*. This, too, was hailed as a momentous step forward, yet we still see students with disabilities struggling in public schools. The heavy testing requirements of the *No Child Left Behind Act* (2001) were framed as a progressive advancement in accountability. Within just a few years, states were applying for exemptions from the essentialist constraints of narrowly focused, high stakes test instruments.

To be fair, these dynamics did not just appear in the 20th century. Immigrants fleeing oppression in England became the oppressors themselves in Puritan New England. Over and over in history, and in our current times, we see systems of oppression and exclusion, often orchestrated by those who have been oppressed and excluded themselves (Friere, 1970). Socio-economic status, race, ethnicity, intellectual capacity, and physical differences... all are dimensions that can either divide us or provide opportunities for us to see and appreciate the beautiful complexity and capacity in each other.

INCLUSIVE LEADERSHIP DEFINED

As we planned for this book, we wanted to honor the Council of Professors of Instructional Supervision (COPIS) tradition of grappling with these complicated ideas. Thomas Sergiovanni wrote about moral leadership, and even admitted that he had changed some of his thinking later in his career (2007). Ed Pajak argued that relationships were fundamental in most dimensions of supervision (1990). Don Beach often referred to the thorny challenges as Gordian Knots.

We, the editors of this book, have long advocated for inclusive leadership, even before we really knew what to call it. As a doctoral student, Sheryl chose to follow six students who were overlooked in a large high school for a full school year. She found that some of their teachers could not tell her anything about the students beyond their names and class grades. The students shared keen insights into how the school projected an inclusive image that many students never experienced. Sheryl saw this as an opportunity to inform leadership practice, but she had to argue for her work to be included in a leadership program of study. As an administrator, Rolandria brought DEI initiatives to the staff and school-belonging initiatives to the students and families to ensure that every individual experienced a sense of community. While these initiatives were not always welcomed, she understood that the importance of connection and inclusion outweighed any hesitation.

Finding the work of the Collaborating for Educator Effectiveness Development and Reform Center (CEEDAR) and CCSSO's National Collaborative for Inclusive Principal Leadership (NCIPL) felt like coming home. What a joy to find educators and policy makers viewing their work through similar inclusive lenses. Sheryl had the opportunity to participate with NCIPL in the creation of a *Guide for Inclusive Leadership* (2018) and to lead a work group for revisions several years later. Knowing the careful process to compile this work, it was an easy decision to use the NCIPL definition of inclusive leadership to ground this book:

> Inclusive principals create strong school cultures and distribute leadership across staff to serve all learners well and ensure all students feel safe, supported, and valued in school. In promoting equity for "all," inclusive principals must respond effectively to the potential and needs of each student. Inclusive principals ensure high expectations and appropriate supports so that each student—across race, gender, ethnicity, language, disability, sexual orientation, family background, and/or family income—can excel in school. (National Collaborative on Inclusive Principal Leadership, Council of Chief State School Officers 2018)

We argue that inclusive practices are good for all students, for each student. Thus, readers will find chapters addressing students with disabilities throughout this book rather than in one section. Our goal is for inclusive leadership to be a way of seeing the world rather than an item on a checklist of tasks. Seeing the world through an inclusive lens changes motivations, actions, and attitudes.

We have encountered critics who assert that an inclusive mindset leads to coddling or lowered expectations. We see the exact opposite in theory and in practice. Inclusive leaders have high expectations with scaffolded support. They understand the importance of Vygotsky's Zone of Proximal Development (1998) and recognize that growth does not happen without

Introduction • **xvii**

some discomfort. They embrace the idea of allowing their faculty and students to experience the dignity of risk and the lessons of failure.

Inclusive leaders also understand the concept of selective isolation. Some people are naturally introverted, and they are happier on the sidelines. Inclusive leaders see the people in their organizations, and they make sure that selective isolation is not a façade for exclusion.

Words are powerful. Since we began work on this book, several states have backed away from terms like equity and inclusion as those words have become politically charged. We make no apologies for encouraging a leadership style that is messy. We believe that a messy process that expects questions, seeks out alternate points of view, and continually considers who needs to be at the table leads to a healthier and more productive school climate. This vision is illustrated in Figure I.1.

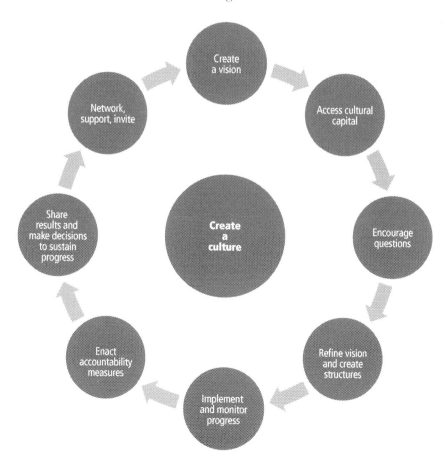

Figure I.1 Model of inclusive leadership. Source: Sheryl Cowart Moss, 2020.

STRUCTURE OF THE BOOK

This book is the second volume in a series endorsed by the Council of Professors of Instructional Supervision (COPIS). As mentioned previously, COPIS members have wrestled with theories of supervision and ideas of inclusion for many years. In this volume, we wanted to give established and emerging scholars a platform to share their work and thoughts on the bridge from theory to practice. We need models to help us understand complex ideas. We need strategies for bringing ideas and theories to life. We need stories from people who have done the work. With these thoughts in mind, we posed these questions in our call for chapters:

- How might we build theory in inclusive leadership through research that seeks to inform practice?
- How do special education, social justice, and cultural proficiency inform the constructs of inclusive leadership?
- How can school administrators mold their practices to authentically create inclusive climates and practices?
- What are generative conduits for future scholarship on inclusive practices for education leaders?

OVERVIEW OF SECTION I

In Section I, we examine findings of research into several facets of inclusive practices. In Chapter 1, McCray and colleagues describe how principals who embrace an inclusive mindset support beginning special education teachers, who are all too often adrift with numerous expectations and little support in their schools. In Chapter 2, Robertson provides a look at the essence of inclusive leaders in New Zealand. Robertson explores not just what these principals do, but who they are. Chapter 3 finds Dominello, et. al. exploring how principals define and perceive inclusive leadership. They delve into and discuss how these personal definitions impact actions to create successful environments for students with disabilities.

Principals are molded and influenced in large part by their preparation programs. Hunter et.al. examine a university and district partnership through the lens of reflections on bridging theory and practice in teacher leadership in Chapter 4. Finally, Zoll et. al. conclude this section in Chapter 5 with a look at student feedback on incorporating the notion of "the in-between" for inclusive leaders in their leadership preparation program.

Introduction ▪ **xix**

OVERVIEW OF SECTION II

In Section II we shift from research studies to explore practical applications of inclusive leadership tenets. These chapters provide insight into experiences, strategies, and tools for practicing leadership with an inclusive mindset. McGhee begins this section in Chapter 6 with a description of intentional coaching dialogs to support building teacher leaders. In Chapter 7, Toni Barton invites us to explore the notion of systemic disruption in the pursuit of authentic inclusion and equity. Evans details her work with equity labs and auditing data with an emphasis on equity and inclusion in Chapter 8. Ciemenski and Melloy conclude this section in Chapter 9, where they describe the actions of leaders who embrace an inclusive mindset with cultural responsiveness and social justice.

OVERVIEW OF SECTION III

Our final section provides insight into personal narratives that illuminate the ideas of being seen and discovering one's own inclusive leadership skills. In this section our authors share the embodiment of what these leaders experience, believe, and walk out. In Chapter 10, Haberlin and Mette provide deeply personal views of their practice of Tonglen as a vehicle to embrace and enact inclusive leadership from the inside out. In Chapter 11, Bryant and colleagues delve into personal stories from their graduate students as they describe their experiences with learning about inclusive leadership and reacting to leading in a pandemic. Willams and Snow share the experiences of inclusive leaders who seek to break down the silos that often exist between leading and learning in Chapter 12. Finally, in Chapter 13, Taylor Barton shares a vivid narrative portrait of Latinx leader, Rafael, giving us insight into his intense experiences of coming to this country, finding his tribe when he did not fit into typical "boxes," and fiercely committing to succeed while offering a helping hand to others.

SUMMARY

There are threads and common themes woven throughout these chapters, and each chapter can stand on its own. The book lends itself to overall study as well as self-contained experiences in each chapter. We hope this design will encourage readers to experience a hermeneutic circle of sorts. We value the life experiences each author and each reader brings, and we

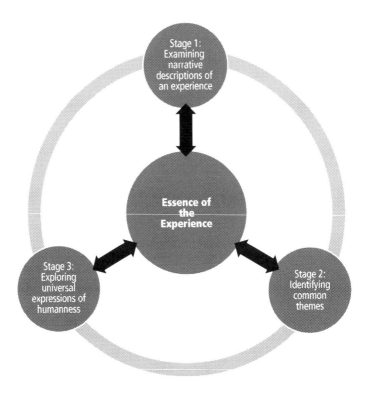

Figure I.2 Heidegger's hermeneutic circle.

celebrate each perspective. We would love for our book to be a resource for leaders like Ms. Hope, and others.

We hope readers will look at the entire book, then take it apart chapter by chapter, looking for common themes, and finally put it all back together, coming away with new understandings that will impact new life experiences. Given our belief that inclusive leadership must be understood and practiced contextually, we hope that readers will find new meaning and understanding over and over as their leadership journeys unfold. Figure I.2 show's Heidegger's representation of the Hermeneutic process (1972)

GUIDING QUESTIONS AS YOU READ

1. How might we continue to build theory in inclusive leadership through research that seeks to inform practice?
2. How can school administrators mold their practices to authentically create inclusive climates and practices?

3. What are your thoughts on the political influences that impact the idea of inclusive leadership? What does this mean for leaders who want to lead with an inclusive lens?
4. What are your thoughts for future scholarship on inclusive practices for educational leaders?

—**Sheryl Cowart Moss**
Georgia State University

Rolandria Justice Emenuga
Justice Consulting Group

REFERENCES

Act, The education for all handicapped children. (1975).

Act, No child left behind. (2001).

Berry, J. R., Cowart Moss, S., & Gore, P. (2019). Leadership in high-needs/high performing schools: Success stories from an urban school district. In E. Murakami, D. Gurr, & R. Notman (Eds.), *Educational leadership, culture, and success in high-needs schools* (pp. 131–148). Information Age Publishing.

CEEDAR Center. (n.d.). *Inclusive education.* http://ceedar.education.ufl.edu/cems/inclusive-education/

Council of Chief State School Officers. (2018). *Supporting inclusive schools for the success of each child: a guide for states on principal leadership.* https://ccssoinclusiveprincipalsguide.org/state-strategies/

Council for Exceptional Children & CEEDAR Center. (2019). *Introducing high-leverage practices in special education: A professional development guide for school leaders.* https://highleveragepractices.org/wp-content/uploads/2019/02/A-Look-at-Instruction.pdf

Cowart Moss, S. (2020, Winter). Infusing inclusive leadership into a program redesign at Georgia State University. *UCEA Review,* 17–19.

DeMatthews, D., Carrola, P., Reyes, P., & Knight, D. (2021) School leadership burnout and job-related stress: Recommendations for district administrators and principals. *The Clearing House: A Journal of Educational Strategies, Issues and Ideas, 94*(4), 159–167. https://doi.org/10.1080/00098655.2021.1894083

Dewey, J. (938) *Experience and education.* Macmillan.

Evans, R. (2001).*The human side of school change: Reform, resistance, and the real-life problems of innovation.* Jossey Bass.

Friere, P. (1970). *Pedagogy of the oppressed.* Seaberry Press.

Gardener, D., et al., (1983). *A nation at risk: The imperative for educational reform. An open letter to the American people.* (ED226006). ERIC. https://eric.ed.gov/?id=ED226006.

Martin, W. (1972, Spring). The hermeneutic circle and the art of interpretation. *Comparative Literature, 24*(2), 97–117. https://www.jstor.org/stable/1769963

McDaniel, T., & Gruenert, S. (2018, June). The making of a weak principal: Actions conscious and unconscious by central administration can limit the effectiveness of school leaders. *AASA School Administrator.* https://my.aasa.org/AASA/Resources/SAMag/2018/Jun18/McDaniel_Gruenert.aspx#:~:text=The%20principal%2C%20while%20desiring%20to,will%20make%20about%20300%20decisions.

Pajak, E. (1990). Dimensions of supervision. *Educational Leadership, 48*(1), 78–80.

Sergiovanni, T. (2007). *Rethinking leadership: A collection of articles.* (2nd ed.) Corwin Press.

Taylor, F. (1919). *The principles of scientific management.* Harper & Brothers.

The Education for All Handicapped Children Act. 1975.

Vygotsky, L. (1998a). The problem of age. In Rieber, R. (Ed.) *The collected works of L. S. Vygotsky.* (Vol. 5). Plenum.

SECTION I

EXAMINING THE INFLUENCES OF RESEARCH
IN DISABILITY SERVICES, SOCIAL JUSTICE LEADERSHIP
CULTURAL PROFICIENCY, AND PROGRAM DESIGN

CHAPTER 1

BEYOND "HANG IN THERE"

A Qualitative Examination of How Inclusive Principals Support Beginning Special Education Teachers

Erica D. McCray
The University of Florida

Margaret L. Kamman
The University of Florida

Maya Israel
The University of Florida

Alexandria N. Harvey
The University of Florida

Emily Crews
The University of Florida

P–12 public schools are complex settings established to meet the learning needs of all students, including students with disabilities. To comply with the law (i.e., Individuals with Disabilities Education Act [IDEA], Every Student

Succeeds Act [ESSA]), school leaders, teachers, and support professionals must collaborate to design and deliver instruction to meet the needs of diverse students. Principals are expected to meet federal mandates, ensuring students with disabilities access the general education curriculum and are meaningfully included in general education settings (ESSA, 2015; IDEA 2014; McLeskey et al., 2014). Inclusive education is complicated by an unstable special educator workforce and expectations that general educators can address the needs of learners with disabilities.

Principals provide instructional leadership for general and special education teachers, creating learning environments that facilitate instruction in inclusive settings (McCray et al., 2014). Leithwood et al. (2008) identified basic leadership practices enacted by successful leaders and noted these practices aligned with Yukl's (1989) taxonomy of managerial behaviors. They identified four categories of leadership qualities: (a) building vision and setting directions, (b) understanding and developing people, (c) redesigning the organization, and (d) managing the teaching and learning program. Leithwood et al.'s synthesis provided a foundation for more recent publications including: (1) *Professional Standards for Education Leaders* (PSEL; NPBEA, 2015); and (2) *Principal Leadership for Inclusive and Effective Schools for Students With Disabilities* (Council of Chief State School Officers [CCSSO] & the Collaboration for Effective Educator Development, Accountability, and Reform [CEEDAR] Center, 2017). Despite the importance of principals establishing inclusive environments, little is known about how they do so. This study aimed to learn from principals who were highly regarded for maintaining inclusive environments and supporting beginning special education teachers. We begin with a brief literature review to illustrate inclusive leadership qualities outlined by Leithwood and colleagues (2008).

Establishing Vision and Setting Direction

An instructional leader must establish a clear and compelling vision and direction (e.g., PSEL Standard #1: *Mission, Vision, and Core Values*; NPBEA, 2015). Setting aspirational, yet achievable goals, and supporting each staff member is critical for organizational success. It is essential for school leaders to attend to culture (MacNeil et al., 2009). Specifically, "School leaders must build a shared vision for inclusive schools that focuses on high expectations and improved achievement for all students, including those with disabilities" (Billingsley et al., 2017, p. 69).

DeMatthews and Mawhinney (2013) defined social justice leadership as an awareness of marginalized groups and action to eliminate inequities. Inclusion was defined as an ideal and as a policy to provide students with disabilities educational rights and privileges offered in general education. Taken together, inclusive leaders are intentional to redress inequities and create equitable opportunities for teaching and learning as a matter of social justice.

Understanding and Developing People

Leaders must know staff, students, and their needs to proactively provide appropriate resources. Human resources in school leadership includes selection, development, and retention of effective staff (Donaldson, 2013; Ellis et al., 2017). Providing opportunities for staff to engage in significant, purposeful work fortifies commitment to the vision and mission. Leaders who empower their staff develop their commitment and capacity to promote academic success and well-being for each student (NPBEA, 2017).

Working conditions, including role clarity or ambiguity, mediate teachers' opportunities to teach effectively (Bettini et al., 2016). Leaders can reduce the role ambiguity special education teachers often face by carefully attending to intentional job design. McCray et al. (2014) discussed the importance of job design in inclusive schools, as poor job design can lead to frustration, stress, and attrition. Focusing on the unique needs of the school, a principal can appropriately determine job parameters, which can lead to increased job satisfaction, motivation, and involvement (Bettini et al., 2015).Teacher burnout and attrition often result from teachers feeling underprepared, unsupported, and unable to meet expectations (Billingsley & Bettini, 2019; Garcia & Weiss, 2019; Israel et al., 2014). Coaching and mentoring can address causes of burnout and attrition (Israel et al., 2014; Reitman & Karge, 2019).

Redesigning the Organization

School leaders must support organizational redesigns. They must foster collaboration, encourage supportive working conditions, and practice supportive and shared leadership (Billingsley et al., 2017; CCSSO & CEEDAR Center, 2017; Hitt & Tucker, 2016; NPBEA, 2017). Youngs (2007) and colleagues (Jones et al., 2013) found that principals can best help novice teachers through direct and indirect mentorship from veteran teachers and grade-level team members. Billingsley et al. (2020) challenged school and district leaders to implement structures for effective instruction and assessment, ongoing progress monitoring, and collaboration among educators serving students with disabilities.

Distributing leadership and tapping expertise leads to increased teacher capacity (Leithwood & Mascall, 2008). In a systematic literature review Jambo and Hongde (2020) found distributed leadership has an indirect, yet positive effect on students' achievement. Thus, principals should share power and authority. In this way, inclusive leadership serves both students and professionals.

Managing the Teaching and Learning Program

Principals manage teaching and learning in their buildings. An instructional leader's work is complex—and context-specific, (Seashore Louis et al., 2010; Bettini et al., 2015), yet it is foundational to ensuring a tight focus on student learning and academic achievement (Hitt & Tucker, 2016). The principal is ultimately responsible for curriculum and instruction (PSEL Standard #3: *Equity and Cultural Responsiveness*, NPBEA, 2015). They must remove barriers to rigorous curriculum and instruction and ensure monitoring and assessment of instruction through multi-tiered systems of support (CCSSO & CEEDAR Center, 2017).

Specialized Skills for Special Education

Early career experiences are critical to teacher satisfaction and retention. Research suggests that principals receive limited preparation to supervise special education (Sun & Xin, 2019; Pazey & Cole, 2012). For instance, Sun and Xin (2019) investigated knowledge, skills, and leadership roles of principals for supporting students with disabilities. They found principals have limited special education knowledge, leading them to less engagement. Principals who are more familiar with special education better understand parental roles and are more engaged for students with disabilities (Templeton, 2017).

Addressing teacher and student needs simultaneously is no small task. Principals must rely on professionals in and outside of their schools to bolster teacher effectiveness and student achievement (Seashore Louis, et al., 2010). Additionally, principals must identify, hire, orient, and provide induction support to new talent. This cannot be taken lightly.

In this study, we examined how principals in two school districts supported beginning special education teachers using foundational concepts, the PSEL Standards (NPBEA, 2015), and guidance specific to students with disabilities (CCSSO & CEEDAR Center, 2017). We found little examination of how principals influence experiences of beginning teachers, particularly special education teachers (Correa & Wagner, 2012; DiPaola et al.,

2004; Holland, 2008–2009; Youngs, 2007). Shaping leadership preparation and evolving roles of inclusive school leaders requires an understanding of managing and leading increasingly complex school environments.

METHODS

We aimed to understand principals' perceived roles in supporting beginning special education teachers. District-level administrators identified the leaders of inclusive schools who were especially effective in supporting beginning special education teachers. We sought to answer the following:

1. What roles do building principals identified as effective in supporting novices play in supporting beginning special education teachers?
2. How do they engage other professionals to ensure adequate support is provided to beginning special education teachers?

This study included interview findings from two districts in the midwestern United States (see Table 1.1). District A served close to 23,000 P–12 students with disabilities across seven sub-districts. This public school district provided special education services to partner schools across a sizable service area. District B was a full-service public school district with close to 35,000 students in P–12. We chose this district because its mentoring program centered on structured evaluations, which might be controversial, as evaluative mentors are often discouraged.

TABLE 1.1 Participant Demographics

School level	Race	Gender	Years Experience as Principal
District A			
K–6	White	Female	2
9–12	White	Male	1
9–12	Black	Female	1
K–5	Black	Female	1
K–8	White	Female	5
PK–6	Black	Female	9
District B			
K–5	White	Female	4
6–8	Black	Male	8
PK–6	White	Female	13
6–8	White	Female	4

We interviewed ten principals across the two settings. They led schools serving students pre-kindergarten through twelfth grade. All had teaching experience. At the time of data collection their experience as principals ranged from 1–13 years.

Data Collection and Analysis

We collected data during the 2009–2010 school year. The research team developed interview protocols grounded in literature on induction and mentoring of beginning teachers in general and special education. Questions focused on principals' perceptions of induction and mentoring for beginning teachers, their role in support, and their perspective on beginning teachers' needs, including special education teachers. Each audio-recorded semi-structured interview was transcribed verbatim (Creswell & Poth, 2018).

We conducted manual preliminary analysis to memo and begin initial coding (Saldaña, 2013). Through multiple readings we developed 32 initial codes. Next, we entered transcripts and codes in HyperRESEARCH (version 3.7.5, ResearchWare, 2015), for focused coding. After coding and review, we discussed discrepancies and came to consensus on code assignments and meaning. Finally, we identified and agreed upon themes.

Credibility

To increase credibility (Tracy, 2010), we collaboratively developed the interview protocols, conducting member checks of transcripts and our initial interpretations of the data. Peer debriefing occurred after preliminary analysis and development of initial codes. We reviewed focused coding and segments of text to ensure consistent interpretations. It is noteworthy that we are former public school special education teachers now engaged in teacher development. Two of us also have training and professional experience as school- and district-level leaders.

FINDINGS

We gained insights into how principals viewed their roles. We organized findings as: (a) managing and supervising building and personnel, (b) promoting an inclusive school climate, (c) providing instructional leadership, and (d) contextualizing beginning teachers' supports with district-level induction and mentoring programs.

Managing the Building and Supporting Personnel

Principals are usually on-site human resources and facilities management officials. They interview and hire staff, schedule classes, and assign physical space, sometimes assisted by a leadership team. PSEL Standards (NPBEA, 2015) #6: *Professional Capacity of School Personnel* and #9: *Operations & Management* and guidance documents (CCSSO & CEEDAR Center, 2017) indicate that effective school leaders ensure faculty and staff have capacity, resources, and conditions to work effectively. Principals indicated they wrestled with challenges of having final accountability to leadership above them and to people in their buildings. They stressed that they attempted to facilitate teachers' work rather than deliver mandates by "trying to wear more than one hat." One principal shared how she changed relating to a teacher by shifting from confrontational to supportive. She shared, "I had to be the 'boss' and tough luck, this is how it is going to happen... and over time the teacher got it and now says, 'I am going to have a conversation with so-and-so could you please be there?'" Another principal shared that not all co-teaching relationships begin with clear understandings. He met with teachers to remind "both sides this is your role, you're responsible."

Providing in/visible support for teachers appeared frequently, particularly in special education teachers' consultation and collaboration with general education teachers. Research on inclusive schools suggests the need for infrastructure to support collaboration (McLeskey et al., 2014). Principals indicated they were intentional with scheduling and reducing new teachers' caseloads, and with assigning physical space. A principal indicated that, "some of the things are sort of invisible things that support... setting up a schedule where they have common planning time during the day." Another provided time for teachers to mesh by maintaining pairings, allowing sufficient time to build rapport and true collaboration.

Effective school leaders must maintain a macro- (school level) and micro- (classroom) view. These principals hired individuals and set them up for success by thinking about them as part of the whole. They created schedules, assigned collaborators, and designated space with intention. Because they viewed individuals as part of the whole school, they were positioned to promote an inclusive climate and success for all.

Promoting an Inclusive School Climate

Inclusive schools are characterized by supportive climates and community for all faculty and staff, which in turn supports student, family, and community engagement (McCart et al., 2014). Every principal stressed the importance of orientation for new teachers. Even principals with limited experience took steps to ensure faculty and staff understood the vision and the importance of all teachers serving all students well. One school leader, completing his first year in a school with systemic school-wide challenges, disclosed, "We're in the process of re-establishing our identity after a couple of years languishing [under former principal's leadership], so I've spent this year creating [policies and procedures]." His focus on school improvement aligned with PSEL Standard #10: *School Improvement* (NPBEA, 2015). Most principals discussed having formal orientations for new teachers, addressing ethos and expectations. One secondary principal expounded,

> I really do an orientation at the beginning of the school year with a group of new teachers, separate from the whole staff, and that gives you the opportunity to share the mission of the building so to speak... Then, expectations with how we work with our kids, the idea of being team-based can be kind of challenging at the high school level for some people.

Another high school principal discussed the importance of manageable workloads for special education teachers (Billingsley et al., 2017). He indicated, "We limited the number of teachers an intervention specialist should have to work with because we know that every additional teacher they have to work with is another layer of communication." This team-based approach allowed interventionists to support fewer teachers and students, thus providing the best individualized education programs possible in an inclusive setting.

Each principal expressed commitment to inclusive environments for students *and* teachers, and teaming was significant at each level. Illustrating PSEL Standard #7: *Professional Community for Teachers and Staff* (NPBEA, 2015), one principal was proud of their "community meetings" where they emphasized commitment to each other. Another principal described how teams were important for collegiality and data-based decision making to meet students' needs. He stated, "Each team has a special educator as part of the general education team. They have their planning time, their data collection time, and they do data teams and collaborative planning together." By working together consistently, IEP development, documentation, and completion were executed well and on time.

Principals set an inclusive tone and employed teams to support teachers and students. They provided instructional leadership, empowering teachers to do their jobs efficiently and effectively. One succinctly stated that she makes it a point to "map out expectations, making sure that's clear for new teachers–how to meet them."

Providing Instructional Leadership

Principals must ensure learning for their students and teachers. Instructional leadership centers on supporting effective delivery and use of curriculum, instruction, and assessment (PSEL Standard #4: *Curriculum, Instruction, & Assessment*; NPBEA, 2015). Principals did this through: (a) active involvement and observation, (b) distributed leadership and teacher empowerment, and (c) intentional mentoring.

Active Involvement and Observation

Principals stressed the importance of their visibility to students and teachers. They were regularly in classrooms, not just during formal observations. Admittedly, their time was divided among many responsibilities, but they believed their presence is vital to "helping them before they really sink." One principal viewed these opportunities as providing support along the way. She explained, "I don't think it's good to jump into the evaluation without setting up the situation and expectations and doing some of the coaching." In the same vein, a principal said observations provide opportunities to collaboratively identify growth opportunities. Regular feedback helped teachers stop seeing evaluation as a "gotcha thing."

One principal wanted to spend more time in classrooms, sharing with her supervisor, "When it comes to one of my kids, I have to be there... It's the same thing with the teachers... staying in that moment and in that classroom to support that teacher." This principal also wanted to more demonstratively show appreciation. She suggested, "You need to find ways to thank them. I'm writing thank-you letters to them about this year with something that stuck out—something special they did." Thus, principals took steps to normalize interactions with teachers and students so communication would feel more comfortable. Specifically, principals were nurturing professional capacity and community (NPBEA, 2015). Such a community creates space for distributed and teacher leadership.

Distributed Leadership and Teacher Empowerment

Principals found ways to tap into teachers' strength to be effective in their many roles. A principal shared that team leaders were trained in specific walk-through observation protocols. Another indicated the team leaders asked to visit other teachers' classrooms to learn from and support each other (Wenner & Todd, 2017). Additionally, team leaders acted as liaisons to school leadership, quasi-administrators. At times, they could provide better support because of their specific knowledge and skills. One principal described a train-the-trainer approach, explaining she "coached them [team leaders] on what kinds of conversations you could have in your teams...." Empowering teacher leaders required "remembering how to delegate to others and feeling comfortable that it will get finished." Teacher-to-teacher supports included formal and informal mentoring.

Intentional Mentoring

Principals relied on mentors inside and outside of the building to meet different needs and ensure ongoing teacher development (Israel et al., 2014). Every principal shared their views about school-based and district-based mentors. The bottom line was to make "sure that we have mentors who really want that responsibility and are really good role models." One principal shared his thinking about a specific mentor match:

> I intentionally hooked my novice [special education] teacher up with a mentor teacher I wanted her to work with.... She was very familiar with the ins and outs of the building and with the student services department, and where to get the resources and what not... I wanted someone she could work with who was very nurturing, very you know, "if you need anything I'm here." I told my beginner, talk to your mentor, talk to me, we will talk with each other and between the three of us we'll get you through this and she did.

Depending on beginning teachers' needs and assignments, principals considered seeking support externally. One principal contacted a principal at a nearby school to identify teachers their novices could be paired with and observe.

Principals coordinating with the "parallel" district serving special education discussed the importance of communicating with mentor-coaches who were not in the building every day. They discussed the importance of those special education teachers having a mentor in the building who was in touch with the principal to support the external mentor-coach.

All of the principals we spoke with demonstrated qualities of instructional leaders who prioritized learning for students and teachers. They clearly emphasized the importance of providing layered support from multiple sources.

Extending and Contextualizing Induction and Mentoring Support

Induction and mentoring are often discussed as a singular, nebulous aspect of beginning teacher experiences. Induction programs are umbrella infrastructures providing new teachers with support and orientation to the profession, district, and school (Ingersoll & Strong, 2011). Mentoring is a program element; ideally principals purposefully designate person(s) to provide psycho-social and/or professional support (Israel et al., 2014). The principals in this study highlighted the importance of mentoring in a comprehensive induction program. One elementary principal explained the importance of:

> ...making sure that they have support from a variety of sources, and I think that the strength is using the expertise and knowledge that someone has and helping a new teacher to...there's so many things to learn. You know, the management piece, the communicating with parents, different strategies for students, that whole differentiation piece, helping learn the curriculum. So, I think that's really overwhelming to a new person so having a support system in place is really helpful.

At times, principals served as mentors. Some principals indicated they met with their beginning teachers even when they had assigned mentors. Despite limited time, one principal emphasized that dedicated time is critical. Several echoed the value of regularly scheduled time to meet with beginning teachers. One school leader was brutally honest in sharing, "I found out from one teacher that I had missed the mark about something, I should have helped her more. I had to do some self-reflection and not take it personally."

Because of the team structures and inclusive cultures, they established, principals expected teachers to "develop a great relationship within their community of peers." This was true of all teachers, general and special education. Principals believed that in most ways, beginning teachers all need similar supports. They acknowledged; however, the special educators may require more intensive support for managing time and responsibilities, managing relationships with peers and families, and ensuring IEP implementation and compliance (Billingsley et al., 2019). One principal admitted, "I think they're similar in every way except that they have to be knowledgeable of the intervention process, time management, how to balance their time, and I think there is more pressure on the intervention specialist teachers."

Managing Responsibilities

Regardless of their preservice preparation or experience, new special education teachers are often perceived as experts. This is particularly true in schools with few or only one special education teacher. Principals identified this issue along with challenges faced by beginning special education teachers as they take immediate responsibility, with limited preparation, for supervising paraprofessionals who are often older and have more classroom experience (French, 2001). One principal reflected on a beginning special education teacher's experience, "There were times she was completely overwhelmed with everything ...and she would sit down in this chair in tears." These early experiences can lead to burnout and attrition. One participant was frank with a teacher suggesting, "just take one thing at a time, you can't do it all at once and I don't expect you to... [mentor] would sit down and say 'come on, we'll do this first, then this, then this.'" Support from the mentor and principal was necessary to assist the beginner with organizing and prioritizing responsibilities.

Managing Relationships

All teachers must manage professional relationships, but special education teachers often bear a greater burden in collaborating with general education teachers (Lamar-Dukes & Dukes, 2005). This is common for inclusive education as they "push in" to general education classrooms or consult with teachers to ensure student progress toward IEP goals. A principal characterized it as, "this dance, between what the teacher prepares and what the interventionist should prepare, what the student is being asked to do, and what the IEP requires them to do... There needs to be flexibility, this 'roll with it' attitude." Possibly, the preparation program may not have adequately prepared beginning special education teachers to advocate for themselves or their students (Rainforth, 2000; Shepherd et al., 2016). Further, few general or special education teachers are prepared to implement co-teaching models effectively or paired well to co-lead in classrooms (Scruggs & Mastropieri, 2017).As, a school leader noted, "especially in co-teaching models to really know how to co-teach. How to plan and then go into a classroom where there are two educators-and usually their partner in that classroom has been around longer—to know how to value themselves so that they just don't become kind of the assistant." Even with deficiencies in preparation or pairing, principals, "expect that when they're having a discussion as a team that they are sharing their expertise."

Special education teachers must work with families and caregivers. Some interactions might call for administrators to intervene. As one principal noted, they keep constant communication because, "some parents are a little difficult and challenging," and they want to be proactive in managing conflict.

Developing and Monitoring IEPs

IEP development, implementation, and monitoring are key to providing students with disabilities a Free and Appropriate Public Education (FAPE), as guaranteed by law (Yell & Bateman, 2020). The IEP process requires special education teachers to provide direct services and facilitate services through other professionals in conjunction with families. Administrators have different levels of involvement in monitoring IEP compliance, possibly entrusting oversight to special education teachers and/or department heads. One principal shared that either she or the assistant principal goes to every IEP meeting, affording awareness about IEP development and monitoring. Because of active involvement in classrooms and the IEP process, one middle school principal described the ways he steps in with out-of-the-box support. He hired a substitute teacher for a day so a teacher of a student with significant disabilities could observe various therapies and learn to better meet her needs. Another principal summed it up, "It's this dance between what the general education teacher prepares and the [special education] interventionist prepares... there needs to be flexibility and this dogged insistence" that a child is supported to do what they need to do.

Ultimately, principals were committed to ongoing student and teacher learning. They demonstrated reflective practice, setting goals for themselves to better meet teacher needs. Principals held high expectations, were actively engaged, and provided supports directly and indirectly to all teachers. Additionally, they matched beginning teachers with mentors, attended to schedules, and were intentional about optimizing space allocations to enable success. School leaders recognized the roles and responsibilities of the beginning special education teachers and provided additional supports so they could serve as experts as expected.

DISCUSSION

Principals juggle multiple responsibilities including the day-to-day management of teaching and learning, federal and state accountability mandates, hiring staff, and communicating with families (Smith et al., 2010). In this study, principals indicated they were challenged by these multiple demands as they attempted to balance their roles as school-wide leaders for teachers and students with diverse needs. Given the high attrition rate of teachers, the principals were responsible for supporting new special and general education teachers every year. These supports are often provided within the context of mentoring and induction (Ingersoll & Strong, 2011; Israel et al., 2014). Despite principals' roles in induction and mentoring, little research delineates how they support these efforts. This study, therefore, aimed to illuminate how inclusive school principals envisioned mentoring and induction.

All principals in this study viewed one of their responsibilities as supporting new special and general education teachers. They noted connections between that support and teacher success. They attempted to ameliorate the challenges described in the literature wherein teachers often work in isolation (e.g., Ingersoll & Strong, 2011; Johnson & Birkeland, 2003). Interestingly, many tasks described by the principals aligned with standards and guidance advanced in the PSEL Standards (NPBEA, 2015) and CCSSO and the CEEDAR Center's (2017) document with specific indicators for ensuring the success of students with disabilities.

Establishing a Vision for Inclusive Education

Each principal discussed the need for shared vision, including the expectations that all teachers were responsible for inclusive instruction to each student, including students with disabilities. This vision resulted in a wide range of supports, setting the stage for successful implementation of inclusion.

Principals noted that new special education teachers often needed supports similar to their general education colleagues including understanding school cultures, roles and responsibilities, and how to best manage time. However, the principals acknowledged the unique roles of special education teachers in managing IEPs, collaborating with general education teachers and other specialists, supervising paraeducators, and working with families. This acknowledgement is consistent with previous studies that highlighted the multiple roles special education teachers enact and the competing demands for their time (Cancio, 2018; Shepherd et al., 2016). To address these responsibilities, principals adjusted caseloads and provided support directly or indirectly through experienced teachers, mentors, and department heads.

Understanding and Developing People

Principals shared that they understood the complexities of teaching students with disabilities. They recognized that even with strong teacher preparation, new teachers could not possibly have the knowledge and skills necessary to assume their positions without support. Consequently, they worked towards educating and supporting new teachers while empowering experienced teachers to support them. Through mentoring, they ensured that new teachers received relevant professional development, felt valued, and supported students with disabilities (Benedict et al., 2013; Israel et al., 2014). This involved promoting leadership skills amongst faculty and modeling positive dispositions such as resilience and commitment to inclusive educational practices. These leaders facilitated professional learning with faculty and noted that "support with follow-up is critical" and can take on different formats.

Redesigning Organizations

Principals discussed their commitment to promoting professional learning through distributed leadership (Leithwood & Mascall, 2008) and to sharing induction and mentoring responsibilities with teachers interested in leadership roles. They encouraged veteran teachers to assume teacher leadership roles. For example, teacher leaders were often treated as quasi-administrators with responsibilities for conducting classroom walk-throughs and attending meetings. This focus on shared leadership (Billingsley et al., 2017) resulted in a supportive environment where teachers felt that they contributed both within their classrooms and to the greater school community. This was especially important for beginning teachers establishing relationships to effectively implement inclusion.

Managing the Teaching and Learning Program

Principals acknowledged they were ultimately responsible for student learning. When describing their accountability for student learning, principals often referred to the importance of supporting their teachers both in visible ways (e.g., setting up professional development) and invisible ways (e.g., ensuring that teachers have common planning time). The ultimate aim was to ensure that teachers had the tools to include and provide access to learning for each student. At the same time, this focus on building capacity was closely tied to the principals' roles as evaluators for the teachers in their buildings. The principals indicated that they viewed evaluation as an opportunity to encourage teacher growth rather than as a punitive process. They highlighted the need to ensure that teachers are comfortable with feedback and evaluation focused on student learning. Thus, the principals carefully balanced encouraging teacher trust and providing meaningful feedback that fostered increased instructional capacity. These findings were consistent with Seashore Louis and colleagues' (2010) findings that principals primarily impact student learning and achievement through supporting teachers' work conditions and morale.

Limitations

This study utilized self-reported data from 10 principals. Although we made efforts to improve the authenticity of data (e.g., refining interview protocols to reduce bias and encourage accurate reporting), there are still unavoidable limitations with self-reported data. Despite this limitation, the principals provided potentially transferable information about their experiences and strategies.

CONCLUSIONS AND IMPLICATIONS

Principals in this study were identified as effectively supporting beginning teachers, particularly beginning special education teachers. Our findings suggest enabling teachers to deliver inclusive education requires principals to proactively support beginning teachers with direct involvement orchestrate layers of support. These include conducting observations and providing timely feedback, assigning knowledgeable mentors, and structuring opportunities to observe other teachers and specialists such as occupational and speech/language therapists. Novices should be paired with veteran teachers in the building if possible or from other schools or district-level offices. Special education teachers are often considered experts regardless of experience or specialization, so it is important to intentionally match them with suitable general educators for co-teaching and for working with paraprofessionals. Ideally, schedules should allow for co-planning, and classrooms should be assigned with proximity to mentors and/or co-teachers.

Future research should triangulate principal interviews with other data sources such as teacher and parent interviews and school-wide observations. This extension would illuminate multiple stakeholder perspectives to better understand the principal's role in facilitating effective teacher support and inclusion within multiple school settings. Future research should also investigate school-level and principal-level variables that may influence activities principals can facilitate to promote inclusive environments. Lastly, given the demands on principals to engage in both teacher support and teacher evaluation, researchers should consider ways of investigating this relationship.

The importance of an effective, inclusive principal cannot be underestimated. Their ability to recruit, develop, and allocate resources to novice teachers is paramount to their success and retention. Thus, their role is critical in ensuring all students, including students with disabilities, have effective teachers and an equitable opportunity to learn.

REFERENCES

Benedict, A. E., Park, Y., Brownell, M. T., Lauterbach, A. A., & Kiely, M. T. (2013). Using lesson study to align elementary literacy instruction within the RTI framework. *Teaching Exceptional Children, 45*(5), 22–30.

Bettini, E. A., Cheyney, K., Wang, J., & Leko, C. (2015). Job design: An administrator's guide to supporting and retaining special educators. *Intervention in School and Clinic, 50*(4), 221–225.

Bettini, E., Crockett, J. B., Brownell, M. T., & Merrill, K. L. (2016). Relationships between working conditions and special educators' instruction. *The Journal of Special Education, 50*(3), 178–190. *The Journal of Special Education, 50*(3), 178–190. https://doi.org/10.1177/0022466916644425

Billingsley, B., & Bettini, E. (2019). Special education teacher attrition and retention: A review of the literature. *Review of Educational Research, 89*(5), 697–744.

Billingsley, B., Bettini, E., & Jones, N.D. (2019). Supporting special education teacher induction through high-leverage practices. *Remedial and Special Education, 40*(6), 365–379. https://doi.org/10.1177/0741932518816826

Billingsley, B., Bettini, E., Mathews, H. M., & McLeskey, J. (2020). Improving working conditions to support special educators' effectiveness: A call for leadership. *Teacher Education and Special Education, 43*(1), 7–27.

Billingsley, B., McLeskey, J., & Crockett, J. B. (2017). *Principal leadership: Moving toward inclusive and high-achieving schools for students with disabilities* (Document No. IC-8). http://ceedar.education.ufl.edu/tools/innovation-configurations/

Boe, E. E., Cook, L. H., & Sunderland, R. J. (2008). Teacher turnover: Examining exit attrition, teaching area transfer, and school migration. *Exceptional Children, 75*(1), 7–31.

Brown, K. M., & Wynn, S. R. (2007). Teacher retention issues: How some principals are supporting and keeping new teachers. *Journal of School Leadership, 17*(6), 664–698.

Cancio, E. J., Larsen, R., Mathur, S. R., Estes, M. B., Mei Chang, & Johns, B. (2018). Special Education Teacher Stress: Coping Strategies. *Education & Treatment of Children, 41*(4), 457–481.

Council of Chief State School Officers & the Collaboration for Effective Educator Development, Accountability, and Reform Center. (2017). *PSEL 2015 and promoting principal leadership for the success of students with disabilities.* https://www.ccsso.org/sites/default/files/2017-10/PSELforSWDs01252017_0.pdf

Correa, V., & Wagner, J. (2011). Principal's roles in supporting the induction of special education teachers. *Journal of Special Education Leadership, 24*(1), 17–25.

DeMatthews, D., & Mawhinney, H. (2014). Social justice leadership and inclusion: Exploring challenges in an urban district struggling to address inequities. *Educational Administration Quarterly, 50*(5), 844–881.

DiPaola, M., Tschannen-Moran, M., & Walther-Thomas, C. (2004). School principals and special education: Creating the context for academic success. *Focus on Exceptional Children, 37*(1), 1–10.

Donaldson, M. L. (2013). Principals' approaches to cultivating teacher effectiveness: Constraints and opportunities in hiring, assigning, evaluating, and developing teachers. *Educational Administration Quarterly, 49*(5), 838–882.

Ellis, C., Tronosco Skidmore, S., & Combs, J. P. (2017). The hiring process matters: The role of person-job and person-organization markers in teacher satisfaction. *Educational Administration Quarterly, 53*(3), 448–474.

Every Student Succeeds Act of 2015, pub. l. no. 114-95 § 114 stat. 1177 (2015–2016)

French, N. K. (2001). Supervising paraprofessionals: A survey of teacher practices. *The Journal of Special Education, 35*(1), 41–53. https://doi.org/10.1177/002246690103500105

Frick, W. C., Faircloth, S. C., & Little, K. S. (2013). Responding to the collective and individual "best interests of students": Revisiting the tension between administrative practice and ethical imperatives in special education leadership. *Educational Administration Quarterly, 49*(2), 207–242.

Frost, L. A., & Kersten, T. (2011). The role of the elementary principal in the instructional leadership of special education. *International Journal of Educational Leadership Preparation, 6*(2).

Garcia, E., & Weiss, E. (2019). *The teacher shortage is real, large, and growing, and worse than we thought*. Economic Policy Institute. https://www.epi.org/publication/the-teacher-shortage-is-real-large-and-growing-and-worse-than-we-thought-the-first-report-in-the-perfect-storm-in-the-teacher-labor-market-series/

Holland, P. E. (2008–2009). The principal's role in teacher development. *SRATE Journal, 17*(1), 16–24.

Individuals with Disabilities Education Act, 20 U.S.C. § 1400 (2004)

Ingersoll, R. M., & Strong, M. (2011). The impact of induction and mentoring programs for beginning teachers: A critical review of the research. *Review of educational research, 81*(2), 201–233.

Israel, M., Kamman, M. L., McCray, E. D., & Sindelar, P. T. (2014). Mentoring in action: The interplay between professional assistance, emotional support, and teacher evaluation. *Exceptional Children, 81*(4), 45–63.

Jambo, D., & Hongde, L. (2020). The effect of principal's distributed leadership practice on students' academic achievement: A systematic review of the literature. *International Journal of Higher Education, 9*(1), 189–198.

Johnson, S. M., & Birkeland, S. E. (2003). Pursuing a "sense of success": New teachers explain their career decisions. *American Educational Research Journal, 40*(3), 581–617.

Jones, N. D., Youngs, P., & Frank, K. A. (2013). The role of school-based colleagues in shaping the commitment of novice special and general education teachers. *Exceptional Children, 79*(3), 365–383.

Lamar-Dukes, P., & Dukes, C. (2005). Consider the Roles and Responsibilities of the Inclusion Support Teacher. *Intervention in School & Clinic, 41*(1), 55–61. http://lp.hscl.ufl.edu/login?url=http://search.ebscohost.com/login.aspx?direct=true&AuthType=ip,uid&db=slh&AN=17997219&site=eds-live

Leithwood, K., & Mascall, B. (2008). Collective leadership effects on student achievement. *Educational Administration Quarterly, 44*(4), 529–561.

Leithwood, K., Harris, A., & Hopkins, D. (2008). Seven strong claims about successful school leadership. *School Leadership & Management, 28*(1), 27–42.

MacNeil, A. J., Prater, D. L., & Busch, S. (2009). The effects of school culture and climate on student achievement. *International Journal of Leadership in Education, 12*(1), 73–84.

McCart, A. B., Sailor, W. S., Bezdek, J. M., & Satter, A. L. (2014). A framework for inclusive educational delivery systems. *Inclusion, 2*, 252–264. https://doi.org/10.1352/2326-6988-2.4.252

McCray, E. D., Butler, T. W., & Bettini, E. (2014). What are roles of general and special educators in inclusive schools? In J. McLeskey, N.L. Waldron, F. Spooner, & B. Algozzine, (Eds.) *Handbook of research and practice for effective inclusive schools* (pp. 80–93). Routledge.

McLeskey, J., Billingsley, B., & Waldron, N. (2016). Principal leadership for effective inclusive schools. In J. Bakken & F. Obiakor (Eds.). *Advances in special education* (vol. 32, pp. 55–74). Emerald Publishing.

McLeskey, J., Waldron, N. L., & Redd, L. (2014). A case study of a highly effective, inclusive elementary school. *The Journal of Special Education, 48*(1), 59–70. https://doi.org/10.1177/0022466912440455

McLeskey, J., Waldron, N. L., Spooner, F., & Algozzine, B. (2014). What are effective inclusive schools and why are they important? *Handbook of research and practice for effective inclusive schools* (pp. 3–16). Routledge.

Moolenaar, N. M. (2012). A social network perspective on teacher collaboration in schools: Theory, methodology, and applications. *American Journal of Education, 119*, 7–39.

National Policy Board for Educational Administration. (2015). *Professional standards for educational leaders.* https://www.npbea.org/wp-content/uploads/2017/06/Professional-Standards-for-Educational-Leaders_2015.pdf

Pazey, B. L., & Cole, H. A. (2012). The role of special education training in the development of socially just leaders: Building an equity consciousness in educational leadership programs. *Educational Administration Quarterly, 49*(2), 243–271.

Rainforth, B. (2000). Preparing teachers to educate students with severe disabilities in inclusive settings despite contextual constraints. *Journal of the Association for Persons with Severe Handicaps, 25*(2), 83–91.

Reitman, G. C., & Karge, B. D. (2019). Investing in teacher support leads to teacher retention: Six supports administrators should consider for new teachers. *Multicultural Education, 27*(1), 7–18.

ResearchWare, Inc. (2015). *HyperRESEARCH version 3.7.5 computer software.* http://www.researchware.com

Ronfeldt, M., Loeb, S., & Wyckoff, J. (2013). How teacher turnover harms student achievement. *American Educational Research Journal, 50*(1), 4–36.

Saldaña, J. (2013). *The coding manual for qualitative researchers* (2nd ed.). Sage.

Scruggs, T. E., & Mastropieri, M. A. (2017). Making inclusion work with co-teaching. *Teaching Exceptional Children, 49*(4), 284–293. https://doi.org/10.1177/0040059916685065

Seashore Louis, K., Leithwood, K., Wahlstrom, K. L., & Anderson, S.E. (2010). *Learning from leadership: Investigating the links to improved student learning, final report of research findings.* The Wallace Foundation. http://www.wallacefoundation.org/knowledge-center/Documents/Investigating-the-Links-to-Improved-Student-Learning.pdf

Shepherd, K. G., Fowler, S., McCormick, J., Wilson, C. L., & Morgan, D. (2016). The search for role clarity: Challenges and implications for special education teacher preparation. *Teacher Education and Special Education, 39*(2), 83–97 http://lp.hscl.ufl.edu/login?url=http://search.ebscohost.com/login.aspx?direct=true&AuthType=ip,uid&db=eric&AN=EJ1097709&site=eds-live

Smith, D. D., Robb, S. M., West, J., & Tyler, N. C. (2010). The changing education landscape: How special education leadership preparation can make a difference for teachers and their students with disabilities. *Teacher Education and Special Education, 33*(1), 25–43.

Stevenson-Jacobson, R., Jacobson, J., & Hilton, A. (2006). Principals' perceptions of critical skills needed for administration of special education. *Journal of Special Education Leadership, 19*(2), 39–47.

Sun, A., & Xin, J. (2019). School principals' opinions about special education services. *Preventing School Failure: Alternative Education for Children and Youth, 64*(2), 106–115.

Templeton, R. (2017). Special education leadership at the elementary school level: How does knowledge influence leadership? *Journal of Special Education Leadership, 30*(1), 19–30.

Tracy, S. J. (2010). Qualitative quality: Eight "big-tent" criteria for excellent qualitative research. *Qualitative Inquiry, 16*(10), 837–851.

Wallace Foundation (2011). *The school principal as leader: Guiding schools to better teaching and learning.* https://www.wallacefoundation.org/knowledge-center/Documents/The-School-Principal-as-Leader-Guiding-Schools-to-Better-Teaching-and-Learning.pdf

Wenner, J. A., & Campbell, T. (2017). The theoretical and empirical basis of teacher leadership: A review of the literature. *Review of Educational Research, 87*(1), 134–171. https://doi.org/ 10.3102/0034654316653478

Yell, M. L., & Bateman, D. (2020). Defining educational benefit: An update on the U.S. Supreme Court's ruling in *Endrew F. v. Douglas County School District* (2017). *Teaching Exceptional Children, 52*(5), 283–290. https://doi.org/10.1177/0040059920914259

Youngs, P. (2007). How elementary principals' beliefs and actions influence new teachers' experiences. *Educational Administration Quarterly, 43*(1), 101–137.

Yukl, G. (1989). *Leadership in organizations* (2nd ed.). Prentice Hall.

CHAPTER 2

"AND ONLY CONNECT!"

Inclusive Leadership in a New Zealand Context

Sylvia Robertson
The University of Otago, New Zealand

Author's Note: The phrase "only connect" is the epigraph from EM Forster's novel *Howards End*.

BACKGROUND

Greater inequity in New Zealand schools and elsewhere is associated with poverty, race, gender, and disability (Bishop, 2008; Carpenter & Osborne, 2014). There are tensions between neoliberal pressures for accountability in schools, especially in terms of academic outcomes, and a desire to meet the needs of those disenfranchised by our school systems (Bottery, 2012; Cranston, 2013). Driven by growing inequities in their schools, many school leaders fight for social justice for their students and communities. Leadership for social justice is grounded in the principles of "legitimacy, fairness, and welfare" (Ryan, 2006, p. 5). Ryan (2014) later argued that the "idea and practice of inclusion" could be a way of promoting social justice (p. 361). The practice of inclusive leaders might include advocacy, addressing social and systemic inequity, cultural responsiveness, challenging deficit discourses, collective practice, and meeting the needs of diverse students. These practices involve interpersonal skills such as communication and collaboration, and intrapersonal skills such as reflection, persistence, and intentionality. Such leadership is highly relational as evident in the cases explored here where there is an emphasis on relationships, communication, trust, collaboration, and purpose.

The case studies are situated in New Zealand, a country now coming to terms with the changes brought about by the neoliberal reforms of the 1980s. Education was included in these reforms through the adoption of the Tomorrow's Schools (1989) policies. This meant devolution of responsibility to individual schools and newly elected School Boards of Trustees, as regional boards were disbanded. Later a National Curriculum (2007) and National Standards (2010) were introduced that sought to bring accountability and a degree of conformity into the system, although schools could interpret curriculum to best meet the needs of their local context. Perhaps the most influential change brought about by the policy in 1989 was the removal of zoning. Parents were free to choose any school leading to the oversubscription of some schools, while rolls fell in those schools deemed to be less desirable (Gordon, 2016). As a result, zoning or enrolment schemes were reintroduced in the year 2000 and for many living in postcodes perceived as less desirable, choice was no longer an option.

Devolution meant families had more input into their schools. Initially, Boards of Trustees were composed of parents and principals, although later it was acknowledged that school boards needed to draw on outside expertise to address perceived inequities between boards in higher and lower socioeconomic areas (Wylie, 2007). For the first time, diverse learners were included in mainstream school settings. Another significant change was the introduction of Kaupapa Māori Schools or Māori immersion schools based on *tikanga* Māori principles. Māori are the indigenous people of Aotearoa New Zealand. *Tikanga* Māori is the Māori world view; a way of being and doing that is uniquely Māori. This change in policy meant that after almost 200 years of colonization, the right of Māori to be educated in their language (*te reo* Māori) and world view was legitimized. This was a positive result of the Tomorrow's Schools policy although in practice, the small number of these schools and their geographical locations meant this choice was not available to all Māori.

The effect of these changes on school leaders was profound as the school leadership role became increasingly complex. School principals found themselves with greater responsibility for property, finance and a host of other tasks not encountered by principals prior to Tomorrow's Schools. While some reveled in their newfound autonomy, others struggled with the increase in administrative workload (Wylie, 2016). For those who saw their role as a leader of teaching and learning, conflict arose between what they wanted to do and what they had to do to meet Ministry of Education requirements. At this time, the role of the school leader as an instructional leader was promoted by government funded research such as the Best Evidence Synthesis (Robinson et al., 2009). The pressure to be expert in both instructional leadership and managerial leadership was enormous. Very often a sense of struggle emerged as school leaders tried to balance government policy requirements with a desire for more inclusive leadership practices (Wylie, 2016; Robertson, 2018). In this chapter, the principals continue to face this dilemma but with the added complexity of the COVID-19 pandemic.

The Tomorrow's Schools Review Report (2018) contended that although education is highly valued in New Zealand, the performance of the system has slipped during the last three decades. The report identifies a widening gap between advantaged and disadvantaged children, issues with student wellbeing, and variance in quality between schools (Ministry of Education, 2018). In short, the report recommended widespread "structural & cultural transformation" (p. 11). These concerns reflect societal issues arising from the neoliberal reforms of the 1980s and the increased complexity of school leadership.

At this time, a new leadership strategy for New Zealand schools was also released (Teaching Council, 2018). This document conceptualizes leadership as about influence rather than position. This shift in thinking moves towards the collective practice Ryan (2014) advocates. Of nine leadership capabilities outlined, three include capabilities of interest in this study: "Building and sustaining high trust relationships; attending to their own learning as leaders and their own wellbeing; and embodying the organization's values and showing moral purpose, optimism, agency and resilience" (Teaching Council, 2018, pp. 11–18). These capabilities highlight intra and interpersonal skills and, alongside an emphasis on building partnerships, networks, and communities, perhaps indicate a shift away from a hierarchical system to a more relational, inclusive approach.

Similar capabilities are identified in the findings of the International Leadership Development Network (ISLDN). Successful principals of high-needs schools were found to be relational, self-aware, values-based, culturally responsive, responsive to context, hopeful, and to have high expectations (Barnett & Woods, 2021). In the findings and discussion that follows, there is evidence of school leaders living these values, addressing complexity in high-needs contexts, fighting for social justice, and thereby demonstrating inclusive leadership.

RESEARCH DESIGN

Theoretical Framework

The theoretical constructs framing this study were drawn from identity theory, social justice frameworks and the successful leadership of high-needs schools. King and Travers (2017) cite Lalor and Share (2013) who argue that "social justice leaders act "in" and "on" their world and are influenced by it" (p. 152). King and Travers (2017) suggest these complex relationships can be best understood by using Bronfenbrenner's ecological theory. Within this system, the mesosystem comprises "the linkages and processes taking place between two or more settings containing the developing person" (Bronfenbrenner, 1994, p. 1645). When identifying how an inclusive leader develops their practice, it is relevant to look at these linkages and processes rather than simply focusing on what the leader does. McHale et al., (2009) argue the mesosystem represents "points of connection" (p. 7). For school leaders, these connections exist between microsystems such as schools and families and the leader-self. There are further impactful connections between the microsystems, exosystem, and the macrosystem when global situations (such as pandemics) affect society. Yet to be realized will be the pandemic's impact over time on education and school leadership (chronosystem). Argued here is that inclusive leaders are adept at making these connections at all system levels no matter who is involved or what the situation entails.

How do leaders make these connections? This is about more than actions. It is not just doing; it is about *being* the leader that is needed. Berry et al., (2019) argue that leaders must be hypervigilant, contextually aware, and intentional in all that they do. In their high-needs schools leadership model, Berry et al., (2019) bring together the principles of transformational leadership (engagement, core values, and developing people) with the principles of social justice leadership (inclusion, equity, and persistence). In short, leaders must understand their context and the values and beliefs associated with it. In addition to this, there must be some alignment between the leaders' values and those of the school or organization (Kouzes & Posner, 2012). Without this alignment, the leader will find it difficult to make the all-important connections needed to foster transformation for social justice in high-needs contexts.

Understanding personal values involves some identity work. Notman (2008) outlines the importance of interrogating values. Robertson (2017) argues that leader identity is key. Leader identity can be described as four aspects of self: the believing-self, the acting-self, the emotional-self, and the thinking-self. All four aspects interact to form response, for example, the thinking-self can moderate the feeling-self, and values held within the believing-self can be used as a moral yardstick to set purpose. To lead inclusively is complex as it involves making meaningful connections at all system levels, self-awareness, critical reflection, and taking action from a values-base. Using these constructs, this chapter considers not only what leaders *do* but what it is about them, their very *being* as leaders, that enables them to make connections within their school communities resulting in positive school cultures and promotion of equity for all.

Research Methods

Research was carried out in 2020 and 2021. The study followed a qualitative design with a multiple case study approach. Schools were purposively selected that met the criteria of the ISLDN. To be categorized as high needs, schools must feature one or more of eight criteria including: High percentage of individuals from families with incomes below the poverty line; high percentage of indigenous students; high percentage of students with learning difficulties; and situational high-need based on natural or manmade disaster (e.g., COVID-19).

The schools were situated in the southern region of New Zealand. Names of schools and participants are pseudonyms (see Table 2.1). The principals (and their senior leadership teams) were invited to take part and all participants were interviewed at least three times, before the impact of COVID-19, after the initial lockdown, and later during the pandemic. Interviews were audio-recorded and transcribed for analysis. All participants were given copies of their transcripts for verification.

Data were analyzed using constant comparative analysis, an inductive process whereby the researcher identifies themes emerging from the data rather than themes being predetermined (Lincoln & Guba, 1985). Five main themes emerged from the data. The overarching theme was relationships and there were four subthemes: collaboration, communication, trust, and purpose.

FINDINGS

Findings are organized under three main subheadings: School context; the leader's strategies in response to inequity; and the leader's self in leadership as expressed through personal beliefs and values.

Case 1: Ribbonwood School

School Context

Ribbonwood is situated in rural New Zealand. The campus reflects the long history of the school with a mixture of older style and modern

TABLE 2.1 The Study Schools—Demographics

School name	School type	Year group	Approximate age	Number of students	Context	SES	Gender	Maori
Ribbonwood	Composite school	Y1–15	5–19 years	169	Small rural town	low-mid	Co-ed	27%
Swanwood	Contributing primary	Y1–6	5–11 years	130	Outer city suburb	mid	Co-ed	16%
Globewood	Full primary	Y1–8	5–13 years	177	Inner city suburb	low-mid	Co-ed	18%

buildings. Annually, the school roll fluctuates between 160–180 students reflecting the transient nature of employment in the area. Prior to the pandemic, some students studied secondary subjects online as there was not the staffing to cover the subjects required. More than 90% of all students attend the school for both primary and secondary education. Approximately half the students travel by bus to school from out of town each day.

The socio-economic status (SES) of the area has changed from low to mid-SES. As a result, the Ministry of Education has reduced funding. However, just prior to COVID-19, many new families had moved to the town from more urban areas seeking cheaper rental housing. Different ethnicities are now represented and for the school, this resulted in different behavioral issues and lower school achievement. Since the pandemic, some families have left the district to seek employment elsewhere as local businesses fail. The district employs many people on temporary work visas who must maintain employment to stay in the country. The school is addressing these social and demographic changes through more culturally responsive teaching practices.

Principal Rob is a highly experienced principal who has been in his current role for 23 years. Prior to that he was a deputy principal and a class teacher. Rob originally trained as a primary teacher before teaching secondary subjects. As principal, he sees himself first and foremost, as a leader of learning. Rob described his changing situation prior to COVID-19 as "a kind of transition period, where we're having to get our head around different behavioral issues, and different expectations from parents at home about learning." Now these issues have intensified due to the impact of the pandemic.

Leadership Response

The school has the highest number of Māori students in its history and numbers are continuing to climb. Rob says it has been necessary to "make sure that we are being fair, and responsive to the different ethnic groups that we've got in the area." Māori students are poorly represented in New Zealand statistics regarding academic achievement (Carpenter & Osborne, 2014). Rob feels conflicted by requirements to report to parents and the Board of Trustees in terms of achievement rather than his preference of showing progress. He is concerned that his small school size skews results:

> You might have one Māori student in Year 13, and they achieve everything, so you get 100% success. Well, that's as silly as having one Māori student who doesn't get through and we get zero. Look, it's just meaningless stuff.

Rob argues it is better to measure progress towards individually tailored goals as this is something more meaningful. He reports to his Board in terms of tracking individual students and notes this gives them a better idea of progress. He says his teachers prefer this approach too. Rob remains very concerned that students do not feel too much pressure to achieve summative goals as he believes this discourages learning and destroys the essential teacher-student relationship.

Leader-Self

Rob says he is a teaching principal because "that's just the way I've decided that I want to do the job." This decision was based on his values. While he could choose not to teach, he spends about one third of his time in the classroom, seeing this as important for school leadership but also collegiality. He sees many positives in being able to collaborate with teachers about their practice as a practitioner himself.

The school values include engagement, personal excellence, and positive relationships. These values align with Rob's beliefs about teaching and learning. He stresses the importance of making personal connections with students to foster an effective learning relationship. During lockdown, he recalled giving the students more personal feedback online than when in the classroom. Dialogue increased but there were lighter sides too:

> I had kids who were out rounding sheep up or chopping the firewood and they had their phone with them so having a learning conversation. They didn't have their books in front of them, but I thought, for a while this is really good.

Many of these students lived on large rural properties, replacing workers who could not be present under lockdown conditions. Rob was flexible, adapting quickly to the changes the pandemic brought to his teaching context and practice.

Rob was very aware of the needs of his teachers, some of whom lived alone, and the importance of maintaining close social contact with all school staff. He held small online meetings rather than large meetings where he found it difficult to make meaningful, personal contact with everyone. The bleakness of a school without students and teachers was captured when he described the final day before lockdown:

> By four o'clock on Wednesday, I sent all the staff home. And I hung around for another couple of hours to make sure all the parents were sorted. And then, it was deathly quiet, and I still remember that last thing of going out and closing the school gates, which I've never done in my life... I locked the gates and that was it.

This image conveys a sense of how much people and relationships feature in Rob's practice. Throughout the pandemic, he continued to lead inclusively, prioritizing the importance of relationships with all stakeholders, and with a focus on maintaining connections.

Case 2: Swanwood School

School Context
Swanwood has experienced significant roll growth since it opened its doors in 1858 as "a little wooden shack." Today, the school's semi-rural location means it is not uncommon for a student to arrive at school on horseback. The school is well supported by the local community who value its coastal location, but a small school can be problematic in New Zealand as the administrative workload is not diminished.

Tim has led in his current role for 8 years. He reflects that he stepped into the principal role directly from his position as class teacher. While he had little or no experience in middle leadership roles, he did have a well-scaffolded handover from the previous principal, and he valued the opportunity to attend leadership training through the now discontinued First Time Principals Program.

Leadership Response
Under Tim's leadership the school roll has more than doubled. Tim was somewhat disappointed the Ministry of Education did not offer extra buildings (assets) to combat the roll growth but instead introduced an enrolment scheme. This scheme gave priority to local students with only a limited number of places offered to those out of zone. Initially, Tim felt the enrolment scheme was perceived incorrectly, despite his best efforts to communicate it, and his roll dipped in numbers. He wanted people to understand the special nature of the school saying, "we believe very firmly in what we do. We like to share that." Tim wanted families to access the school based on their desire to be part of the community and the values it stood for, rather than just their physical proximity to the school.

Connections within the school community are important to Tim. This was evident in a remark from his deputy principal who said they supported each other but also had their "ears and eyes open for other things that might be going on for other people." This illustrates an awareness of relationships between teachers, teachers and students, and student to student. This awareness pervades the culture of the school and is evident in the playground that does not differentiate areas for older and younger children. Everyone plays together and looks out for each other.

A challenge for Tim was meeting the needs of a diverse teaching staff with appropriate professional learning. He was adamant that "our responsibility is to ensure that all of the teachers are able to deliver an effective, broad curriculum." His concern was that implementation of National Standards resulted in a narrowing of the curriculum to focus on numeracy and literacy. Tim champions a more integrated approach where children learn, for example, aspects of written language, within a meaningful context. In this way, he can better meet the needs of his diverse community.

The Leader-Self

Like Ribbonwood, the school operates from a values base including risk-taking, thinking, collaboration, communication, and self-management. These values underpin all learning and reflect a sense of the semi-rural community. Tim notes:

> We've implemented our vision, and our values, into every aspect of our teaching program, all parts of the curriculum. It's visible, it's on display, it's celebrated... [the students] won't just give lip service and parrot those values; they understand what they mean and how to display them. And the parents do as well.

Tim talked about how the values were conceived; school staff were surveyed first, then the students, and the community. Everyone had ownership of the process as they went through a cycle of reviewing and revising until the important aspects were agreed. He was proud of the level of community engagement, noting that most families are supportive and deeply involved in their children's learning. During the lockdown, Tim described how students followed the scripted learning provided by the teachers and then began developing their own interests and feeding these back into the learning. He was excited as his teachers began to see in practice "what a local curriculum looks like because they [the families] implemented it themselves."

Tim spoke about the need to maintain positivity for his community. He likened his role to a duck gliding serenely along the surface of the water but paddling furiously underneath. This positive, calm attitude combined with transparency in communication resulted in the school becoming a hub for the local community, ironically at a time when no one could be physically present. Tim led inclusively, seeking to connect everyone in his school community with clear communication and a united sense of purpose.

Case 3: Globewood School

School Context

Globewood has a proud history of more than 160 years. It is situated in a low-SES area where many families live in poverty and/or substandard housing. Like Ribbonwood, the area is changing, and the school is now regarded as serving a mid-SES community. SES is important in New Zealand as it is part of the government funding formula for schools and is reflected in a school's decile level. Deciles are not associated with the quality of a school but with the SES of the surrounding community. For Ribbonwood and Globewood, change upwards in decile level means having to address a drop in funding.

Harry is a highly experienced principal of more than 33 years, with 15 years in his current role. He was a principal before the Tomorrow's Schools policy was introduced and has witnessed considerable change during his career. Harry's advice on many matters is often sought by less experienced principals and he is very willing to share his knowledge and experience.

Leadership Response

Globewood's upward shift in decile is a source of frustration for Harry:

> The neat thing about being mid-decile is that we miss out on everything. I'm getting that message through to people that actually, no, we don't have $10,000 of X's books. We're not low enough decile. I've got kids that need the books, but we don't qualify. No, we don't get X's free shoes. We don't get free fruit.

Harry remembers a time before Tomorrow's Schools when he did not have to worry where the money came from. Now he works hard to get grant money to fund the Outdoor Education programs and other things his students need. Another frustration was the struggle to get a new boiler to heat the school. It took two years. He recalled a time "when the Education Board worried about heating my school–not me." In those days, he could devote most of his time to leading teaching and learning. However, Harry is pleased to have the autonomy to spend his professional learning budget where he sees the need.

Harry has embraced a behavioral program that fosters social and emotional wellbeing. The program is part of life for everyone at the school. He says, "we've all bought into it–we're all on this journey." He fosters a positive school culture and notes it is important when getting teachers to shift their thinking, to focus on no more than three goals at a time. There will be a school wide goal, something curriculum focused, and then something more personally tailored to the individual teacher. He says things must be "manageable, doable and sustainable." Harry is intentional: "You've got to keep thinking about what's your core business. What is your purpose?" He sees this as more than a philosophical viewpoint but also as a way of preventing overload, and he applies this thinking to the introduction of new initiatives too.

Harry was very protective of his staff after lockdown when it was time to come back to school, monitoring wellbeing and insisting teachers take a proper break when it was due in July. He was concerned that teachers might be expected to teach online and face-to-face concurrently. He was adamant this would not happen and informed his school community early to set the expectation.

The Leader-Self

Five concepts underpin the behavioral program Harry has adopted for the school. These can be summed up as care for others and self, courage, aspiration, purpose and being sensible. These are the maxims that Harry lives by, and they are reflected in his vocation for teaching and his strong record of community service. He lives by an ethic of care as evidenced when he talked about his struggling families during lockdown. "I was worried about this family when we had that bad weather... I thought 'there goes the winter wood,' because they are at home all day and they've got a freezing cold house." He knew the family would be struggling as he had already provided the children with shoes. His solution was to rally some teachers, pack the caretaker's van with food parcels, and deliver them where needed despite lockdown restrictions. He was in constant touch with support agencies and encouraged his teachers to be aware of their students' needs. Harry continues to lead inclusively focusing on the support and care of everyone within his school community.

DISCUSSION

Five themes were evident across all three case studies: relationships, communication, trust, collaboration, and purpose. These themes demonstrate the interrelationship between successful high-needs leadership and leadership for social justice and they are evident in an inclusive leadership approach. The cases provide insight into the ways leaders make connections, and how their leader-self informs their actions. Although these cases represent a snapshot in time, the inclusive nature of the principals' leadership existed before the pandemic and has continued beyond. They continue to prioritize each of the following:

Relationships

The principals spoke about the importance of maintaining positive, strong relationships between teachers, students, and families. After lockdown, Rob reflected, "some of our teachers hated it and hated the distance between them and the kids—especially our primary teachers." The pandemic raised questions about building and maintaining relationships when teaching online. The study's participants reported a sense of emotional fatigue as teachers worked doubly hard to stay connected with families and students virtually. Welfare of staff was important and staying connected with those who were isolated. Rob had two or three teachers who lived alone. He communicated with them frequently to ensure they were safe and well. During lockdown, the principals set up online social groups where teachers could meet and share experiences. This helped sustain relationships. Tim held online meetings with parents to ensure that expectations about teacher performance were conveyed. In this way, he became a gatekeeper protecting the welfare of his teachers and other nonteaching staff who were coping with their own issues at home.

The leadership of these principals is values-based with a focus on relationships. In the words of Giles (2019) each "lives 'towards' a deep moral and ethical commitment to critical, humane and connected interrelationships" (p. 12). During the pandemic they related to their communities with humanity and compassion. This demonstrates a shift from pedagogical leadership to a more relational approach where, as Ryan (2006) suggests, welfare is a governing principle of leadership.

Communication

Early in the pandemic, the New Zealand government clearly articulated the response required to follow an elimination strategy by introducing four levels: Level 4 Lockdown; Level 3 Restrict; Level 2 Reduce; and Level 1 Prepare. A bubble analogy was adopted quickly by everyone. Mutch (2021) interprets this metaphor as scaling people into 'bubbles' and making sure the bubbles were not 'burst' by allowing other people in. While this worked from a safety perspective, it also meant many people were isolated at a time of heightened anxiety and fear. To combat this anxiety, Tim made connections with his community through clear, concise communication, preferring email to the phone so parents could "attend to things when they had the clear-thinking space." Tim was respectful of his families, their time, and their anxiety levels. He was also modeling what he expected from his community regarding contact with teachers. He reflected:

> They let us into their homes. We know so much more about them. And they felt supported. And they felt the communication was better. So, why isn't it always like that?

Tim planned to continue these improved practices beyond the pandemic.

Both Tim and Harry saw their roles as filtering and disseminating information. This was not to control but rather to support teachers and parent communities who were feeling overwhelmed. Tim used online platforms, websites, and various applications but also many phone calls. Rob decided his school would not follow a normal timetable. He acknowledged that the children (and his teachers) had to deal with "their own bubbles and their issues within their bubbles." Not all families had access to the internet. Indeed, research carried out in 2020 revealed, "a digital divide that exacerbated existing educational inequity" in New Zealand (Mutch, 2021, p. 248). Mutch (2021) noted that 50% of families in New Zealand did not have access to online learning and for those who eventually got it, there was considerable upskilling needed to learn the technology.

Harry spoke of his desperate need to reach everyone. Government packs of educational materials were provided but his teachers had to supplement these with resources to better cater for the diverse learning needs of their students. Government promises that all families would get access to technology did not materialize for his school, and he reluctantly issued the school's devices knowing many would not be returned. Certainly, the learning experiences for students at Harry's school were not equal. Some students thrived in the sheltered environments of their homes while others struggled in overcrowded situations with very limited or no access to technology. All three principals embodied the principle of fairness (Ryan 2006). They were troubled by the inequity that was already present but exacerbated by the pandemic. They used communication as a tool and supplemented supply systems to combat these inequities, attempting to ensure that their students and families in need were reached and supported.

Trust

In New Zealand, decision-making about school closure was driven by the Department of Health and communicated through the Ministry of Education. Coming out of lockdown provided challenges. Harry recalled he had eight staff at school when the school opened at Level 3 and only one child appeared. Gradually, the numbers increased but he was frustrated that he was not trusted to make the decision about when to reopen. Initially, Harry said he was overly strict in his enforcement of the 'track and trace' rules, but he quickly realized he could trust his community to follow the rules. There was also evidence of respect for the school at a time when he worried about possible vandalism. No such event occurred and indeed, even the hastily made laminated signs to warn people off the play equipment were still there six weeks later. Harry reflected, "I felt like the public opinion was there supporting all this." Increase in public support for the teaching profession was evident in Australia too, where it was reported that 41.6% of those surveyed felt "their perceptions of teachers' work had improved as a direct result of COVID-19" (Heffernan et al., 2021). For the principals, the schools quickly became the trusted virtual hubs of the community. Their leadership in this space was successful because of their ability to connect with people in a transparent, trustworthy way.

Collaboration

Each of the school leaders fostered collaboration within their teams at school but also within their communities. However, during the lockdown phase, roles appeared to shift slightly. Positionality was emphasized as decisions were made quickly. Teachers and families looked to the principal for direction while the principals responded to Ministry directives. In a sense, the principals became middle leaders but their influence at this time was profound. They demonstrated the hyper-vigilance identified by Berry et al. (2019). The principals' responsibilities increased as they looked after school property, students and their families, staff and their families, and personal wellbeing. However, true to their core values they remained engaged and persistent in their attempts to do the best for their students, teachers, and families.

Purpose

Throughout the lockdown and in the days that followed, each leader did not lose sight of their vision for school. The intentionality Berry et al. (2019) argue is important for high-needs leadership was enhanced. The focus on inclusion and equity continued and again the core values of each principal drove their hard work. Efforts to support everyone meant addressing connections between the school and community. For Swanwood, the emergence of a 'local curriculum' was driven further by parents and children as they started to adapt curriculum to meet their individual interests. For Ribbonwood, student engagement was enhanced through increased communication, and teaching strategies were diversified as learners became more mobile, taking their devices with them as they worked, and engaging with each other in a variety of different contexts. For Globewood, it was an opportunity to update communication systems within the school. Communication with parents switched from paper to email. Time was spent ensuring families could receive messages, loaning school devices in some instances, and enabling internet connections.

Harry's biggest concern was the social and emotional wellbeing of students and teachers, and his ethic of care continues, evident in his support of teachers and parents throughout the pandemic. Tim shared his primary focus:

> We are accountable to our children first and foremost. And our decisions should be based on that. It's not about, I don't know, looking fancy, attracting enrolments, doing some sort of compliance, making a PTA happy; it's about the kids. And we don't need to apologize for it.

All three principals acknowledge the importance of identifying and interrogating personal values. Their beliefs and values underpinned their moral purpose, and this did not change even in a time of crisis.

Returning to Bronfenbrenner and the mesosystem. It is largely within this system that leaders operate. Inclusive leaders are particularly adept at creating and building connections within the mesosystem. However, they can struggle to find a connection between their systems of values and those they need to connect with. These struggles are evident in the dilemmas revealed in this chapter. So, what makes an inclusive leader successful in this space? As Barnett and Woods (2021) argue, likely it is their determination, their optimism, and a sense of hope that enables them to pursue these connections. Looking at the values espoused by the three leaders, there is a hint of what drives them and a true sense of their moral purpose. This purpose is summed up in Tim's quote above. Everyone in this study agreed that children are at the heart of everything they do. When the microsystems of the school, families and board were in alignment through shared values, the connections fostering these relationships were easy to sustain. However, where there was a disconnect between values and systems (often brought about by pressures from the exo and macrosystems), it became difficult to maintain the connections that enabled the relationships. The leader working within and through the mesosystem is constantly challenged with creating and sustaining these connections. This is the real work of inclusive leaders, and it is frequently invisible.

IMPLICATIONS AND FUTURE RESEARCH

The experiences recorded here provide some insights to take forward. Perhaps a rethink is needed about the capabilities valued in leadership. The principals in this study demonstrated the importance of building and sustaining high trust relationships, strategically thinking and planning, and managing resources to achieve vision and goals (Teaching Council, 2018). However, perhaps most important was the leaders' capacity to show moral purpose, optimism, agency, and resilience. These four characteristics were evident in the thinking, feeling, and acting aspects of the leader-self but were most deeply rooted in the believing aspect of the leader-self. Further work is needed to determine to what extent leaders can be developed and supported in these areas.

Important to any work engaging the leader-self, is the opportunity for leaders to reflect on events and the impacts on themselves, their students, their families and ultimately, their practice. Time is needed for critical reflection to consider new learnings and decide what to hold onto when faced with pressure to return to 'normal' as quickly as possible. To do this, leaders' must make connections in their practice and "this means surfacing, reflecting upon, and making sense of the affective, emotional, personal and physical demands of the work, as well as seeking an alignment between personal values, moral purpose and actions" (Morrison et al., 2017, p. 167). Future research to explore awareness of the leader-self, each of the four aspects, and the connections held within the complex ecological systems Bronfenbrenner describes may provide further insight into the self and practice of the inclusive leader.

This study is limited by size and timeframe. The impact of the pandemic continues, and it will be important to keep returning to the field to understand the long-term consequences of this event for school leadership. For schools, the digital divide is exacerbated, and further research is needed to understand the impact of the pandemic on those already occupying a place of disadvantage in our society. However, research should also target the positives that emerged from this time of adversity to enable reflection and guide discussion about education and the importance of inclusive leadership.

CONCLUSION

To lead inclusively is to truly tackle the complexities of leadership. These leaders demonstrate what it means to *be* a leader as much as what a leader does. Case studies such as these help us understand leadership complexity while providing insight into the different contexts where this important leadership work takes place. The pandemic highlighted the educational and social inequities already in existence in New Zealand. The leaders in this study navigated the crisis by drawing on their values and beliefs. They made powerful, reciprocal connections with students, teachers, and families that allowed their school communities to thrive despite the hardships faced.

REFERENCES

Barnett, B.G., & P.A. Woods, P.A (Eds.). (2021) *Educational leadership for social justice and improving high-needs schools: Findings from 10 years of international collaboration.* Information Age Publishing.

Berry, J. R., Cowart Moss, S., & Gore, P. (2019). Leadership in high-needs/high performing schools: Success stories from an urban school district. In E.

Murakami, D. Gurr, & R. Notman (Eds.), *Educational leadership, culture, and success in high-needs schools*. Information Age Publishing.

Bishop, R. (2008). A culturally responsive pedagogy of relations. In C. McGee & D. Fraser (Eds.), *The professional practice of teaching* (pp. 154–170). Cengage Learning Australia.

Bottery, M. (2012). Leadership, the logic of sufficiency and the sustainability of education. *Educational Management Administration & Leadership, 40*(4), 449–463.

Bronfenbrenner, U. (1994). Ecological models of human development. In T. Husen & T. Postelthwaite (Eds.). *International encyclopaedia of education*, (pp. 1643–1647). Pergamon.

Carpenter, V. M., & Osborne, S. (Eds.). (2014). *Twelve thousand hours: Education and poverty in Aotearoa New Zealand*. Dunmore Publishing Limited.

Cranston, J. (2013). School leaders leading: Professional responsibility not accountability as the key focus. *Educational Management Administration & Leadership, 41*(2), 129–142.

Giles, D. (2019). *Relational leadership in education: A phenomenon of inquiry and practice*. Routledge.

Gordon, L. (2016). "Rich" and "poor" schools revisited. *New Zealand Journal of Educational Studies, 50*(1), 7–21.

Heffernan, A., Magyar, B., Bright, D., & Longmuir, F. (2021). *The impact of COVID-19 on perceptions of Australian schooling: Research brief*. Monash University.

King, F., & Travers, J. (2017) Social justice leadership through the lens of ecological systems theory. In P. S. Angelle (Ed.), *A global perspective of social justice leadership for school principals* (pp. 147–165). Information Age Publishing.

Kouzes, J., & Posner, B. (2012). *The leadership challenge: How to make extraordinary things happen in organizations*. Jossey Bass.

Lincoln, Y. S., & Guba, E.G. (1985). *Naturalistic inquiry*. Sage Publications.

Morrison, M., Notman, R., & McNae, R. (2017). Transcending the personal and political: Provocations. In R. McNae, M. Morrison, & R. Notman (Eds.), *Educational leadership in Aotearoa New Zealand: Issues of context and social justice* (pp. 159–173). NZCER Press.

Mutch, C. A. (2021). COVID-19 and the exacerbation of educational inequalities in New Zealand. *Perspectives in Education, 39*(1), 242–256.

Notman, R. (2008). Leading from within: A values-based model of principal self-development. *Leading and Managing, 14*(1), 1–15.

Robertson (2017). Transformation of professional identity in an experienced primary school principal: A New Zealand case study. *Educational Management Administration & Leadership, 45*(5), 774–789.

Robertson (2018). A New Zealand principal's perceptions of identity and change. *Leading & Managing, 24*(1), 33–46.

Robinson, V., Hohepa, M., & Lloyd, C. (2009). *School leadership and student outcomes: Identifying what works and why*. Crown.

Ryan, J. (2006). Inclusive leadership and social justice for schools. *Leadership and Policy in Schools, 5*, 3–17.

Ryan, J. (2014). Promoting inclusive leadership in diverse schools. In I. Bogotch & C. M. Shields (Eds.), *International handbook of educational leadership and social (in)justice*. Springer. https://doi.org/10.1007/978-94-007-6555-9

Teaching Council. (2018). *The leadership strategy for the teaching profession of Aotearoa New Zealand: Enabling every teacher to develop their leadership capability.* Education Council.

Tomorrow's Schools Independent Taskforce (2018) *Our schooling futures: Stronger together.* https://conversation.education.govt.nz/conversations/tomorrows-schools-review/

Wylie, C. (2007). *School governance in New Zealand—How is it working?* NZCER Press.

Wylie, C., Cosslett, G., & Burgon, J. (2016). New Zealand principals: Autonomy at a cost. In H. Ärlestig, C. Day, & O. Johansson (Eds.), *A decade of research on school principals: Cases from 24 countries.* Springer.

CHAPTER 3

PRINCIPAL INFLUENCE ON SUCCESS FOR STUDENTS WITH DISABILITIES

An Exploration of Educator Perceptions of Inclusive Leadership

Zak Dominello
The University of Northern Colorado

Vanessa Giddings
The University of Northern Colorado

Amie Cieminski
The University of Northern Colorado

The purpose of this chapter is to illuminate inclusive leadership practices which may contribute to improved outcomes for students with disabilities. The chapter begins with a brief overview of the trends in inclusion and achievement for students with disabilities and provides extant literature on leadership needed for inclusive environments. Next, a brief description of the research design and methods is included along with an introduction of the two elementary school settings, student demographics, and principal profiles. We then provide examples of how these two principals exhibited inclusive leadership by demonstrating courageous leadership, instituting systematic instructional leadership, and exemplifying transformational leadership in their pursuit of better outcomes for students with disabilities. The chapter concludes with a summary of practical steps that leaders can take that are aligned with the results of this study and connections to previous studies.

Legislation, Accountability, and the Inclusive Leader

In this chapter, we define inclusion as a schoolwide practice that provides students with disabilities with equitable access and opportunity to general education along with the appropriate resources and support they need (Council of Chief State School Officers, 2020). Inclusive schools and environments are those where educators and leaders ensure that students with disabilities are included in the general classroom setting to the fullest extent possible. As such, inclusive principals and educators are those who make inclusion a priority in their practice.

The current wave of education reform focuses on data, inclusion, equity, and the education of all students. Educational policies such as the *Individuals with Disabilities Education Act* (IDEA, 2004), No Child Left Behind (NCLB, 2001), and the *Every Student Succeeds Act* (ESSA, 2015) aim to promote access and inclusive educational opportunities for all students including those with disabilities. While students with disabilities are spending more time included in the general educational setting, their achievement toward grade-level expectations remains considerably lower than that of their peers (Eckes & Swando, 2009; McFarland et al., 2017; Schulte et al., 2016).

Principal practices should support the success of all students in alignment with policy demands stipulated in IDEA (2004). According to the Council of Chief State School Officers (2020), "Inclusive principals create strong school cultures and distribute leadership across staff to serve all learners well and ensure all students feel safe, supported, and valued in school" ("What is Inclusive Principal Leadership" section). They promote equity for all by ensuring high expectations and appropriate support to meet the needs of each student.

The role of the principal has a significant impact on student achievement (Leithwood et al., 2004). Furthermore, studies indicate that teachers' perceptions of principal behaviors, such as shared leadership and professional community, have an impact on instructional practices (Goddard et al., 2010; Kurşunoğlu & Tanrıöğen, 2009; Wahlstrom & Louis, 2008).

However, there is limited research about the impact of the principal as leader of special education (Day et al., 2016; Hoppey & McLeskey, 2013) as well as limited information about how educators view principal behaviors surrounding successful practices that support students in special education (Goddard et al., 2010).

The Principal as a Leader in Special Education

The responsibility of serving the needs of the general education population, as well as the special education population, begins with the building principal. McHatton et al. (2010) expressed that "principals who have a broader understanding of exceptional student education can foster an environment more conducive to improving outcomes for these students" (p. 16).

When self-reporting confidence of their knowledge within special education, principals have reported feeling most confident in specific district procedures and policy, but less confident in program improvement plans and specific state and legal knowledge of special education (Frost & Kersten, 2011). In another study, practicing principals expressed that their preparation programs severely neglected special education content knowledge, equity, the discipline of students with disabilities, and co-teaching (DeMatthews et al., 2020). These results suggest that principals enter the role with a lack of understanding and knowledge to effectively support students with special needs. DeMatthews et al. (2020) recommended three practices to promote inclusive schools: creating a collaborative school culture, using data to drive instruction, and improving instructional quality, specifically for special education. Similarly, Cobb (2015) identified inclusive programming, staff collaboration, and parental engagement as three important domains of preparation in the field of special education leadership. School principals have reported minimal interactions with special education teachers about improving teaching and learning due to the competing demands of their job (Bays & Crockett, 2007). Principals simultaneously report having limited understanding of what effective instruction for students with disabilities encompasses (Lynch, 2016).

Salisbury (2006) suggested that schools that function inclusively do so as a result of the effective leadership of a principal focused on inclusion. Additionally, an analysis of case studies of effective, inclusive schools suggested that having "strong, active principal leadership to ensure that teachers share core values and an institutional commitment to developing an effective inclusive school," is a critical factor for success (McLeskey & Waldron, 2015). Billingsley et al. (2017) identified four critical components for high-achieving inclusive learning environments for students with disabilities: "(a) building a shared vision and commitment, (b) developing a professional community that shares responsibility for the learning of all students, (c) redesigning the school, and (d) sharing responsibility for inclusive education" (pp. 26–27).

Researchers have suggested a push for inclusion is a necessary direction for educating all students (Hang & Rabren, 2009; Hoppey & McLeskey, 2013; Kirby, 2017; McLeskey et al., 2014; Printy & Williams, 2015); however, the way educational leaders drive for more inclusion is still an area lacking clarity (Lynch, 2016). There are few studies that examine the perceptions of principals, general education teachers, and special education teachers within schools making strides to closing the achievement gap (DeMatthews et al., 2020; Hoppey & McLeskey, 2013). Given that over 10% of the U.S. school-age population are students with disabilities and that outcomes for this group lag behind their neurotypical peers, the purpose of the case study was to explore educator perspectives that influence success for students with disabilities and promote inclusive school environments. We investigated the following research question: What are the leadership behaviors, actions, and characteristics identified by educators regarding the school principal that are crucial to the inclusion and success of special education students?

METHODS

This qualitative, intrinsic case study explored educator perspectives of principal behaviors, actions, and characteristics that influence success for students with disabilities and that promote an inclusive school environment. By selecting two different schools, we examined and compared different perspectives and contexts.

Data collection for the study was the same at both sites and consisted of an open-ended survey given to all staff, a semi-structured interview with each principal, and two focus group interviews (one with general educators and one with special educators) at each school. Data collection focused on school culture, inclusive practices, and leadership contributions to the success of all students, including those with disabilities. Interviews were audio-recorded and transcribed. Two of the researchers coded data from the three sources using first and second cycle coding methods (Saldaña, 2013). Gathering perceptions from various educators allowed for triangulation and increased the trustworthiness of findings (Patton, 1999).

Selected Sites and Participants

We selected two elementary schools that included the majority of their students with disabilities in the general education setting for the majority of the school day. According to state assessment data, the average achievement and annual growth scores for students with disabilities in these schools were higher than the state average. Study participants included 44 licensed teachers, two veteran principals, two assistant principals, four paraprofessional staff, and six student support staff.

Bright Future Elementary School

Bright Future is a public elementary school serving students pre-kindergarten to sixth grade in a middle-class suburb. Bright Future has approximately 430 students, of which 82% identify as Anglo-American, 10% identify as Hispanic, 4% identify as two or more races, 2% identify as African American, 1% identify as Native American, and 1% as Pacific Islander. Currently, 12% of students receive free and reduced lunch services and 12% of students are categorized as students with disabilities.

Anne, the principal of Bright Future for the last five years, worked within the district for several years as a librarian, teacher, and assistant principal. She received no formal training in special education beyond what was required in graduate classes.

At Bright Future, students were educated within grade-level grouping with added support in each classroom based on student needs. Paraprofessional, mental health, and other educational support staff pushed into classrooms to observe, support, and meet the needs of all students. At Bright Future, students who might be in self-contained settings at other schools were included within the general education classrooms to the fullest extent possible.

New Horizon Elementary School

New Horizon is one of eight public elementary schools in a school district that serves 6500 students within a large geographic area. The school serves approximately 380 students, of which 78% identify as Anglo-American, 18% identify as Hispanic, 3% identify as two or more races, 0.2% identify as African American, 0.5% identify as Native American, and 0.5% as Pacific Islander. Thirteen percent of students qualify for free and reduced lunch services and 10% of students are categorized as students with disabilities.

Jane, the principal of New Horizon, was serving her fifth year in the position. Before this, Jane served as a kindergarten and third-grade teacher as well as an assistant principal in two large elementary schools with diverse populations in a different state. While she held no formal degree or certification in special education, she had worked in schools with dual language services and extensive services for exceptional students.

At New Horizon, students participated in a personalized schedule consisting of core academic blocks, elective blocks, and planned intervention/service time to provide students with support without missing core instruction. Special education and general education teachers collaborated with instructional coaches in a weekly professional learning community (PLC) model to develop plans supporting diverse learners. There was a focus on differentiation, scaffolding, and instructional strategies, allowing students to demonstrate learning in a variety of ways.

FINDINGS

Participants' responses reflected three main leadership styles and categories within each style: courageous leadership, systematic instructional leadership, and transformational leadership. Although each school's context and structures were slightly different, both principals exhibited courageous leadership; they embraced a vision for inclusion and demonstrated core beliefs regarding the inclusion of each student. They were determined to act, lead change for the benefit of the students, and hold themselves and others accountable for meeting the unique needs of each student. The principals exhibited a strong focus on instruction as well as an ability to use a systems-thinking approach to build structures that emphasized quality instruction. The leaders worked with staff as they built capacity, established relationships with students and their families, and collaborated with staff.

Courageous Leadership

Courageous leaders hold consistent beliefs ensuring actions align with a common school mission; they seek feedback and collaboration with staff to make informed decisions (Blankstein, 2017). The principals at both campuses demonstrated courageous leadership which involved the passion and persistence to act, lead change, and hold oneself and others accountable.

Core Beliefs About Inclusion
Both principals viewed themselves as educators who believe in creating inclusive school cultures. Anne, the principal of Bright Future, expressed a core belief in taking care of all students as well as all staff taking care of each other. She stated that "the continuous message is that every child here has a place." The faculty and staff made similar observations about Anne's commitment to the success of each student, including those with disabilities. They shared that Anne had non-negotiables about an inclusive school culture and that those core beliefs were mirrored by the faculty and staff. Marie, a special educator, stated:

Our principal Anne always says, "We are just taking good care of kids." It is her quote that she uses a lot for us, and whatever we have to do to just make it work, and take good care of them, and blend our services together to meet all of their individual needs.

This "make it work" attitude was further exemplified regarding individualized plans for every student as well the collaboration and care shown within the common practices of the classroom teams.

Likewise, Jane the principal at New Horizon shared her belief in inclusion and personalized learning:

It's just a mindset of we're going to individualize for everyone. Every one of our kids has a need. We want to support that. I think highlighting that all the time creates an inclusive school because parents hear that, teachers hear that, and that's the message.

A faculty member at New Horizon reinforced Jane's sentiment stating, "Our principal is a passionate advocate for ALL of our students, and we are constantly talking about and sharing ideas for how to grow all of our students and encouraged to try new things if we are not seeing growth."

Kristine, a fourth-grade teacher, highlighted that personalized learning was synonymous with inclusion: "I think that inclusion is a huge part of our mission. I mean personalized learning is the biggest keyword I can think of for the school. But it's the application that is heavily supported and followed through."

Another faculty member noted it was the principal's beliefs that drove the ideas of inclusion in the school stating, "It is ultimately her philosophy that works in connection with general classroom teachers and special education teachers to meet the needs of students with disabilities." In these successful inclusive schools, the leaders believed that all students matter, and that the faculty and staff would do whatever it took to make that a reality for students.

Vision of Inclusion

A visionary leader focuses on the ideal school, driving towards a future vision of the school with a proactive stance (Kowalski, 2008). A vision of inclusion emerged as a category within courageous leadership. The principals demonstrated strong visionary thinking through establishing a shared vision with their staff based on beliefs about inclusion.

At Bright Future, the vision was stated as:

Bright Future is a special place, and a sense of community is what defines us. Working together with our families, we take care of each other, and we support learning. Through this, we create an environment where children achieve and thrive. We invite you to partner with us!

At New Horizon, the vision was written as, "A safe, collaborative and rigorous learning environment in which all students are held to high expectations and are active participants in their learning process." They established a culture of inclusion through developing a vision with faculty, staff, and other stakeholders. A New Horizon survey participant stated, "Our principal leads our school by developing school goals and personal goals around how we are supporting all students including students with disabilities." In each school, participants shared about learning environments where each student had access to and was supported in their general education classroom instruction, which in turn fostered student success.

Marie stated, "I think our principal is so inclusive. We are all so inclusive as a faculty and staff. I think we just see that faculty and staff recognized the principal's beliefs about inclusion were foundational in the schools' vision, something they wanted to support.

Systematic Instructional Leadership

The second leadership style identified at both schools was systematic instructional leadership. Systematic instructional leadership involves a strong focus on instruction and the ability to use systems-thinking to build structures that prioritize instruction (Shaked & Schechter, 2019). In this study, systematic instructional leadership included elements of the traditional instructional leadership and systems thinking to support inclusivity.

Focus on Quality First Instruction

A focus on instruction started with students receiving high-quality first instruction aimed at grade level expectations within their general education classrooms. By maximizing each student's time spent in the general education classroom, these principals reached their goals of high-quality instruction for each student. At Bright Future, Anne expected that students were educated with strategies and accommodations in the classroom to the maximum extent possible while receiving the services of their Individualized Education Program (IEP). She stated, "The piece of saying kids are going to get first instruction in their class as a non-negotiable is one of those important things." Educators shared similar perceptions regarding the importance of maximizing high-quality first instruction within the general education setting.

At New Horizon, the focus group conversations revealed similar mindsets regarding maximizing time in the general education classroom for students with disabilities. Rachael, a special education teacher, stated, "We also try to have a lot of that pushed-in model so that kids aren't being taken out of their class." The drive for inclusion included appropriate and scaffolded instruction as part of quality first instruction. For example, special education teachers assisted with small group instruction, providing it to any student who needed it, so students with disabilities would not be singled out in front of their peers.

Through the focus group discussions at both campuses, it became evident that the educators shared similar perceptions regarding the importance of maximizing quality first instruction within the general education setting. Educators identified that in the past, they may not have been equipped with the skills to assist each student. However, at New Horizon, faculty and staff described professional learning driven by the need for effective classroom practices for quality first instruction. Both schools used Professional Learning Communities (PLCs) as tools to promote quality first instruction and monitor its effects on student progress within the general classrooms. Likewise, both principals mentioned the importance of, effectively utilizing faculty, including paraprofessionals, for quality instruction. This elevated each member's instructional strengths and promoted a mindset that every adult is a teacher. Anne focused on developing her entire faculty and staff's instructional capacity through feedback and support. Likewise, Jane shared, "...our paraprofessionals, I call them teachers...They are teachers. And they work with our kids like anyone does." These principals maximized their human resources to focus on instruction.

System Building

Within the theme of systematic instructional leadership, system-building indicated the principal's strategic focus on establishing systems and maintaining their efficacy through collaboration and staff development. The principals built systems related to scheduling, collaboration, and hiring with inclusion in mind while also maximizing benefit to student success.

Both schools had effective master schedules that promoted inclusion. Principals, faculty, and staff overwhelmingly reported that inclusion required a thoughtfully developed master schedule so that students with disabilities were not "pulled-out" during high-quality first instruction. Jane shared that developing and maintaining a successful inclusive school "starts with scheduling."

In addition to robust PLCs, both schools offered development opportunities built into the day-to-day operation. The PLCs were focused on, but not limited to, school improvement goals of quality instruction and academic growth for each student. Survey respondents described the PLCs as inclusive of all staff, including paraprofessionals, special education team members, and elective teachers. Although the PLCs took different forms, collaboration between special education and general education staff about the goals, supports, and structures necessary within inclusive classrooms was a shared topic. Educators at New Horizon described PLC activities as a combination of learning new practices, sharing resources, and showcasing staff members' expertise for what was working in their classrooms. Additionally, both leaders recognized the importance of creating time for educators to participate in, and give full attention to, their professional learning. Staff from both schools described weekly rotations and built-in scheduling opportunities that allowed for substitute coverage in the classroom, additional time before and after school, and other times for learning and collaboration during the week.

Systematic hiring perpetuated the vision and culture of inclusion at both schools. Hiring practices focused less on previous work experience and more on factors that would contribute to inclusionary practices for students. Both principals focused on the ability of the interviewee to "build relationships" and fit with their overall vision for the school. Anne from Bright Future expressed that potential new hires "will work with children with all levels of need. You don't get to shop at your comfort level." While she described how this hiring approach led to a higher level of demand for training, with the correct systems in place to provide staff support, this approach had worked to "break down silos" within the building. Similarly, Jane from New Horizon focused on hiring people with strong relationship-building and communication skills. Newly hired faculty and staff in both schools strengthened the systems in place, either with expertise or with a collaborative mindset.

Transformational Leadership

Transformational leadership encompasses four leadership actions including inspirational motivation, individualized attention, intellectual stimulation, and idealized influence (Bass, 1985). Facets of transformational leadership as defined by Bass (1985) were realized by the principals in this study through valuing each staff member, relationship building, and capacity building.

Value for Each Staff Member
Across the two school sites, the educators and principals reported similar views of how the staff were treated within the building and how that helped to contribute to the success of their schools. Both principals demonstrated a belief in educator efficacy and a passion for their individual growth and success. Anne, the principal of Bright Future explained:

You must take people where they are at and figure out their strengths and allow them to flourish with their strengths. Different people have different strengths, but people are here for the right reason. Let's honor the fact that they want to make a difference in the lives of children.

Educators from the schools provided a variety of examples about how they felt valued, and many conveyed a culture of openness and growth in which everyone could contribute to the school's success. For example, a faculty member stated:

This is a cornerstone of why our staff is effective in this school with all our kiddos who experience challenges. The staff I work with understand that everyone wants the best for our kiddos. We have a team approach that emphasizes that we all "own" our kids from custodians, paraeducators, to caseworkers and teachers instead of a more compartmentalized mentality of "that kid is in special education" or that they belong to a certain program, which I've experienced in other schools.

Similarly, a general education teacher suggested:

Inclusion works because every individual works hard and works together to make it happen. If something isn't working, our principal is always open to finding a time to sit down, meet as a team, and brainstorm together to find a solution that does work.

The idea that the faculty and staff could try new methods and strategies for inclusion without fear of judgment was common across schools. One teacher indicated:

One of the best things she does is really support and believe in us as teachers. I think it would be very difficult to try new things and take risks ourselves if we felt that she was not supportive.

Overall, the principals recognized the importance of each staff member in their day-to-day push for inclusion. They led their schools with the belief that all staff were valued and were able to grow and take risks while providing an inclusive education for students.

Relationship Building
Both principals of these successful inclusive schools intentionally focused on building relationships with faculty and staff and within the faculty and staff. They saw themselves not only as a leader but as a co-worker and a thought partner with a common goal to educate every student. The principals modeled caring and being part of the team with "kids taking breaks in my office" and daily debriefs over potential issues within the classroom. The

principals expressed that relationship building extended far beyond the way they worked with the faculty and staff and included modeling the behaviors that they wanted teachers to show students and students to show each other.

Anne described the importance of relationships, explaining, "If I don't understand you, and might not know how to work with you, help me to figure it out." Educators anecdotally validated that Anne took time to seek them out, learned their interests and strengths, and used that to help them grow. When asked about support from their principal, the majority of the faculty and staff spoke of how they cared for them, worked together with them, and valued them.

The principals valued relationships with students and families also. One educator reflected that the principal "takes the time to build relationships with students and with families and is very active in building those relationships. I can guarantee you she knows something special about every single kid in this school and that's huge." Additionally, the principals' relationships extended beyond the faculty, staff, and students into the community. Anne explained, "My message to the outer community is that we take care of each other. This is a community school and inclusion fits within that vision." This sentiment was also reflected in the Bright Future mission statement.

Capacity Building

As team-oriented leaders, both principals recognized the importance of building a dedicated and talented team through professional development, accountability, skill-building, and transfer of knowledge. Team members from the schools agreed their individual development took precedence, and their principals were actively engaged in working with them to improve their professional craft.

While capacity building was described in many ways by staff in the two schools, the majority described professional development opportunities, PLCs, and individual coaching conversations as avenues for building capacity. For example, special education faculty was embedded into the school schedule, collaborating alongside general education faculty members to support individualized learning and model instructional strategies in the classroom. Anne explained the team at Bright Future was knowledgeable and used differentiation to teach students with disabilities. Collaboration between general educators and special educators ensured that they were "all on the same page when it comes to best meeting the needs of our students inside and outside of the regular education setting." When presented with professional learning opportunities, the principal would ask, "How does this professional development support the mission and vision of inclusion in the school?" Both schools built capacity through professional development and opportunities to collaborate and discuss practice.

DISCUSSION

This research provided an in-depth look into two outlier cases, in which elementary school faculty and staff improved the academic achievement and growth for students with disabilities, where many other schools saw stagnant results. Similar to previous studies in educational research, this study identified that leadership style impacts the culture and success of schools (Frost & Kersten, 2011; Leithwood & Riehl, 2005; Waters et al., 2003). This study's data and findings supported much of the current research which suggests that key practices such as data-based decision making, shared decision making, capacity building, and professional development are important for student growth and achievement in inclusive schools (Hoppey & McLeskey, 2013; Kirby, 2017; McLeskey et al., 2014). Furthermore, educator perceptions were consistent with practices DeMatthews et al. (2020) identified by suggesting that an instructional leader can promote successful inclusion by creating a collaborative school culture, using data to drive instruction, and improving instructional quality.

According to the Council of Chief State School Officers (2020), inclusive principals create strong school cultures to serve all students well. Our study sheds light on *how* principals might do this by illuminating three specific leadership styles and associated actions that created cultures in which students with disabilities flourished. These three leadership styles could serve as a guide for future leaders when considering practices and systems to benefit students with disabilities through courageous leadership, systematic instructional leadership, and transformational leadership, as represented by Figure 3.1. The visual was created to represent the findings of the study and leadership styles exhibited by these inclusive principals. The three types of leadership provide areas for educational leaders working towards the collaborative culture necessary for growth and achievement for all students.

Courageous leadership, as reported by educators in this study, and supported by research, includes core beliefs for student success and an unwavering vision for making it happen. Participants reported intentional goal setting and staff development tied to the central mission of the school with constant feedback and encouragement directed towards educating each student. This suggests successfully implementing inclusion within a school not only takes a vision regarding inclusionary practices, but a core belief that all students belong in the general education classroom to the maximum extent possible. This was evident in most responses explaining some variation of a sentiment expressed by Anne that "inclusion is not a choice. It is part of the culture. It is just the way it is." The courageous leaders in these schools demonstrated that when the school recognized the diversity of the students (Blankstein, 2017) and aimed to abolish labels (Kirby, 2017), an inclusive culture can support each student.

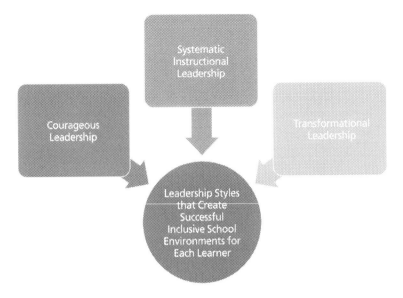

Figure 3.1 Leadership styles for inclusive school environments.

Instructional leadership has been shown to have a direct effect on student achievement (Waters et al., 2003), and established systems within schools have a positive impact on instruction (Shaked & Schechter, 2019). Educators and principals at both schools identified systematic instructional leadership as a significant leadership style. Within these successful inclusive schools, the principals focused on instructional leadership while implementing structures and schedules, so the faculty was able to provide high-quality first instruction within grade-level classrooms with minimal pull-out instruction and support. Educators noted the intentional building of collaborative systems specifically assisted them in meeting the needs of students with disabilities in the general education classroom. Both schools also enacted PLC systems to meld general education and special education best practice.

Research has indicated that 85% of special education students can master general education grade-level content when provided with the correct support (Thurlow et al., 2011). Furthermore, an increase in class time with general education peers has been shown to increase engagement, maintenance of support, and student outcomes for students with disabilities (Bui et al., 2010). Both successful inclusive schools in this study collectively built schedules between general educators, special educators, and support staff to ensure students were receiving quality first instruction in the general student milieu. This study's findings are consistent with the research regarding the benefits of initial instruction taking place with the primary teacher

(Bui et al., 2010). However, these findings also emphasize the importance of collective and collaborative scheduling to ensure the representation of all staff voices to support students.

Lastly, principals and educators recognized qualities of transformational leadership that contributed to success for students with special needs. Both principals focused on relationship building, enacting beliefs regarding staff efficacy, as well as building capacity. Many team members highlighted the ability to learn and grow in a safe environment that encouraged risk-taking. The school teams also reported their motivation was influenced by inspiration and charisma of the building leader and their beliefs regarding inclusion. This finding was consistent with research about the effects of transformational leadership on school achievement (Bass, 1985; Leithwood & Jantzi, 2005).

CONCLUSIONS AND RECOMMENDATIONS FOR PRACTICE

Current educational reform focuses on data, inclusion, equity, and the education of all students. National educational policies, including the *Every Child Succeeds Act* (2015), promote access and inclusive educational opportunities for all students. Overall, students with disabilities are spending more time included within the general education setting, yet their achievement toward grade-level expectations is considerably lower than their peers (Eckes & Swando, 2009; McFarland et al., 2017; Schulte et al., 2016).

The primary contribution of this study is the exploration of the leadership practices important to the success of special education students as perceived by educators within the public school setting. While research has identified theories and practices of inclusion and special education leadership (Billingsley et al., 2017; Cobb, 2015; DeMatthews et al., 2020; McLeskey & Waldron, 2015), these results provide possible tangible and applicable practices.

Leadership Style

Principals of these successful inclusive schools utilized a combination of leadership styles to inspire and motivate all staff to rally around each student. Policy demands for increased accountability have shifted the role of the principal over the years from building manager to instructional and transformational leader (Day et al., 2016). The principals of two effective inclusive schools drew upon a variety of leadership styles including courageous leadership, inclusive leadership, systematic instructional leadership, and transformational leadership. For both principals within the study, the combination of these three styles yielded success for each student.

Faculty and Staff Perceptions

We found limited existing research on educator perceptions regarding principal practices, skills, and beliefs that contribute to successful inclusive schools for students with disabilities (Goddard et al., 2010). This study contributed to the research by exploring the ways educators view their principal's leadership in relation to inclusive practices for students with disabilities. Through focus groups and surveys, study participants repeatedly shared that principals believed in each student, set clear and high expectations for staff and students grounded in this belief, developed systems that supported quality instruction for each student, and valued relationships with all stakeholders. The participants relayed that their principals believed in each team member and held high confidence in their ability to help each student find success.

Recommendations for Practice

This multi-case study provides recommendations for educational leadership preparation programs as well as the principal recruitment hiring. The review of existing literature exposed a lack of preparation for principals as leaders of special education (DeMatthews et al., 2020; Frost & Kersten, 2011; Melloy et al., 2021) and indicated that formal preparation in special education did not necessarily yield success (Schulze & Boscardin, 2018). Although the principals in this study did not have formal backgrounds in special education, their schools were successful inclusive elementary schools. Given that these principals utilized a combination of leadership styles to motivate and inspire their school community, we recommend that principal preparation programs focus efforts on developing principals who can apply and blend these styles effectively. It was the combination of leadership styles that yielded success at these two campuses.

Previous research has shown that principals' core beliefs impact developing an inclusive school culture (Billingsley, et al., 2017). The principals in this study had clearly defined core beliefs that focused on creating welcoming environments for all students, families, and staff. Each principals' beliefs set the vision for the school and defined actions for educators in their schools. They had courage and tenacity to act upon their core beliefs. We recommend that school district leaders take care to recruit and hire principals who hold firm beliefs grounded in inclusive practices with the courage to hold others accountable to the same commitment. Hiring principals with a vision and heart for supporting each learner may grow the number of successful inclusive schools across the nation.

Final Thought

Each student deserves an educational champion within the school setting pushing for their individual growth and development. As inclusive practices within schools become the norm, it will take talented and dedicated leaders to ensure that students with disabilities are receiving adequate support within general education classrooms. One quote from an anonymous survey respondent embodied the attitude necessary to lead a successful inclusive school: "Inclusion does not happen by accident. It is a purposeful, daily dedication, and it must be demonstrated child by child at every moment to work successfully within a school environment."

REFERENCES

Bass, B. M. (1985). *Leadership and performance beyond expectations*. Free Press.

Bays, D. A., & Crockett, J. B. (2007). Investigating instructional leadership for special education. *Exceptionality, 15*(3), 143–161. https://doi.org/10.1080/09362830701503495

Billingsley, B., McLeskey, J., & Crockett, J. B. (2017). *Principal leadership: Moving toward inclusive and high-achieving schools for students with disabilities* (Document No. IC-8). Collaboration for Effective Educator Development, Accountability, and Reform Center. http://ceedar.education.ufl.edu/tools/innovation-configurations/

Blankstein, A. M. (2017). Courageous and uplifting leadership. *The Education Digest, 83*, 38–42.

Bui, X., Quirk, C., Almazan, S. and Valenti, M. (2010). *Inclusion works!* Maryland Coalition for Inclusive Education. https://www.mcie.org/_files/ugd/34e35e_0f6d9a16276648a2b68181b800d9e3e2.pdf

Cobb, C. (2015). Principals play many parts: A review of the research on school principals as special education leaders 2001–2011, *International Journal of Inclusive Education, 19*(3), 213–234, https://doi.org/10.1080/13603116.2014.916354

Council of Chief State School Officers. (2020). *Supporting inclusive schools for the success of each child*. https://ccssoinclusiveprincipalsguide.org/

Day, C., Gu, Q., & Sammons, P. (2016). The impact of leadership on student outcomes: How successful school leaders use transformational and instructional strategies to make a difference. *Education Administration Quarterly, 52*(2) 221–258. https://doi.org/10.1177/0013161X15616863

DeMatthews, D. E., Kotok, S., & Serafini, A. (2020). Leadership preparation for special education and inclusive schools: Beliefs and recommendations from successful principals. *Journal of Research on Leadership Education*, 15(4), 1–27. https://doi.org/10.1177/1942775119838308

Eckes, S. E., & Swando, J. (2009). Special education subgroups under NCLB: Issues to consider. *Teachers College Record*, 111, 2479–2504.

Every Student Succeeds Act, 20 USC § 6301. (2015). https://www.congress.gov/bill/114th-congress/senate-bill/1177

Frost, L. A., & Kersten, T. (2011). The role of the elementary principal in the instructional leadership of special education. *International Journal of Educational Leadership Preparation*, 6(2), 1–21.

Goddard, Y. L., Neumerski, C. M., Goddard, R. D., Salloum, S. J., & Berebitsky, D. (2010). A multilevel exploratory study of the relationship between teachers' perceptions of principals' instructional support and group norms for instruction in elementary schools. *The Elementary School Journal*, 111(2), 336–357.

Hang, Q., & Rabren, K. (2009). An examination of co-teaching: Perspectives and efficacy indicators. *Remedial and Special Education* 30(5), 259–268. https://doi.org/10.1177/0741932508321018

Hoppey, D., & McLeskey, J. (2013). A case study of principal leadership in an effective inclusive school. *The Journal of Special Education* 46(4), 245–256. https://doi.org/10.1177/0022466910390507

Individuals with Disabilities Education Act of 2004, 20 USC § 1400 *et seq.* (2004).

Kirby, M. (2017). Implicit assumptions in special education policy: Promoting full inclusion for students with learning disabilities. *Child Youth Care Forum*, 46, 175–191. https://doi.org/10.1007/s10566-016-9382-x

Kowalski, T. J. (2008). *The school principal: Visionary leadership and competent management*. Routledge.

Kurşunoğlu, A., & Tanrıöğen, A. (2009). The relationship between teachers' perceptions towards instructional leadership behaviors of their principals and teachers' attitudes towards change. *Procedia Social and Behavioral Sciences*, 1, 252–258.

Leithwood, K., & Jantzi, D. (2005). A Review of Transformational School Leadership Research 1996–2005. *Leadership and Policy in Schools*, 4(3), 177–199. https://doi.org/10.1080/15700760500244769

Leithwood, K., Louis, K., Anderson, S., & Wahlstrom, K. (2004). *How leadership influences student learning*. https://www.wallacefoundation.org/knowledge-center/documents/how-leadership-influences-student-learning.pdf

Leithwood, K., & Riehl, C. (2005). *What we know about successful school leadership*. American Educational Research Association. http://olms.cte.jhu.edu/olms2/data/ck/file/What_we_know_about_SchoolLeadership.pdf

Lynch, J. M. (2016). Effective Instruction for Students with Disabilities: Perceptions of Rural Middle School Principals. *Rural Special Education Quarterly*, 35(4), 18–28. https://doi.org/10.1177/875687051603500404

McFarland, J., Hussar, B., de Brey, C., Snyder, T., Wang, X., Wilkinson-Flicker, S., Gebrekristos, S., Zhang, J., Rathbun, A., Barmer, A., Bullock Mann, F., & Hinz, S. (2017). *The Condition of Education 2017* (NCES 2017- 144). U.S. Department of Education. National Center for Education Statistics. https://nces.ed.gov/pubsearch/pubsinfo.asp?pubid=2017144

McHatton, P. A., Boyer, N. R., Shaunessy, E., Terry, P. M., & Farmer, J. L. (2010). Principals' perceptions of preparation and practice in gifted and special education content: Are we doing enough? *Journal of Research on Leadership Education*, 5(1), 1–22. https://doi.org/10.1177/194277511000500101

McLeskey, J., & Waldron, N. L. (2015). Effective leadership makes schools truly inclusive. *Phi Delta Kappan*, 96(5), 68–73. https://doi.org/10.1177/0031721715569474

McLeskey, J., Waldron, N. L., & Redd, L. (2014). A case study of a highly effective inclusive elementary school. *The Journal of Special Education*, 48(1), 59–70. https://doi.org/10.1177/0022466912440455

Melloy, K. J., Cieminski, A. B., & Sundeen, T. (2021). Accepting educational responsibility: Preparing administrators to lead inclusive schools. *Journal of Research in Leadership Education*.

No Child Left Behind Act. (2001). Pub. L. No. 107-110.

Patton, M. Q. (1999). Enhancing the quality and credibility of qualitative analysis. *Health Services Research*, 34(5 Pt 2), 1189–1208.

Printy, S. M., & Williams, S. M. (2015). Principals' decisions: Implementing response to intervention. *Educational Policy*, 29(1), 179–201. https://doi.org/10.1177/0895904814556757

Saldaña, J. (2013). *The coding manual for qualitative researchers.* SAGE Publications.

Salisbury, C. (2006). Principals' perspectives on inclusive elementary schools. *Research and Practice for Persons with Severe Disabilities*, 31(1), 70–82. https://doi.org/10.2511/rpsd.31.1.70

Schulte, A. C., Stevens, J. J., Elliott, S. N., Tindal, G., & Nese, J. F. T. (2016). Achievement gaps for students with disabilities: Stable, widening, or narrowing on a state-wide reading comprehension test? *Journal of Educational Psychology*, 108(7), 925–942. https://doi.org/10.1037/edu0000107

Schulze, R., & Boscardin, M. L. (2018). Leadership perceptions of principals with and without special education backgrounds. *Journal of School Leadership*, 28(1), 4–30. https://doi.org/10.1177/105268461802800101

Shaked, H., & Schechter, C. (2019). Exploring systems thinking in school principals' decision-making. *International Journal of Leadership in Education*, 22(5), 573–596. https://doi.org/10.1080/13603124.2018.1481533

Thurlow, M. L., Quenemoen, R. F., & Lazarus, S. S. (2011). *Meeting the needs of special education students: Recommendations for the Race to the Top consortia and states.* National Center on Educational Outcomes. https://nceo.umn.edu/docs/OnlinePubs/Martha_Thurlow-Meeting_the_Needs_of_Special_Education_students.pdf

Wahlstrom, K., & Louis, K. S. (2008). How teachers experience principal leadership: The roles of professional community, trust, efficacy, and shared responsibility. *Educational Administration Quarterly*, 44(4) 458–495. https://doi.org/10.1177/0013161X08321502

Waters, T., Marzano, R. J., & McNulty, B. (2003). *Balanced leadership: What 30 years of research tells us about the effect of leadership on student achievement* (Working Paper). https://www.mcrel.org/wp-content/uploads/2016/06/Balanced-Leadership%C2%AE-What-30-Years-of-Research-Tells-Us-about-the-Effect-of-Leadership-on-Student-Achievement.pdf

CHAPTER 4

INCLUSIVE TEACHER EDUCATOR LEADERSHIP

Situating Reflective Practice Within Theory, Partnerships, and Equity in an Undergraduate Dual Licensure Educational Preparation Program

William Hunter
The University of Memphis

Wesam Salem
The University of Memphis

Keishana Barnes
The University of Memphis

Logan Caldwell
The University of Memphis

Jennifer Bubrig
The University of Memphis

Educator Preparation Programs (EPP) have a history of preparing teachers for realities of the 21st century classrooms while providing strategies to improve academic and behavioral outcomes of diverse students. However, EPPs grounded in traditional models have garnered reputations for "doing a mediocre job of preparing teachers for the realities of the 21st century classroom" (Duncan, 2010, p.13). Traditionally coursework is taught by tenure-track faculty members, usually grounded in theory and research. Practicum components are taught by clinical faculty or supervisors. Traditional frameworks seldom bridge research and practice; thus, they are often described as "disjointed, fragmented and confusing methods courses...disconnected from curriculum courses...and both [being] disconnected from the practice of teaching" (Bullough & Gitlin, 2001, p. 1). Often, these models are fragmented, haphazard experiences due to gaps between theory, coursework, and practice. Moreover, many EPPs maintain separate concentrations for general education and special education, even when programs intentionally focus on diversity and equity (Robinson, 2017, p. 165). Traditional programs deviate from inclusive pedagogy models (McIntyre, 2009), where schools and universities provide integrated and diverse learning experiences. This model brings theory into practice, setting high expectations for inclusive teaching with rich learning communities for all learners (Florian & Black-Hawkins, 2011). Within the inclusive pedagogy model, P–12 teachers and university professors have different and equally valued roles and responsibilities. They commit to consensual academic language and discourse, bridging the gap between school and university. The inclusive pedagogy model creates a forum where student teachers recognize their capacity to teach students from diverse backgrounds (Florian & Linklater, 2010). Teachers receive equitable training in general education and special education intertwined within their clinical work.

Although traditional teacher preparation coursework remains impactful, colleges are recognizing the crucial role of high impact and research-evident clinical experiences in producing highly effective teachers. In fact, in-service teachers credit student teaching and clinical experiences with the greatest impact on their teaching practice (Borko & Mayfield, 1995; Cochran-Smith & Zeichner, 2005). Some research suggests the most effective teacher preparation includes high-quality, relevant curriculum, high-impact student teaching/clinical placement, and a program improvement culture and process with ongoing district and university partner dialog (Yendol-Hoppey & Hoppey, 2018). Hence, it is incumbent on P–12 districts and EPPs to form authentic partnerships addressing divides between theory and practice in development of preservice teachers (PSTs) while meeting the changing realities of diverse classrooms (Zeichner, 2010). Such purposeful EPP structure and P–12 partnerships have been the impetus for dual licensure programs in colleges of education (Leko et al., 2015). Clinical experiences purposefully connect theory to practice (Yendol-Hoppey & Hoppey, 2018), and P–12 school leaders select high-quality mentor teachers (Mark & Nolan, 2018) who collaborate with clinical supervisors to cultivate hands-on, supportive environments for PSTs.

Dual Licensure

Dual Licensure programs create a forum for co-planning/co-teaching as major themes (Blanton & Pugach, 2011), and for expanding P–12 partnerships. There are emergent teacher-based practices in general and special education preservice programs (Leko et al., 2015) clinical experience practices are connected to preservice courses through High Leverage Practices (HLPs) created by the Council for Exceptional Children (CEC) and Collaboration for Effective Educator Development Accountability and Reform (CEEDAR). HLPs are designed to improve student learning across content areas, grade levels, and abilities. HLPs can teach evidence-based practices within a Multi-Tiered Systems of Support (McLeskey et al., 2017). Dual License programs create the forum for HLP's within clinical practice components, providing opportunities for PSTs to use evidence-based practices.

Clinical Practice

The variance of opinions on clinical application of methodologies concerns EPPs. In traditional EPPs, there is often a disconnection from methodologies and the teaching practice (Bullough & Gitlin, 2001). Methods courses should be taught in conjunction with rich clinical experiences with connected theories and practices. While learning theories and methodologies, PSTs have opportunities to observe, practice, and reflect on applications. Candidates are able to develop their pedagogical knowledge alongside their content knowledge in a reflective context (Bullough & Gitlin, 2001).

Bridging theory and practice requires deliberate and explicit connections between theory and P–12 classrooms. PSTs must spend time in schools and develop strong relationships with school partners. Strong relationships, common knowledge, and shared beliefs are links to sustaining successful university/school partnerships (Darling-Hammond, 2006), including students, faculty, and school administration. Through this experience PSTs can understand historical, political, and social contexts of communities where they learn and work. These practices should emphasize pedagogical process and development.

In the practicum, a teacher candidate, a mentor teacher, and a clinical faculty member form a cooperative learning triad, cited as critical in beginning teacher development (Steadman & Brown, 2011). The clinical faculty is vital in bridging theory and practice and university-school divides (CAEP, 2013). The clinical faculty, the university representative, forms a partnership with the principal to support PSTs. Within the partnership, clinical faculty field supervisors emphasize the need for PSTs to engage in co-teaching structures supporting students with exceptionalities (Chesley et al., 2007).

THE ROLE OF INCLUSIVE LEADERSHIP WITHIN THE UNIVERSITY AND SCHOOL PARTNERSHIP

Direct collaboration among clinical supervisors, mentor teachers, and PSTs provides an opportunity for principals to promote inclusion, emphasizing the necessity of culturally responsive education, and breaking down barriers to student equity (Berry, Cowart Moss, & Gore, 2019). Stakeholder collaboration aids with developing shared leadership and practice, crucial characteristics of successful inclusive principals (Berry et al., 2019). It is essential for principals to practice inclusive leadership, cultivating cultures where each child and adult feels safe, supported, and valued.

Using HLP's (McLeskey et al., 2017), inclusive leaders can lead conversations to promote equity, facilitate collaboration between general and special educators, and focus on social/emotional behavior, thereby embedding constructs within clinical experiences. As mentor teachers, PSTs, and clinical faculty engage in reflective practices, inclusive school leaders can facilitate this process from a school community perspective (Berry et al., 2019). Therefore, inclusive leaders maintain attention and focus on social justice to solve real-world problems and empower students.

Theoretical Framework/Purpose

Using change theory (Fullan, 2006) and partnerships (AACTE, 2018) as conceptual frameworks, this chapter highlights how our College of Education (COE) adopted the dual licensure model alongside a P–12 school-university partnership to enhance clinical experiences. We argue this model has potential for meaningful clinical experiences, yielding highly effective and well-prepared teachers. This model positively impacts both preservice and in-service teachers and, most importantly, P–12 student growth and achievement.

Using narrative inquiry (Chase, 2011), we illuminate voices of leaders and highlight author experiences as clinical supervisors. Using journal entries, Professional Learning Community (PLC) meeting minutes, clinical faculty's reflective journals, and lesson plan documents, the authors share four vignettes to represent four emerging themes. This information can support the work of inclusive school leaders in cultivating community partnerships.

CLINICAL SUPERVISOR REFLECTIONS

VIGNETTE 1: RECOGNIZING, RESPECTING, AND TAKING ROOT: CULTURALLY RELEVANT PEDAGOGY AND DIVERSE LEARNERS.

Ashlyn is an excited college junior in an educator preparation program. Her courses have focused on equity-based practices and pedagogies. In many ways, she fits the "typical" future teacher. She is female, white, and "ready to make a difference." This semester's clinical experience will be her first opportunity in a school as a prospective teacher. Her placement is a large elementary school serving students zoned to the school, as well as students accepted to a separate program within the school. This special program does not have unique requirements for admission. Ashlyn's Mentor Teacher is Mrs. Baril, an African American, highly qualified teacher, reaching a level 5 on the state's Level of Overall Effectiveness (LOE) Scale. Her pedagogy and student achievement earned the highest possible scores. Mrs. Baril is an attentive Mentor Teacher, taking immense pride in her roles. She is particularly proud of her attention to student data, often referencing her data wall when Ashlyn's Clinical Supervisor visits. Mrs. Baril often reminds Ashlyn ,"data is what the principal wants when it comes to teachers' evaluations." One day, Ashlyn informs her Clinical Supervisor she will need to change her upcoming observation, because she would be teaching the "zoned kids," leaning in to tell her Clinical Supervisor, " you know how they are..." Ashlyn stated matter-of-factly that the zoned students likely could not complete the planned lesson, therefore her "data" would not look good. Mrs. Baril told Ashlyn this while explaining the importance of showing students' academic growth toward the grade level standards. Not wanting to look "bad," Ashlyn relayed her understanding from her Mentor Teacher that data reflect her skill as a teacher. Ashlyn's Clinical Supervisor was concerned this mindset was being passed on to Ashlyn, and the students themselves.

While school leaders consistently report desire and intention to establish and maintain a culture where all students have equitable opportunities, actual school cultures frequently promote the opposite (Nadelson et al., 2020). When principals allow anticipating or permitting lower performance from any group of children, they create an inequitable school (Shields, 2004). Whether in schools with tracking, schools with magnet programs, or schools with certain classes for students with and without IEPs, systemically excluding subgroups of students from educational opportunities can eventually become a self-fulfilling prophecy. Students in excluded groups inevitably *do* perform and respond differently. Emphasis on student performance is especially significant given the priority on academic data, a message that trickles down from district leaders, to principals, to in-service and preservice teachers. Data brings funding, influences teacher evaluations, and keeps some schools open while closing others (Ladd, 2012; Brummett, 2014; Lee & Lubienski, 2016). Consequently, teachers might be tempted to focus on students who are guaranteed to produce good numbers.

To counter this, principals must examine themselves. Theoharis and Haddix (2011) found white, urban principals' commitment to "create more equitable and excellent schools, in particular for students from marginalized communities" (p. 1333), should begin with examining "…emotional and intellectual undertakings about their own racial identities and histories, their privilege, and the presence of institutional racism" (p. 1347). Principals must examine their specific school cultures to unpack quantitative and qualitative data to better understand how systems of exclusion may be present.

After multiple classroom observations and discussions with other Mentor Teachers, Ashlyn's Clinical Supervisor discovered this binary interpretation of "zoned school students" vs. "special program students" was indeed persistent in many classrooms. There was common acceptance that students in the special program were brighter and worked harder than students who were simply attending their zoned school. Though much of Ashlyn's coursework was equity-minded, the influence of her Mentor Teacher and clinical school had a clear impact on her attitude and actions. The principal could have created different conditions by committing to "monitoring teacher-student interactions for fairness and cultural sensitivity" (Athanasesa & Martin, 2006, p. 628).

Mrs. Baril specifically made sure Ashlyn understood the value of Data Walls. Using data within Culturally Relevant Pedagogy could equip principals to actively promote cultures where all students are seen and known as valued members of the school community. Principals should work to cultivate what Nadelson, et. al (2020) call an "education equity mindset," allowing "the embrace of a philosophy that motivates engagement in actions that increase opportunities for all students to achieve to their highest capacity" (p. 1). When working in schools with persistent cultures of exclusion, principals should "embrace and support transformative learning and work toward changing perceptions of fixed abilities and expectations to a mindset of inclusiveness, reflection, and achievement" (p. 4). Specifically, principals may consider the following steps as outlined by Galloway and Ishimaru (2020) :

1. framing disparities and action through organizational routines for professional learning (p. 114)

2. shifting power and constructing leadership as collective activity (p. 117)
3. ongoing inquiry on equity-focused improvement (p. 119)

School leaders should then ask themselves: How do *I* know? How will *my teachers* know? How can/should my teachers' 'Data Walls' help communicate this?

Endim (2016) reminds us, "without teachers [and school leaders] recognizing the biases they hold and how these biases impact the ways they see and teach students, there is no starting point to changing the dismal statistics related to the academic underperformance of urban youth" (p. 43). Principals must do this challenging work by interrogating themselves and their teachers' attitudes toward student achievement for each student.

VIGNETTE 2: EXPOSURE TO CONTENT AND BEST PRACTICES IN ELEMENTARY SCIENCE EDUCATION

During a reflection on personal experiences with science, five of seven field-based preservice teachers associated science from their elementary schooling as reading books or completing worksheets if they remembered any science learning at all. Specifically, Dana said, "I don't remember any actual science, like dedicated time. It's not until I went to middle school when it was like a whole class period." Unfortunately, in my experience as a site coordinator and science methods instructor, this lack of exposure creates anxiety for pre-service candidates, causing them to self-identify as "bad at science" or, as Dana said, "Me and science aren't friends." Tawana, who remembered no science instruction until middle grades, stated, "I was nervous about [teaching my lesson] as science is not my strong suit. I don't remember learning about landforms. I was nervous about it and, to be honest, I learned quite a bit while I was creating my lesson. It made me realize I'm going to be learning along with my students." Similarly, Julia's elementary school had a science lab and dedicated science teacher who, "did a ton of experiments, but they didn't necessarily connect. Other than that, it was just worksheets, honestly." She reported, "Science is probably my weakest subject, so I did have to prepare a little more for [my science lesson]." She practiced her science lesson at home prior to teaching it. She did not do this for any other content areas. The two teacher candidates in this small group who expressed confidence in teaching science and self-identified as "a science person," are also the only ones who reported specific hands-on experiences in elementary school as early as 3rd and 4th grade.

When discussing science experiences in their elementary clinical placements, most reported little to none occurred during their once-a-week visits. Julia saw science modeling, "Not very much. The way her schedule is supposed to go is she teaches math for part of the day and then science. We got to science three [out of 11] days I observed. My mentor's math lessons just always ran over, so they would just not do science.." She didn't see any evidence of the class getting to science other than what she observed. Only one mentor teacher specifically addressed why science was rarely observed, "My mentor said, with science, unfortunately, if there's not enough time, it isn't focused on. If we must omit something, we will just take science." Britni stated "Every time I've seen her, she does language arts and math for the majority of the day. She will do a science lesson at the end, but you can tell it's not like the time she devotes to language arts or math. It just doesn't seem as well-planned, and her energy level is low."

This was another commonality, as all preservice teachers who saw some science in their mentor's classroom reported it occurred at the end of the day or the end of the class period. The preservice teachers began to connect that not only is the likelihood of running out of time greater, but the students' (and teacher's) energy levels are lower, and it could send a message that science is not as important.

Britni and Jessica noted their mentor teachers expressed gratitude for them teaching science. "My mentor teacher was happy because she did not have to plan for it." Jessica's teacher mentioned that it was valuable for her to see someone else teach science. Both preservice teachers perceived their science lesson increased student motivation. Jessica said, "[My students] were so excited." Britni, who did not observe science, reflected, "I think that was a plus [for me] doing a science lesson. [The students] seemed to really enjoy it." With the limited exposure in science in her elementary schooling, she recognized the motivation science can create in a classroom environment when time is dedicated.

Disconnects between previous science education experience, coursework, and P–12 field experiences exist, in addition to lack of access to real-world science experiences that promote inclusion. Using the tenets of inclusive leadership, P–12 partners and universities have an opportunity to elevate pre-service teacher preparation, break down barriers to equitable access to science, and design opportunities to empower students. Collaborative partnerships can begin to bridge those teaching science self-efficacy (TSSE) gaps:

> ...principals reported that the [school-university] partnerships were a catalyst for science content growth for both their students and teachers. This growth stemmed from the collaboration within and across partner groups: the two-way communication needed for developing and maintaining trust, acknowledgment of the risks, and in achieving reciprocity where each partner

was willing to contribute to meeting the needs of the other." (Gilbert et al., 2018, p. 79)

Principals must focus and advocate for more classroom time dedicated to culturally responsive science learning. They must provide professional development in teaching science to increase self-efficacy for in-service teachers. The university should simultaneously train preservice teachers on best practices for collaborating with mentors in inclusive co-teaching models.

Only 38% of fourth-graders, 34% of eighth graders, and 22% of twelfth graders earned proficient or advanced on the 2015 National Assessment of Educational Progress (NAEP) Science test (National Center for Education Statistics, 2015). This data indicates most U.S. students are not proficient in science. Inclusive leaders can collaboratively and purposefully address this data by enhancing P–12 science experiences and reinforcing scientific teaching while applying effective, culturally responsive science learning practices.

National reports continue to indicate teachers' self-efficacy is lowest in science. Self-efficacy is defined as one's perceptions of their capabilities to perform in specific instances (Bandura, 1977). TSSE is defined as a teacher's belief that they have the capability to effectively teach science and affect student performance (Enochs & Riggs, 1990). Eighty-one percent of elementary school teachers report feeling prepared to teach language arts, yet only 39% report this in science (Trygstad, 2013). Low teacher self-efficacy is associated with low student achievement. Incoming teachers' self-efficacy is lowest in science, resulting in less time dedicated to science in the classroom (Bergman & Morphew, 2015), as evidenced in the preservice teachers' discussion above. Research suggests "[t]here is a logical connection between teachers' attitudes toward a subject and student outcome, both in terms of impacting students' opportunities to learn science and their own developing attitudes" (Riegle-Crumb et al., 2015, p. 823). Many factors play a role in the low TSSE ratings, including inadequate content training, resulting in weak scientific background knowledge (Enoch & Riggs, 1990; Knaggs & Sondergeld, 2015; Menon & Sadler, 2018; Rice & Roychoudhury, 2003; Trundle et al., 2007), deficient science experiences as a student (Avery & Meyer, 2012; Bautista, 2011; Kazempour & Sadler, 2015; Rockinson-Szapkiw & Caldwell, 2019); and inadequate modeling of effective instructional strategies in science methods courses (Bautista, 2011; Menon & Sadler, 2018; Rice & Roychuldhury, 2003). Furthermore, research shows a child's encounters in elementary school science are clear indicators of both interest and assurance of future ability to teach science. In other words, if a teacher was inadequately taught science as a child, the teacher tends to teach science inadequately (Hattie, 2012; Jarrett, 1999; Riegle-Crumb et al., 2015).

A good elementary school experience, starting with a good school leader, appears to be especially important in fostering inclusivity and later interest in science and in providing models for teaching that enhance prospective teachers' self-confidence (Riegle-Crumb et al., 2015; Rockinson-Szapkiw & Caldwell, 2019). Inclusive leaders are situated to address this cycle of ineffective science teaching by maintaining the focus of social justice, modeling effective science teaching strategies, providing meaningful, real-world opportunities for preservice and in-service teachers, and tackling low incoming teachers' science self-efficacy.

> **VIGNETTE 3: PARTNERSHIPS AT HEART OF TRANSFORMED MODEL**
>
> Quote from partner school Principal:
>
> > "The relationship cultivated in my partnership with the University of Memphis has afforded me the opportunity to see the inner workings of an awesome program that truly invests in the success of educators. Together, we have fostered a relationship that includes open dialogue about practical needs to support students in their transition to the K–12 teaching environment. Our partnership is one of support and authenticity. We rely on each other to build and support teachers, so they are ready for teaching."
>
> Our school partners and coaches play an integral part in preparing future teachers. The vignette below describes our transformation and how it became apparent inclusive leadership was paramount in teacher preparation. Our school partners' inclusive leadership paved the way for cultivating authentic partnerships resulting in each child having a highly prepared teacher.
>
> I still recall the transformation our program embarked on in 2015 to ensure a more practiced-based approach to teacher education during our pre-residency (Junior year) of program study. Like many other EPP transformations/redesigns, our efforts focused on growing and sustaining relationships with our local school district. When I reflect on the many benefits of the transformation over the last six years, the part in the word Partnership stands out to me. To truly embark on transformative work in teacher education, parts (roles) are redefined for faculty and school partners.
>
> At the time of our transformation, we already had an existing dual licensure program and first focused work on resequencing courses to have a mix of both general and special education method courses in our junior year program of study. Our program also housed a yearlong senior experience for our residency teacher candidates. For our teacher candidates to be engaged in a yearlong residency experience, we needed to move elementary and special education method courses to the junior year. Then, we structured

course offerings in a block schedule to allow for a bell-to-bell experience.

Observations of practice were no longer short bursts occurring for only one to two hours. Our candidates reported to their schools for the first bell, and they spent the entire day immersed in observation of practice and co-teaching with mentor teachers until the final bell of the day. Having a full day of clinical observation revealed the importance of partnership for obvious reasons, necessitating a powerful learning triad involving teacher candidates, mentor teachers, and clinical faculty members. Clinical faculty were assigned school cohorts and committed to weekly site visits. As junior teacher candidates were assigned to a partner school, they began to understand their role in co-teaching, practicing, and supporting students in their assigned classroom and also in establishing their identity within the school culture.

The transformation created a need for all junior methods course faculty to meet monthly for professional learning community (PLC) team meetings to collaborate on clinical course assignments and receive updates and data from clinical faculty. The PLC partnership completed the learning triad and extended the continuum of the clinical teaching and learning experience to junior faculty. The relationships formed during the PLC time between my colleagues and myself continues to sustain our passion for education. About two years into the transformation, the partnerships clearly became the beating heart of the work.

To create learning triads and cultivate authentic partnerships, school administrators had to pave the way for the work to begin. This work went far beyond selecting mentor teachers who embraced the opportunity to lead and model best practices. The heart of the work was the authentic relationships between partner school administrators, who lead with inclusivity, and identified mentor teachers to work in unison with clinical faculty. The relationships were grounded in mutual respect and understanding of our profession. Clinical faculty and school administrators bonded by ensuring each child has a highly prepared teacher.

School administrators knew the impact would be much greater if mentor teachers embraced the aspects and benefits of the partnership, understanding how having a junior teacher candidate could affect overall student achievement. With time and intentionality, clinical faculty were a constant presence in the partner schools observing and supporting candidates in classrooms. Mentor teachers could immediately see the benefits of having clinical faculty coach candidates and define best practices in action. They trusted clinical faculty to be engaged in the learning in their classrooms, even welcoming co-teaching with them. Candidates would feel an unspoken sense of belonging when they entered their partner schools. As faculty, we realized how powerful the connection to theory and practice could be for pre-service candidates at a critical time in their pedagogical development. Not only did we hear the immediate feedback from candidates, but clinical faculty could see those connections each week in their candidates' practice.

Traditional university teacher preparation models have received national attention for "doing a mediocre job of preparing teachers for the realities of the 21st-century classroom" (Duncan, 2010, p.13). America's traditional programs need revolutionary change because of educational challenges in our country (Duncan, 2010). The vignette presented above highlights critical components of our EPP's transformation journey and how inclusive leadership by our partners truly impacted both in-service and preservice teachers. The school leaders promoted inclusion and equity by articulating the common language of practice and foregrounding inclusive pedagogies (McLeskey et al., 2017). Using Darling-Hammond's framework (2006), I highlighted three critical components we implemented to create a more effective program: cohesiveness and alignment in course and clinical work, closely supervised clinical work grounded in theory to practice, and building authentic university-school partnerships that serve diverse learners.

While our transformation will always be a work in progress, there is no doubt about positive gains for our program. This includes relationships with district partners and university faculty, methods courses that ensure cohesiveness and alignment to practice, and candidate opportunities to practice skills, knowledge, and dispositions during their pedagogical development. When teacher education partnerships are redefined and transformed, the impact inevitably leads to highly prepared teachers ready to meet the needs of all students.

VIGNETTE 4: EQUITY, ACCESS, AND OPPORTUNITY IN MATHEMATICS EDUCATION

"The school follows a scripted curriculum.," shared Rachel, one of my preservice teachers (PSTs) as she pondered her dilemma. Rachel is a white female junior. On a Math Autobiography assignment at the beginning of the semester, she indicated she was never a "math person" and "hated math." Nonetheless, when the semester unfolded, she occasionally mentioned seeing the relevance of mathematics representations and conceptual understanding. Rachel was one of the PSTs who experienced a shift in their own positionality as math learners and doers. Hence, she created her clinical lesson plan to provide her third-grade students with access to "rich and meaningful mathematics,."

Drawing from five equity-based practices (Aguirre et al., 2013) we discussed in class, her lesson focused on Practice 1: Going Deep with Mathematics. She employed the 3-Act Math practice, opening with a short high-interest video to provide the context, followed by students working on multiple-entry tasks, and ending with student discussion and thinking. The lesson focused on teaching multiplication conceptually, using contextual problems and mathematical representations. When her mentor teacher reviewed the lesson, she indicated that they followed the Eureka textbooks script, completing two lessons in one session. Rachel's plan required a whole session, leaving no time to complete scripted problems. "What's the point of learning all these high leverage practices when we will be unable to use them?," I pondered. "How can we navigate the bureaucratic system to find openings for teaching mathematics conceptually as opposed to procedurally?" "What is the role of the school's principal in supporting these efforts?"

I realized that there is more to provide PSTs in my methods course beyond the walls of our class. While I oriented the course pedagogy to center conceptual learning and equitable teaching practices, some public schools use traditional procedural approaches to teaching mathematics. Not only did the scripted curriculum disrupt progress towards providing students with access to rich and meaningful mathematics, but it also demotivated the PSTs and forced them away from using creative, research-based practices. Apparently, my methods course embodied practices not privileged or celebrated in some public schools. As I grappled with finding ways to help PSTs, I considered the idea of "creative insubordination" (Gutiérrez, 2016) where teachers become advocates for their students' success. Can methods courses teach PSTs creative insubordination or political knowledge to make them agents of change?

With growing diversity in U.S. schools, concerns for inequitable practices brought attention to social justice projects and examinations of students' identities in mathematics. Research suggests strong interconnectedness between issues of equity, power, sociopolitical context, culture, and development of mathematics identities (Ladson-Billings, 1997; Martin, 2000; Nasir, 2012). Cobb & Hodge (2010) posit that the "concept of equity encompasses a complex range of concerns that emerge when people who are members of various local communities and broader groups within society act and interact in the mathematics classroom" (p. 180). These concerns include access to mathematics learning opportunities; societal function of schooling; and students' development of robust mathematics identities. Therefore, equity and mathematics identity development inform each other and cannot be separated.

Similarly, educator preparation programs (EPPs) are increasingly preparing preservice teachers (PSTs) to teach mathematics with equity and social justice. The current political and social climate demands highlighting inequities and injustices in society, particularly regarding opportunities, access, and outcomes based on race, gender, culture, and language. EPPs must support PSTs to cultivate instructional practices with equity and social justice, empowering students and informing positive mathematics learning and identity development. Sustaining and supporting these practices in schools is equally important. New teachers' support entails amplifying culturally relevant practices and pedagogical knowledge to sustain and develop teaching capacity.

As instructional leaders who profoundly impact instruction and student learning (Branch et al., 2013), principals are key in supporting new teachers, promoting practices of equity and social justice, and catalyzing "teacher focus on affording students with opportunities to make connections, think analytically, [&] solve problems" (Nelson et al., 2020, p. 2). Hence, inclusive, and social justice school leadership gained considerable attention in research on principal's practices creating and sustaining the work in schools and communities (DeMatthews, 2016). With stark differences in academic successes between historically marginalized student populations and their counterparts, school leadership and EPPs must align reforming efforts to ensure development and sustainability of equity (Gay, 2002).

Principals face numerous challenges from increased emphasis on high-stakes testing and standards-focused instruction. Coupled with perceptions that many new teachers are unprepared by inadequate EPPs (Darling-Hammond, 2010), adopting scripted or narrowed curriculum appears a natural consequence of "helping" teachers teach" (Milner, 2013). Scripted or narrowed curriculum overshadows students' meaning-making and eliminates opportunities to engage with the content. Most importantly, scripted curriculum dismisses sociopolitical context that informs and shapes learning identities and positionalities. Hence, students' culture, race, religion, ethnicities, language, and gender are collapsed and deemed irrelevant to teaching. High stakes education and packaged reforms stifle teachers' advocacy, teaching with equity and promoting social justice. These challenges become even more profound in urban school settings with underserved and historically marginalized students. When learning occurs in narrow and formalized "figured worlds" (Holland et al., 1998), students' agency is limited, leading them to reject mathematics or "*disidentify*" with school (Nasir, 2012, p. 13, emphasis in original).

Nonetheless, students' ability to succeed in mathematics is not enough for the development of positive mathematics identities. Positive mathematics identities come from engagement and participation in authentic mathematics events where students see themselves as mathematical learners and doers (Nasir, 2012). As such, school principals should support theories and the necessary pedagogy to teach mathematics conceptually. Scripted curriculum emphasizes procedural and unattainable mathematical learning versus conceptual learning enabling students to make connections and make sense of the world around them.

EMERGING THEMES

Clinical field supervisors and principals should promote tenets of inclusive leadership, which include promoting inclusion, heightening collaboration, and focusing on student equity in and out of classrooms. Inclusive leaders can help eliminate deficit thinking and embrace cultural competence. Cultural competence involves encouraging students to learn about themselves and the world around them, and become community contributors (Milner, 2010). Deficit thinking means educators hold negative, stereotypical, and counterproductive views about pupils from diverse cultural and linguistic backgrounds (Ford & Grantham, 2003). Culturally relevant educators appreciate a community of learners and social interaction, which has a positive impact on academics and behavior (Ladson-Billings, 1992). Culturally relevant pedagogy involves awareness of broader social, economic, and political contexts in education, linking principles of learning with deep understanding of individual pupils' cultures (Ladson-Billings, 2014). Best practices can be highlighted within content areas, and inclusive leaders can create pathways to enhance teacher self-efficacy through collaboration and professional development.

CONCLUSION

The four vignettes can inform the principals' practices to enhance their capacities as inclusive leaders. The literature review illustrates the importance of building partnerships between higher education and P–12 partners to enhance teaching and learning for preservice teachers and P–12 student achievement. There is increasing attention on building partnerships, especially with the dual licensure focus. With increasing pressure to produce highly effective teachers, preparation programs should build collaborations with P–12 partners to meet the diverse needs of teacher candidates and P–12 students. Creating space for collaboration and communication with principals is essential in supporting their efforts to be inclusive leaders.

REFERENCES

Aguirre, J., Mayfield-Ingram, K., & Martin, D. (2013). *The impact of identity in K–8 mathematics: Rethinking equity-based practices*. The National Council of Teachers of Mathematics.

American Association of Colleges for Teacher Education (AACTE). (2018). A pivot toward clinical practice, its lexicon, and the renewal of educator preparation. *A report of the AACTE Clinical Practice Commission.*

Athanasesa, S., & Martin, K. (2006). Learning to advocate for educational equity in a teacher credential program. *Teaching and Teacher Education, 22,* 627–646. https://doi.org/10.1016/j.tate.2006.03.008

Avery, L. M., & Meyer, D. Z. (2012). Teaching science as science is practiced: Opportunities and limits for enhancing preservice elementary teachers' self-efficacy for science and science teaching. *School Science and Mathematics, 112*(7), 395–409.

Bandura, A. (1977). Self-efficacy. Toward a unifying theory of behavioral change. *Psychological Review, 84*(2), 191–215.

Bautista, N. U. (2011). Investigating the use of vicarious and mastery experiences in influencing early childhood education majors' self-efficacy beliefs. *Journal of Science Teacher Education, 22*(4), 333–349.

Bergman, D., & Morphew, J. (2015). Effects of a science content course on elementary preservice teachers' self-efficacy of teaching science. *Journal of College Science Teaching, 44*(3), 73–81.

Berry, J. R., Moss, S. C., & Gore, P. (2019). Leadership in high-needs/high performing schools. In E. Murakami, D. Gurr, & R. Notman (Eds.), *Educational leadership, culture, and success in high-need schools* (pp. 131–148). Information Age Publishing.

Borko, H., & Mayfield, V. (1995). The roles of the cooperating teacher and university supervisor in learning to teach. *Teaching and Teacher Education, 11*(5), 501–518.

Branch, G., Hanushek, E., & Rivkin, S. (2013). School leaders matter. *Education Next, 13*(1), 62–69. Retrieved from http://educationnext.org/school-leaders-matter

Brummet, Q. (2014). The effect of school closings on student achievement. *Journal of Public Economics, 119,* 108–124. https://doi.org/10.1016/j.jpubeco.2014.06.010

Bullough, R., & Gitlin, A. (2001). *Becoming a student: Linking knowledge production and practice of teaching.*

Chase, S. E. (2011). Narrative inquiry: Multiple lenses, approaches, voices. In N. K. Denzin & Y. S. Lincoln (Eds.), *The sage handbook of qualitative research* (4th ed., pp. 421–434). Sage Publications, Inc.

Chesley, G. M., & Jordan, J. (2012). What's missing from teacher prep. *Educational Leadership, 69*(8), 41–45.

Cochran-Smith, M., & Zeichner, K. (2005). *Studying teacher education: The report of the AERA panel on research and teacher education.* Lawrence Erlbaum.

Darling-Hammond, L. (2006). Constructing 21st-century teacher education. *Journal of Teacher Education, 57*(3), 300–314.

Darling-Hammond, L. (2010). Teacher education and the American future. *Journal of Teacher Education, 61*(1–2), 35–47.

DeMatthews, D. (2016). Social justice dilemmas: Evidence on the successes and shortcomings of three principals trying to make a difference. *International*

Journal of Leadership in Education, 1–15. https://doi.org/10.1080/13603124.2016.1206972

Duncan, A. (2010). Teacher preparation: Reforming the uncertain profession. *Education Digest,* 75(5), 13–22.

Enochs, L. G., & Riggs, I. M. (1990). Further development of an elementary science teaching belief instrument: A preservice elementary scale. *School Science and Mathematics,* 90(8), 694–706.

Florian, L., & Black-Hawkins, K. (2011), Exploring inclusive pedagogy. *British Educational Research Journal,* 37(5), 813–828. https://doi.org/10.1080/01411926.2010.501096

Florian, L., & Linklater, H. (2010). Preparing teachers for inclusive education: using inclusive pedagogy to enhance teaching and learning for all. *Cambridge Journal of Education,* 40(4), 369–386.

Ford, D. Y., & Grantham, T. C. (2003). Providing access for culturally diverse gifted students: From deficit to dynamic thinking. *Theory Into Practice,* 42(3), 217–225.

Fullan, M. (2006). The future of educational change: System thinkers in action. *Journal of Educational Change,* 7(3), 113–122.

Gay, G. (2002). Preparing for culturally responsive teaching. *Journal of Teacher Education,* 53(2), 106–116.

Gilbert, A., Hobbs, L., Kenny, J., Jones, M., Campbell, C., Chittleborough, G., & Redman, C. (2018). Principal perceptions regarding the impact of school-university partnerships in primary science contexts. *School–University Partnerships,* 11(2), 73–83.

Gutiérrez, R. (2016). Strategies for creative insubordination in mathematics teaching. *Special Issue Mathematics Education: Through the Lens of Social Justice.* 7(1), 52–60.

Hattie, J. (2012). *Visible learning for teachers. Maximizing impact on learning.* Routledge.

Jarrett, O. S. (1999). Science interest and confidence among preservice elementary teachers. *Journal of Elementary Science Education,* 11(1), 49—59.

Kazempour, M., & Sadler, T. D. (2015). Pre-service teachers' science beliefs, attitudes, and self-efficacy: A multi-case study. *Teaching Education,* 26(3), 247–271.

Knaggs, C. M., & Sondergeld, T. A. (2015). Science as a learner and as a teacher: Measuring science self-efficacy of elementary preservice teachers. *School Science and Mathematics,* 115(3), 117–128.

Ladd, H. (2012). Presidential address: Education and poverty: Confronting the evidence. *Journal of Policy Analysis and Management,* 31(2), 203–227.

Ladson-Billings, G. (1992). Culturally relevant teaching: The key to making multicultural education work. In C. A. Grant (Ed.), *Research and multicultural education: From the margins to the mainstream* (pp. 106–121). Routledge.

Ladson-Billings, G. (2014) Culturally Relevant Pedagogy 2.0: a.k.a. the Remix. *Harvard Educational Review,* 84(1), 74–84.

Lee, J., & Lubienski, C. (2016), The Impact of School Closures on Equity of Access in Chicago. *Education and Urban Society,* 49(1), 53–80. https://doi.org/10.1177/0013124516630601

McLeskey, J., Barringer, M. D., Billingsley, B., Brownell, M., Jackson, D., Kennedy, M., Lewis, T., Maheady, L., Rodriguez, J., Scheeler, M. C., Winn, J., & Ziegler,

D. (2017). *High-leverage practices in special education*. Council for Exceptional Children & CEEDAR Center.

Menon, D., & Sadler, T. D. (2016). Preservice elementary teachers' science self-efficacy beliefs and science content knowledge. *Journal of Science Teacher Education, 27*(6), 649–673.

Milner IV, H. R. (2010). What does teacher education have to do with teaching? Implications for diversity studies. *Journal of Teacher Education, 61*(1–2), 118–131.

Milner, H. R. (2013). Scripted and narrowed curriculum reform in urban schools. *Urban Education, 48*(2), 163–170. https://doi.org/10.1177/0042085913478022

Nadelson, L., Albritton, S., Couture1, V., Green, C., Loyless, S., & Shaw, E. (2020). Principals' perceptions of education equity: A mindset for practice. *Journal of Education and Learning, 9*(1), 1–15. https://doi.org/10.5539/jel.v9n1p1

Nasir, N. S. (2012). *Racialized identities: Race and achievement among African American youth*. Stanford University Press.

National Center for Education Statistics. (2015). *The nation's report card*. Retrieved from https://www.nationsreportcard.gov/

Rice, D. C., & Roychoudhury, A. (2003). Preparing more confident preservice elementary science teachers: One elementary science methods teacher's self-study. *Journal of Science Teacher Education, 14*(2), 97–126.

Riegle-Crumb, C., Morton, K., Moore, C., Chimonidou, A., Labrake, C., & Kopp, S. (2015). Do inquiring minds have positive attitudes? The science education of preservice elementary teachers. *Science Education, 99*(5), 819–836.

Robinson, D. (2017). Effective inclusive teacher education for special educational needs and disabilities: Some more thoughts on the way forward. *Teaching and Teacher Education, 61*, 164–178. https://doi.org/10.1016/j.tate.2016.09.007

Rockinson-Szapkiw, A. J., & Caldwell, L. R. (2019). Improving STEM career aspirations in underrepresented populations: Strategies for urban elementary school professionals. In *K–12 STEM education in urban learning environments* (pp. 208–237). IGI Global.

Shields, C. M. (2004). Dialogic leadership for social justice: Overcoming pathologies of silence. *Educational Administration Quarterly, 40*, 109–132.

Steadman, S. C., & Brown, S. D. (2011). Defining the job university supervisor: A department-wide study of university supervisors' practices. *Issues in Teacher Education, 20*(1), 51–68.

Theoharis, G., & Haddix, M. (2011). Undermining racism and a whiteness ideology: White principals living a commitment to equitable and excellent schools. *Urban Education, 46*(6), 1332–1351. https://doi.org/10.1177/0042085911416012

Trundle, K. C., Atwood, R. K., & Christopher, J. E. (2007). A longitudinal study of conceptual change: Preservice elementary teachers' conceptions of moon phases. *Journal of Research in Science Teaching: The Official Journal of the National Association for Research in Science Teaching, 44*(2), 303–326.

Trygstad, P. J. (2013). *2012 National survey of science and mathematics education: Status of elementary school science*. Horizon Research, Inc.

Yendol-Hoppey, D., & Hoppey, D. T. (Eds.). (2018). *Outcomes of high-quality clinical practice in teacher education*. Information Age Publishing.

CHAPTER 5

NAVIGATING THE IN-BETWEEN

Defining the Third Space for Educational Leadership Programs

James A. Zoll
The University of North Georgia

Sheri Hardee
The University of North Georgia

Catherine Rosa
The University of North Georgia

Administrators face multiple challenges with the increased enrollment of students whose first language is not English, who come from backgrounds of poverty, or who belong to underrepresented identities and cultures. These include combating systemic racism, oppressive policies, questions of power and privilege, and ensuring social justice and advocacy for all. Principals need the capacity to create inclusive learning environments meeting the needs of all students. While scholars have argued for such spaces in P–12 classrooms, we found little work on expanding this idea to Principal Preparation Programs (PPPs) and, in turn, to the work of the school (O'Meara et al., 2019; Pereira, 2019; Steele, 2017; Zeichner, 2010). Using a concept theorized by Bhabha (1994) and expanded on by scholars such as Anzaldúa (1998), we envisioned our PPP and the first years of leadership as literal and metaphorical third spaces, a decolonizing linguistic space. As this chapter will demonstrate, this is not an easy space in which to exist, but it is necessary to deconstruct and examine binaries and move toward inclusive leadership.

In the research for this chapter, we expanded on a qualitative case study of a PPP working with aspiring and current assistant principals one year after their program completion, utilizing surveys and focus groups. In our original study, we discovered that PPPs and the first years could be viewed as a third space to inspire inclusive leadership. First, leaders need this space to explore the self-as-leader and the self-in-relation to others. Completers stated that while they felt success in their coursework, they faced uncertainty in their new roles. Candidates also experienced a transition of thinking in the in-between. Working with adults is an unanticipated challenge, and encouraging reluctant teachers to accept change is difficult. Moreover, candidates began to recognize the complexity of the work. While the third space should be a place of learning and growth, leaders navigate a role that by its own definition, is "in-between," often difficult and uncomfortable. This is a binary that should not exist, but one where leaders must become comfortable if they are to lead inclusive settings (Zoll et al., 2020).

We have since expanded this work to examine the steps that come after this initial self-exploration. Once leaders became more comfortable with the self-as-leader, they transitioned to creating their own third spaces within the context of the school, which included exploring the concepts of holistic education, inclusion, multiple perspectives, culture, and climate. While most of our completers noted they felt comfortable with their understanding of culture and its relationship to schooling (88.89%), their conversations reveal a lack of cultural awareness or depth of understanding. Their feelings of uncertainty regarding their roles limit their abilities to act as change agents or advocates for students, parents, or teachers within their schools. The national demographics of our leadership do not correlate with the students for whom they are working. It is critical that we take time to live within these third spaces so that our leaders can help create inclusive learning spaces for their school communities. We hope that our chapter can provide a foundation or starting point for other PPPs.

LITERATURE REVIEW

In examining exemplary PPPs, several components were noted consistently, including student-centered instruction with a problem-based focus, a mix of theory and practice, and job-embedded internships supervised by university and site leaders. Additionally, faculty should be experts in the field or practitioners, curriculum should be aligned with state and national leadership standards, and recruitment should be selective, with the goal of finding "school leaders who are knowledgeable, highly skilled and relentless" (Mitgang, 2012, p.10). Perhaps more than any other component, the literature is clear that school leadership has a strong impact on student achievement, second only to classroom instruction in school-controlled variables (Leithwood et al., 2008; Marzano et al., 2005). As instructional leaders, principals set high expectations, develop and support mission and vision, and protect learning time. They provide necessary resources, instructional support, and professional learning (Blase & Blase, 1999; Hallinger & Heck, 1996; Hattie 2009; McEwan, 2009).

In reviewing years of research on effective principal leadership, four leadership behaviors emerge (Grissom et al., 2021). These are important to our conversation regarding themes discovered through this study. The four behaviors include engaging in conversation around meaningful instruction with teachers, building a productive and engaging culture and climate, providing an environment that allows for collaboration through professional learning communities, and managing resources and personnel effectively to support student learning.

In addition to this emerging framework is an ethical lens to magnify the "principal's role in producing equitable outcomes across students from historically marginalized and non-marginalized groups" (Grissom et al., 2021, p.73). Indeed, the Professional Standards for Educational Leaders (PSEL) standard three states that leaders should "strive for equity of educational opportunity and culturally responsive practices to promote each student's academic success and well-being" (NPBEA, 2015, p. 11). Additionally, several states adopted the definition of inclusive leadership developed by the National Collaborative on Inclusive Principal Leadership (Council of Chief State School Officers 2018):

> Inclusive principals create strong school cultures and distribute leadership across staff to serve all learners well and ensure all students feel safe, supported, and valued in school. In promoting equity for "all," inclusive principals must respond effectively to the potential and needs of each student. Inclusive principals ensure high expectations and appropriate supports so that each

student—across race, gender, ethnicity, language, disability, sexual orientation, family background, and/or family income—can excel in school.

Inclusive principals set high expectations for all students, provide access to higher-level courses, develop professional learning communities focusing on data surrounding diversity, and prioritize diversity in the teacher workforce. Leaders must have anti-racist competencies, a mindset devoid of deficit perspectives (Hong, 2019). They must address topics such as poverty, bullying, and increased enrollment of underrepresented students and students whose first language is not English. Candidates in our program can articulate the importance of inclusivity and identify barriers; however, as they enter the new space of leadership, they face challenges in ensuring that they meet the needs of all. They are challenged to realize components of inclusive leadership.

THEORETICAL FRAMEWORK

To examine leadership with a specific focus on diversity, equity, and inclusion, we utilized postcolonial theories of the third space and borderland as the foundation for our program. We also argue this space is a necessary component to the first years of leadership and the leader's conceptualization of the school space (Anzaldúa, 1998; Bhabha, 1994). The development of metaphorical and literal third spaces allow us to create more inclusive leadership models for PPPs and provides new principals opportunities to create more inclusive spaces. In explaining the creation of borders, Anzaldúa (1998) wrote, "[b]orders are set up to define the places that are safe and unsafe, to distinguish us from them. A border is a dividing line, a narrow strip along a steep edge" (p. 25). The dominant culture produces power polarities such as white/Black, wealthy/impoverished, male/female, and so forth, where one group maintains power over, categorizes, and defines the second. In these dichotomies, this need to classify and define the "other" is the dominant group's way to both name and maintain its own group identity and position. Some students and families become marginalized or relegated outside of these borders in the process.

Thus, the development of third spaces or borderlands for marginalized individuals becomes key to survival—these are spaces where educators, students, families, teachers, and stakeholders can examine the development of their own identities and begin to deconstruct those false dichotomies created by dominant cultures. In its basic definition, this third space or borderland becomes a "community of resistance" (hooks, 1990, p. 149). This is a space where change can occur, a space of exploration and understanding, and a space to reclaim history and create newness. As Giroux (1991) described, "[t]here are no unified subjects here, only students whose multilayered and often contradictory voices and experiences intermingle with the weight of particular histories that will not fit easily into the master narrative of a monolithic culture" (p. 515).

For this study, we see two layers to this third space. The PPP itself is a third space, in which candidates can dialogue, reflect on, and explore the complexity of their programmatic third space without judgment. Once they are in their leadership roles, their school becomes a third space where they explore inclusive leadership and encourage the development of their school as a borderland for students, teachers, families, and the community. These emerging leaders, then, have the potential to create spaces of change for their stakeholders.

METHODOLOGY

This two-year qualitative case study included focus groups with graduates one year after completion and survey data from in-program participants and completers. We selected a case-study approach because the model aligns itself with the framing of the third space. Indeed, the center of a case study is a system that has well-defined borders (Merriam, 1998). The third space is the place between these boundaries, yet it also has walls and is "fenced in," per se, by the surrounding spaces (although these borders are porous). While this case study provides a "slice of life" from the participants' experiences, we hope our work can tell others a great deal about how PPPs and inclusive leadership function as well as how individuals interact and survive within these systems (Guba & Lincoln, 1982, p. 247). The "situated knowledges" of our participants can provide means for developing more inclusive programs and potentially more inclusive mentorship programs for new leaders (Haraway, as cited in Hesse-Biber, Leavy, & Yaiser, 2004, pp. 12–13).

In terms of data sources, surveys included Likert-scale questions based on state and national standards and program logistics and included open-ended questions on program improvement. Focus groups occurred in two rounds. In 2020, we interviewed six 2019 completers in two focus groups, and then in 2021, we interviewed nine program completers in three groups. To garner participation, program coordinators emailed all program completers from the 2019 and 2020 years to ask who would be willing to partake in a focus group, and all volunteers were included.

For data analysis, we began with initial and elaborative coding, based on a previous research study, and then we met to discuss initial codes prior to developing themes and moving to more focused coding (Saldaña, 2016). These focused areas consisted of (1) inclusion or feeling included, (2) multiple perspectives, (3) holistic approaches, (4) and culture and climate. The fourth code, culture and climate, was further divided into subcodes including safety, communication, and relationships. After we re-coded all transcripts, we isolated quotations centered on each code into their own document. We examined and discussed instances where we coded similarly.

We previously determined that while our candidates embraced new roles, there was discomfort in this new area, what we call the "in-between." We expanded on this idea of the third space to become one where participants take important steps toward inclusive leadership. As our participants grappled with inclusion, multiple perspectives, holistic approaches, and culture and climate, our findings demonstrated these were primary areas where growth in relation to inclusive practices and theories was emerging.

FINDINGS

Feeling Included in the In-Between

To be an inclusive leader, new leaders must feel included themselves, one of the first steps toward the development of supportive third spaces. As candidates transitioned into this "in-between," they found themselves in a liminal space where they questioned their identities as leaders while trying to understand their new roles (Zoll et al., 2020). Their sense of self was challenged as they navigated this uncertain territory. Feeling included in previously unfamiliar areas was invigorating and intimidating. One candidate stated, "I'm in those [leadership] conversations for the first time, and I knew that would happen. It still feels very unexpected when they do. I'm not sure why." We can see this leader feels that sense of inclusivity from her administrators. Being part of these deeper conversations opens a new world, and the idea of "shared leadership" is something that she can hopefully extend to teachers.

Inclusion begins with a strong orientation and mentoring systems. Our findings in this area were dichotomous, with some claiming strong support and others minimal. Expressing strong support, one participant stated:

> I continue to be impressed with my county. So, you could ask those questions in that safe space. So, we have that each month. We also were given a coach. We meet with our coach once a month. Then we also have a mentor that we meet with just more periodically.

While coaching, mentoring, and a safe place to learn and grow was the norm for this candidate, another responded, "There's no formal induction or even informal. I was thrown to the wolves. I was also hired at a time of huge turnover." Lack of support makes creating inclusive environments more difficult. Leaders who do not feel included may be less likely to understand how to extend a sense of inclusiveness to others.

Despite the quality of their orientation, leaders sought their own support systems. A new assistant principal stated:

> So, I kind of sought out my own mentors and people to help guide me. And I've kind of told them, I'm like, "You're going to mentor me." I mean, they're people that I have a good rapport with. They're people that I know, and I trust very well, but I make a point of referring to them as my mentor, because I'm like, "I need you to help me. I trust you. I respect you."

Yet another participant declared, "I've had to branch out and get out of my comfort zone and reach out to people I don't know and ask questions." Building on their knowledge and experience, these leaders forged their own inclusive support systems to support growth in their role and their leadership capacity. Sense-of-self as a new leader is expanded by feeling included in the total school process. This necessitates creating those third spaces where mentorship can occur, and new leaders can expand their knowledge of leadership roles and responsibilities.

Recognizing and Valuing Multiple Perspectives in the In-Between

Another theme that emerged in this study of new leaders operating in the third space was the PPP played a significant role in expanding the perspective of emerging leaders, especially in the context of readiness for building equitable and inclusive schools. Adapting and navigating through changing societal norms and creating inclusive engaging learning environments while balancing the needs of the community are necessary skills for effective leaders (Wise, 2015). One challenge to widening this lens was that it was not always possible for participants to be in diverse settings. This inhibited learning in the school environment due to a lack of background in issues surrounding diversity, equity, and inclusion. Indeed, biases about underrepresented students can impact leaders' approaches so they operate from a deficit framework rather than seeing the assets that all students bring to the school environment (Hong, 2019; Salomone, 2010). As one participant stated, "There's always a bias. We bring our own biases to it, and I wish that wasn't the case, but we're in the business of people." Too often, if administrators are part of the dominant group, and their experiences are not in schools with diverse student populations, they do not think about inclusivity and equity issues.

In these cases, it was important to gain multiple perspectives from their peers and colleagues, and there was evidence that participants gained perspective from one another, professors, guest speakers, and the program of study. The participants valued this knowledge as necessary to navigate the demands of the position using a wider lens and understanding the value that multiple ideas can bring to be table. Indeed, leaders need to be empathetic, think from an equity standpoint, and have an appreciation of and respect for students' unique backgrounds (Dinnan, 2009). As one participant stated, "I think one thing I was thankful for with the program was that there were certain things that we had to do that were outside of our comfort zone." The content in the program was a way for participants to expand their knowledge and to make equity and inclusion priorities. As one participant remarked, "I'm making sure that I'm really trying to dig down into what is going on with a particular kid or family, and really trying to make sure that we're being equitable." For most participants, contributions made by other members of the cohort, who had experiences in diverse school settings, helped to expand their own perspectives.

Throughout the program, exposure to multiple perspectives was intentional, allowing candidates to use a constructive approach to gain knowledge to build relationships in their districts. As one participant stated, "I had so many valuable conversations, because I met with so many different types of principals in different socio-economics than where I was that it really helped me understand the context of a lot of things I was learning." For many, the content extended their perspective, as stated by this participant:

> I didn't really know a lot about ESOL. Our school doesn't have a big ESOL population. So, when I did an activity that was surrounding what ESOL encompasses and what you have to do, and the funding for it, it really helped me to get a better understanding for ESOL.... Okay. It was enlightening because it gives you different perspectives.

Overall, participants came to the important realization that they needed to extend their understanding of cultures other than their own. Thus, the participants became aware of the value of multiple perspectives and the importance to effective leadership, as seen in the following quotation:

> I felt like we did discuss that a lot in the program, just being equitable and talking about how using the cultures and the diversity of our groups and as far as how that affects the community.... It helped bring that to light for me, because it may not have been something I noticed before.

Participants began to see the benefits of inclusiveness and to see their roles as change agents responsible for broadening the lens used by their teachers, who, like them, might not have given much thought to inclusiveness. As one participant claimed,

> I actually think that being involved in this program and kind of getting more of the awareness has helped me more in dealing with staff because our staff is not necessarily used to dealing with a diverse population...you help your staff navigate through.

Participants are beginning to navigate the in-between with intentional consideration to widening their lenses and interacting with all stakeholders:

> You're always talking with different groups of people, whether that's PLCs, whether that's an individual teacher, whether that's community members and you're having to really think about what's in front of you and how you're going to respond, because whatever you say is going to have a weight to that.

These new leaders are beginning to understand the powerful impact of their words and actions and are recognizing the need for schools and districts to train school leaders and staff to meet the needs of all students.

Developing a Holistic View in the In-Between

With this wider lens, leaders begin to see the broader school environment in different ways. Having a holistic view allows new leaders to better create those third spaces of support for students, faculty, and parents. This is a vital component to inclusive leadership enabling the leader to recognize what is not working in their school. Indeed, one candidate outlined steps learned in the PPP to ensure the needs of all students were met.

> One, going back into what we worked on, ethics and law, and really understanding what policies are in place that need to be carried out so that all students' needs are met academically. Two is really relying on those standards and frameworks to help guide us to ensure that we're not missing. There's not something that we're missing. There's not a component that we're overlooking but relying on those frameworks to guide us so that we can measure and that all students' needs are being met. And then, the last one is providing and analyzing data. Those are my three takeaways that I still utilize for students' academic needs.

As seen here, she has outlined steps needed for a holistic viewpoint of education, which is necessary for development of inclusive third spaces. Yet another candidate emphasized the social emotional needs of students as a vital component to holistic spaces:

I think for me, I took more away embedded into our climate and culture. And from the (PPP), I think I identified more the development of climate and culture as also developing alongside that meeting the social emotional needs of students. Even on a broader scale, meeting the social emotional needs of several stakeholders.

New leaders expressed frustration that while they see the holistic view, teachers are often focused more on the curriculum:

...high school teachers are very, very curriculum and content-oriented, so it's very important to them, whereas the whole child is very important to me. So, it's just kind of breaking down that, "You're not teaching math. You're teaching a child." And helping them to see that, that geometry shouldn't be the end-all, be-all to that kid's education.

And even administrators sometimes lack a holistic view of all students, as captured by this new assistant principal:

...just making sure that we're [administrators] not labeling kids based on whatever label they may have, and not limiting what they're able to do. Again, just going back to those high expectations, and making sure that we're pushing kids, regardless of what a number on a test says or anything like that. What is this kid actually able to do, and how can we get them just a little bit further and closer to their goal?

These quotations show the importance of teachers and administrators viewing all children as "at-promise" rather than "at-risk." The "at-risk" label comes from a deficit perspective and certainly has an impact on students. The desire to meet the needs of all students, though, is embedded in the completers in our PPP. In the third space, candidates and new leaders may develop confidence to address issues of support, access, and equity with their colleagues in a way that results in change.

Strengthening Climate and Culture in the In-Between: Application to Practice

Lastly, a major part of the process of existing in the "in-between" involves creating similar spaces within each school. Being in the third space is not a negative. It provides important time for reflection and community-building, whereby stakeholders can develop survival tools for moving outside the bounds of the third space. Members of this space do not exist solely within the borderland, but they learn to become boundary crossers, navigating in and out dependent upon their individual situations. For communities of underrepresented students and families, these spaces are vital. We know that borders were developed to divide people (Anzaldúa, 1998; Mignolo, 2000). As Giroux (1991) stated,

> It also speaks to the need to create pedagogical conditions in which students become border-crossers in order to understand otherness in its own terms, and to further create borderlands in which diverse cultural resources allow for the fashioning of new identities within existing configurations of power. (p. 510)

Part of the way in which new leaders can assist with this is through thoughtful development of school culture and climate that supports self-reflection and dialogic practices. Several of the new leaders interviewed for this study noted the difficulty of creating this space, especially while coming to terms with their new roles. As one participant noted, "when you're just in your classroom and it's within your four walls, you can really control the culture of your little space." As noted previously, we found more research on creating borderlands within classroom spaces than research centered on the school community as a third space.

The school is a much larger space with an increased number of stakeholders and increased risks in terms of navigating these spaces. The steps toward development of the school as a third space often begin with an awareness of, understanding of, and reflection on one's role as a leader within this space. As one participant described this recognition of role:

> ...a leader of building can be very influential to achievement and especially to the culture of the building. I do think I'm more realistic now about the day-to-days of leadership and often it's very difficult. It's very easy to get bogged down in the day-to-day operations and lose sight of that bigger vision of the school. So, I'm more realistic about everything, but I think those core beliefs are still there.

Indeed, the creation of the third space becomes more difficult in the larger context of the schools and within the confines of the daily logistics of the position of leader.

In addition to reflecting on and understanding one's role, the second step is understanding one's current environment. All participants interviewed recognized the importance of forming strong relationships across stakeholders and the significance of listening and communication. One participant stated the following regarding listening to students:

> ...the relationship-building is key. And I think you have to keep reminding kids, or reminding the people in the building that you're working

with... They're still children. They're in big bodies, but they're still really children. And you don't know what they come to school with.

Some tools for navigating as border crossers include learning to listen and respond accordingly. As leaders in the third space, our participants are both becoming border crossers themselves and modeling this for the students with whom they work.

Strengthening relationships with guardians and community members was mentioned by almost every participant. As one participant stated, "just being that voice in the community... I'm going to be somebody who's helpful and willing to listen." The emphasis here is on the importance of listening and "being that voice in the community." In some ways, this is a positive step. Conversely, the candidate must learn their role is not necessarily to be the voice, but to provide spaces for those voices to be heard. Another participant echoed this same sentiment in highlighting the importance of "thinking about the role that the administrator plays with the community, with connecting families to services and resources, with keeping the public informed." They are beginning to recognize the ways their leadership roles require them to step outside the traditional space of the school.

As another part of this process of creating safe, supportive cultures and climates, participants recognized the need to assess the current climate and the school's readiness for change. As one participant summed this up:

> I think that one thing that I took away from the (PPP) is we worked on understanding readiness and readiness to receive change. And through that exercise and through that discussion, I was able to have a better appreciation for when you're initiating change or you're building a climate and culture is to really understand the process of developing that change or that environment or building that environment, and how to understand readiness.

The third space within the PPP for participants to dialogue and collaborate enabled the exploration of the concept of "readiness" together. As a new leader, it is difficult to enter a position and make changes of any kind, but it is vital to understand the current climate prior to implementing changes. It is also vital that stakeholders participate in the development of necessary changes. Change takes time, reflection, and planning. It requires creating spaces where this work can safely occur. In reference to these borderlands, hooks (1990) noted, "'the 'politics of location' necessarily calls those of us who would participate in the formation of counter-hegemonic cultural practice to identify the spaces where we begin the process of re-vision" (p. 145). We know the culture and climate of schools does not always support underrepresented students, and we want our graduates to become inclusive leaders who specifically focus on supporting students who have been marginalized. After all, as Apple (2003) stated, "much of the problem in education is not only about educating the oppressed but re-educating those who were and are in dominance" (p. 113).

IMPLICATIONS AND DISCUSSION

In preparing candidates for leadership positions, it is important to make them aware of the existence of this third space and to promote the development of literal and metaphorical borderlands within their programs and within those first years of leadership. Through simulation and case study, future leaders experience the nuance of the third space and, at the same time, begin to realize the importance of this collaborative area, eventually finding comfort in the space. As they enter their new roles, this comfort can be enhanced by feeling included through mentorship, recognizing multiple perspectives, seeing the bigger picture, and understanding their role in developing the culture and climate of their schools. These combined tasks will make for better prepared leaders.

Emerging leaders in this study began to feel comfort in the third space when they felt included. This is a powerful reminder of the need for the third space, which was originally conceived as a space for communities not accepted by the dominant culture. As Anzaldúa (1999) wrote, "[a] borderland is a vague and undetermined place created by the emotional residue of an unnatural boundary. It is in a constant state of transition. The prohibited and forbidden are its inhabitants" (Anzaldúa, 1999, p. 25). The very need for the borderland, then, was as a space for communities and individuals not accepted into dominant culture. While not comparable in terms of the level of exclusion that underrepresented communities experience from dominant culture, these newly minted administrators experience a small part of what it is like to feel they are in a space where they may feel uncomfortable or initially unwelcome.

Although we could argue that these spaces are sacred to those who have experienced exclusion based on their cultures and backgrounds, what we want to highlight is the conceptual work that goes on in these third spaces. These are spaces where we challenge the idea of "culture as a homogenizing, unifying force, authenticated by the original Past, kept alive in the national tradition of the People" (Bhabha, 1995, p. 208). As Bhabha (1995) continued, within the borderland, "the disruptive temporality of enunciation displaces the narrative of the Western nation" (p. 208), and our hope is that these new leaders can learn the power of third space to help them change the course of action within their schools. The power of dialogue and listening creates new contexts within the third space aimed at improving the educational experience for all students.

We see a need to maintain the relationships with their cohort and grow relationships with other leaders within the district, as they build a network of support before moving into the principalship. Participants need to cultivate the ability to cross borders and make new meaning, followed by continual professional development. Without the ability to navigate this space and successfully cross borders, the potential for inclusive leadership is minimized. While there are certainly other steps necessary on the journey to inclusive leadership, we argue the creation, articulation, and maintenance of the third space is an essential first step for principal preparation programs in developing inclusive leaders. Through both self-reflection and collective action within these spaces, the borderland can be a place where candidates develop courage to take and share responsibility, become aware of interconnectedness and the value of others, create shared vision for change, and build relationships, all aspects important to inclusive leadership (Bortini et al., n.d.).

Holistically, it appears that educators are more adaptable to changing situations than once thought and are driven by taking care of the whole child. While managing push back and resistance to an inclusive vision was an area of frustration for these new leaders, they are beginning to recognize the importance of bringing all voices to the table. Helping candidates manage these conversations is a vital component of leadership education. Focusing on crucial conversations in the PPP and the mentoring process is essential. After all, "[t]hat society's problems play out in schools means that schools also offer an opportunity to open a dialogue about race and equality, yet this dialogue is never easy" (Jervis, 1996, p. 548).

Developing an inclusive climate and culture should be a precept of any PPP. Forming professional learning communities, viewing data with an ethical lens, assuring elevated expectations including access to higher level courses and opportunities, and assuring cultural competency as the norm are non-negotiable acts. (Grissom et al., 2021). Leaders must be able to have an anti-racist mindset and avoid deficit-based approaches to education (Hong, 2019). However, as new leaders enter this third space, their impact on the previously created culture and climate is limited. Some contexts may be limited in approaching the borders of inclusive leadership, especially when the borders are closed, are not considered, or other administrators and teachers are against ideas of inclusion for all students. That said, the new leader can be a role model in the third space as stakeholders are watching to see what the leader values as important. New leaders have the fundamental obligation to be intentional about building relationships, while learning how to communicate effectively.

Educational leaders face the challenges of oppressive policies and legislation, systemic racism, discussions of power and privilege, and issues with social justice and equity for all students. Commitment to the tenets of inclusive leadership must be paramount to PPPs to combat these challenges and assure leaders can cross linguistic and dialogic borders. For these new leaders, the third space or in-between provides opportunity. New leaders existing in the in-between can learn to create such spaces for their schools, students, and families. As Delgado-Bernal (2002) noted:

> The Eurocentric perspective has for too long viewed the experiential knowledge of students of color as deficit or ignored it all together.... To recognize all students as holders and creators of knowledge, it is imperative that the histories, experiences, cultures, and languages of students of color are recognized and valued in schools. (p. 121)

CONCLUSION

This chapter explored the components of a successful PPP, the implementation of tenets of diversity, equity, and inclusion in the program, and the lived experiences of candidates transitioning from the PPP to the demands of the work as instructional leaders. In particular, it is the definition of inclusive leadership (Council of Chief State School Officers 2018) that framed this study. Leaders must view their school through an ethical lens to assure they are creating school cultures and environments that support each student. Without the ethical lens, a leader has diminished ability to confront social injustice and meet the demands of inclusive leadership.

These new leaders faced challenges related to a lack of social justice, systemic and systematic racism, the impacts of poverty, increased enrollment of students whose primary language is not English, and oppression of underrepresented identities and cultures. As these new leaders emerged in their roles, they questioned their sense of identity, expanded their knowledge and understanding of the role, and navigated through new complexities of the work. They recognized a binary between their previous work as teachers and the role of leadership, a binary that should not exist. They found themselves in what Bhabba (1994) terms as the third space, a decolonizing and linguistic space. The space is uncomfortable and challenging, yet also an area where collaborative leadership expands, and change can occur. Indeed, as they grew into their sense of identity in their new roles, these emerging leaders developed views of holistic education and recognized the multiple perspectives surrounding inclusive leadership.

Yet while the desire to make change is real, the ability to maneuver through entrenched beliefs and opposition is a struggle, even in this third space. Though candidates in our PPP are better prepared for the challenges of the job, it is evident there is room for improvement. Indeed, PPPs must provide opportunities to grow and nurture multiple perspectives leading to inclusive leadership, a difficult process when the leaders uphold dominant perspectives. Awareness of the third space and the ability to understand and cross borders are imperative. For many of our candidates, the schools where they work do not mirror the national demographics, meaning PPPs should provide diverse experiences in internships. Additionally, mentoring is crucial for the new leader to adapt to the third space. It was clear that leaders who had significant on-site induction programs adapted more readily to the challenges of the job. In-program candidates receive mentoring and coaching from a university professor and their site mentor; however, this may not continue at their new place of employment. Possible extension of mentorship for these beginning years is a topic for further exploration. At a minimum, conversation between the university and the district partnership is pivotal, particularly mentoring relationships embedded in the tenets of inclusive leadership.

Finally, we return to the argument that the definition of inclusive leadership must be the umbrella over the program and should be a basis for other PPPs. While students have exposure to examining bias and interacting through case study or simulation, elements of inclusive leadership, social justice, and equity for all need to be expanded and interwoven through courses and internship experiences. Knowledge and understanding of the third space will help PPPs to better prepare future leaders to handle their difficult roles, equipping them to expand and enhance them. It is essential that our candidates know how to interact in these spaces to better prepare each P–12 student and to prepare themselves to successfully interact within the school climate and community.

REFERENCES

Apple, M. W. (2003). Freire and the politics of race in education. *International Journal of Leadership in Education, 6*(2), 107–118.
Anzaldúa, G. (1998). *Borderlands/La frontera: The new Mestiza.* Aunt Lute Books.
Bhabha, H. (1994). *The location of culture.* Routledge.
Blase, J., & Blase, J. (1999). Principals' instructional leadership and teacher development: Teachers' perspectives. *Educational Administration Quarterly, 35*(3), 349–378. https://doi.org/10.1177/0013161X99353003
Bortini, P., Paci, A., Rise, A., & Rojnik. (n.d.). Inclusion leadership: Theoretical framework. https://www.academia.edu/36862490/INCLUSIVE_LEADERSHIP
Council of Chief State School Officers. (2018, June 1). *Why inclusive leadership.* https://ccssoinclusiveprincipalsguide.org/why-inclusive-leadership/.
Delgado-Bernal, D. (2002). Critical race theory, Latino critical theory, and critical raced-gendered epistemologies: Recognizing students of color as holders and creators of knowledge. *Qualitative Inquiry, 8*(105), 105–126.

Dinnan, P. J. (2009). *The effects of a short-term cultural immersion experience to Mexico on school leaders.* Retrieved from ScholarWorks @ Georgia State University website, Department of Educational Policy Studies: https://scholarworks.gsu.edu/cgi/viewcontent.cgi?referer=https://scholar.google.com/&httpsredir=1&article=1049&context=eps_diss

Guba, E. G., & Lincoln Y. S. (1982). Epistemological and methodological bases of naturalistic inquiry. *Educational Communication and Technology, 30*(4), 233–252. https://www.jstor.org/stable/30219846

Giroux, H. A. (1991). Democracy and the discourse of cultural difference: Towards a politics of border pedagogy. *British Journal of Sociology of Education, 12*(4), 501–519.

Grissom, J. A., Egalite, A. J., & Lindsay, C. A. (2021). *How principals affect students and schools: A systematic synthesis of two decades of research.* The Wallace Foundation. http://www.wallacefoundation.org/principalsynthesis.

Hallinger, P., & Heck, R. H. (1996). Reassessing the principal's role in school effectiveness: A review of empirical research, 1980–1995. *Educational Administration Quarterly, 32*(1), 5–44. https://doi.org/10.1177/0013161X96032001002

Hattie, J. (2009). *Visible learning: A synthesis of over 800 meta-analyses relating to achievement.* Routledge.

Hesse-Biber, S. N., Leavy, P., & Yaiser, M. L. (2004). Feminist approaches to research as a process: Reconceptualizing epistemology, methodology, and method. In S. N. Hesse-Biber, & M. L. Yaiser (Eds.), *Feminist perspectives on social research* (pp. 3–26). Oxford University Press.

hooks, b. (1990). *Yearning: Race, gender, and cultural politics.* South End Press.

Hong, S. (2019). *Natural allies: Hope and possibility in teacher–family partnerships.* Harvard Education Publishing Group.

Jervis, K. (Fall, 1996). "How come there are no brothers on that list?": Hearing the hard questions children ask. *Harvard Educational Review, 66*(3), 546–576.

Leithwood, K., Harris, A., & Hopkins, D. (2008). Seven strong claims about successful school leadership. *School Leadership & Management, 28*(1), 27–42. https://dera.ioe.ac.uk/6967/1/download%3Fid=17387&filename=seven-claims-about-successful-school-leadership.pdf

Marzano, R. J., Waters, T., & McNulty, B. A. (2005). *School leadership that works: From research to results.* Association for Supervision and Curriculum Development. http://www.eric.ed.gov/ERICWebPortal/detail?accno=ED509055

McEwan, E. (2009). *10 traits of highly effective schools.* Corwin Press.

Merriam, S. B. (1998). *Qualitative research and case study applications in education.* Jossey-Bass Publishers.

Mignolo, W. D. (2000). *Local histories/Global designs: Coloniality, subaltern knowledges, and border thinking.* Princeton University Press

Mitgang, L. (2012). *The making of the principal: Five lessons in leadership training.* Wallace Foundation, 34. https://www.wallacefoundation.org/knowledge-center/Documents/The-Making-of-the-Principal-Five-Lessons-in-Leadership-Training.pdf

National Policy Board for Educational Administration (2015). Professional Standards for Educational Leaders 2015. Reston, VA: Author.

O'Meara, K., Griffin, K. A., Nyunt, G., & Lounder, A. (2019). Disrupting ruling relations: The role of the PROMISE program as a third space. *Journal of Diversity in Higher Education, 12*(3), 205–218. https://doi.org/10.1037/dhe0000095

Pereira, F. (2019). Teacher education, teachers' work, and justice in education: Third space and mediation epistemology. *Australian Journal of Teacher Education 44*(3), 77.

Saldaña, J. (2016). *The coding manual for qualitative researchers* (3rd ed.). SAGE.

Salomone, R. (2010). *True American language, identity, and the education of immigrant children*. Harvard University Press.

Steele, A. R. (2017). An alternative collaborative supervision practice between university-based teachers and school-based teachers. *Educational Research, 27*(3), 582–599. http://www.iier.org.au/iier27/steele.pdf

Wise, D. (2015). Emerging challenges facing school principals. *NCPEA Education Leadership Review, 16*(2). https://www.ncpeapublications.org/index.php/volume-16-number-2-fall-2015/701-emerging-challenges-facing-school-principals

Zeichner, K. (2010). New epistemologies in teacher education: Rethinking the connections between the subjects of the campus and the experiences of practices in the training of teacher staff in the University. *Interuniversity Journal of Teacher Education, 24*(2), 123–149. https://core.ac.uk/download/pdf/41577215.pdf

Zoll, J., Hardee, S., & Rosa, C. (2020). Navigating the in-between: Defining the third space for educational leadership programs. *Education Leadership Review, 21*(1), 99–131.

SECTION II

PRACTICAL APPLICATIONS:
INCLUSIVE LEADERSHIP IN ACTION

CHAPTER 6

PRACTICING INCLUSIVE LEADERSHIP BY NURTURING AND DEVELOPING TEACHER LEADERS

Marla McGhee
Texas Christian University, Retired

This chapter describes the inclusive leader's role as it relates to developing and utilizing other leaders—those within the teaching ranks. Principals and assistant principals must come to understand that they are not alone when shouldering leadership tasks and duties, and including faculty members who are capable and willing to lead, means they can begin to turn their attention and energies to other priorities. Identifying and nurturing teacher leaders requires thoughtful administrative involvement and action and is not simply a function of principals stepping aside or taking a backseat. Once teacher leadership is successfully started, it can profoundly impact the school in a multitude of positive ways.

GUIDING QUESTIONS

- How does teacher leadership promote inclusive instructional leadership?
- What is the role of teacher leadership in school improvement?
- What do inclusive leaders do to operationalize teacher leadership?
- How can inclusive administrators model effective followership?
- What lessons can we learn from successful teacher leadership projects?

Schools are unique organizations. While sharing attributes with other well-known institutions, the purpose, mission, and function of schools distinguishes them from businesses, congregations, or hospitals. Moreover, schools are patently human enterprises. Mature human beings—who never cease to grow and develop—work together to grow and develop *other* human beings. Quite simply, that is what schools do. And, because schools are characterized by this human dynamic, interactions and relationships are central to their operation. School leaders who are sensitive to human relations within their organization and work from a "relationally-responsive orientation," respect others, nurture trust, and honor and promote expression (Cunliffe & Eriksen, 2011). Donaldson (2007), notes that schools are perfect places to practice *relational leadership* (as compared to hierarchical leadership). "This model starts by recognizing that relationships already exist among teachers, principals, specialists, counselors, and support staff... Leadership is a particular type of relationship—one that mobilizes other people to improve practice" (p. 27). When principals and assistant principals recognize, promote, and nurture leadership among their teaching faculties, they are strengthening the instructional mission of the school (McLester, 2018) while practicing inclusive leadership.

WHY TEACHER LEADERSHIP?

Teacher leadership enhances an inclusive school environment in significant ways. The examples outlined below show how teacher leadership can eclipse positional power and legal authority by shaping campus culture, contributing to site-level problem solving, and informing the professional literature on teaching and learning. Instead of top-down processes or change by administrative fiat, teacher leaders have their fingers on the pulse of the formal and informal structures and can use their relational capital to influence others (Safir, 2018; Lattimer, 2012).

Teachers are Powerful and Effective Role Models for One Another

Because of their expertise, credibility, and impact, teachers can shape educational activities regardless of the formal positions they assume. When teachers regularly interact with one another and share leadership responsibilities across the teaching ranks and with campus administrators, strongly held inclusive values begin to develop.

Over time these norms represent the standard way of doing business. Teachers come to expect a level of commitment and coherence from their instructional peers, holding "each other accountable to the social contract that emerges in the course of day-to-day practice" (Printy & Marks, 2006, p. 129). In such situations, teachers have little patience with or regard for colleagues who operate outside the cultural norms and educational expectations of the school. "Slack is not tolerated, and nonconforming teachers are largely ignored or pressured to leave" (p. 129).

Teachers Can Provide Valuable Ideas for Solving School-Based Problems

When faced with educational challenges or dilemmas, teachers are uniquely situated to think through and offer innovative solutions (Printy & Marks, 2006). Moreover, when teachers are directly involved in generating ways to address situations, they often assume greater responsibility for making the solution work. At an elementary campus in Austin, Texas it became common practice to inclusively prepare the master schedule for the coming academic year. This was accomplished by having grade level representatives present in a meeting to express the needs (or desires) of their peers to the whole group. At the annual collaborative gathering—hosted by the principal—each team communicated the wishes of their grade level via their selected representative. Through whole group dialogue and compromise, solutions were generated, and the schedule was ultimately crafted. Because this became an annual event, groups who were called on to "give a little" one year were on the "get a little" end of things the next.

Teacher Voice Can Influence Policy and Practice

When a colleague and I made a site visit to PS 290 (The Manhattan New School) in New York City to witness firsthand their successful literacy and writing practices, I experienced many impressive things. One issue in particular made an immediate impression as we walked through the auditorium doors. Each visitor was handed a colorful flyer entitled "Books by our Faculty." Several of the titles I recognized right away as well regarded, authoritative volumes published by one of the nation's leading sources on reading, writing, and literacy practices. These "teaching authors" were exercising leadership far beyond the walls of their school by contributing to the extant literature on literacy learning best practices.

TEACHER LEADER STYLES

"Although school administrators play a vital role in these efforts [making learning better for all students], teachers are uniquely positioned to contribute special assets to the school leadership mix..." (Donaldson, 2007, p. 27). There are a variety of leadership roles teachers can assume without undertaking a formal administrative post, including school improvement team member, department head, grade level chairperson, mentor, staff developer, and curriculum writer. In my experience as principal, I encountered several unique teacher leader archetypes. Each had distinct qualities or assets essential to an inclusive atmosphere because of the roles they assumed. What was critical about seeing and understanding these contrasting styles is each required a varied approach from me as I encouraged the teacher to assume or assist with leadership tasks (Smith, 2017).

The Front and Center Teacher Leader

This teacher is completely confident and competent in front of others, especially large groups, enjoys teaching and working with peers and does not hesitate to assume leadership roles when approached. This individual seems to possess natural communication and human relations skills and abilities. She often volunteers or steps forward for leadership tasks with little prompting. The *front and center teacher leader* may also approach colleagues or formal leaders on the campus or district about starting an initiative or pursuing a special project.

The Initially Reluctant Teacher Leader

Though capable, this teacher may not perceive herself as a leader or have ever considered a leadership role. Because she is reluctant at the onset, they may require gentle coaxing, encouragement, or convincing to assume leadership roles. Such teachers generally become more confident and comfortable with leadership activities over time. With success and experience, this teacher leader may ultimately become a front and center or recognized teacher leader.

The Behind-the-Scenes Teacher Leader

While utterly capable, this individual does not enjoy being singled out or publicly recognized as a leader in front of her peers. This teacher does not feel comfortable working with or being in front of large groups and may be naturally introverted, quiet, or reserved. Regardless of these proclivities, this individual is a highly effective leader with smaller teams or in one-on-one situations. She responds best to leadership invitations when approached in a private setting or closed-door meeting. Although successful as a leader, this teacher may always be most comfortable working "behind the scenes" rather than in a more public forum.

TEACHER LEADERSHIP AND SCHOOL IMPROVEMENT

"Effective or purposeful leadership is generally accepted as being a central component in securing and sustaining school improvement" (Muijs & Harris, 2007, p. 111). Although formal leadership certainly matters when it comes to improving schools, evidence indicates that teachers strongly influence the effectiveness of schools. However, teacher leadership does not simply happen. It requires deliberate planning and action on the part of principals and assistant principals. Without thoughtful and intentional actions, the impact of teacher leadership will be uneven, haphazard, and never realize systemic potential.

As noted in Muijs and Harris (2007), "The data we collected suggests that teacher leadership can only flourish where both school culture and associated structures allow it to develop" (p. 131). For the administrative team, this means promoting a spirit of collaboration and trust, providing resources that promote and enable teacher leadership, and offering the professional development necessary for teachers to assume leadership roles.

The Importance of Being Deliberate and Taking Strategic Action

Abdicating leadership or simply stepping aside hoping that others will fill the leadership gap does little to promote teachers as leaders. In fact, when leaders do not make parameters clear or choose not to act when faced with a leadership challenge, teachers can be confused about boundaries and become frustrated when unhealthy situations are allowed to languish. While one might believe that weak principal leadership would promote or encourage teacher leadership, it tends to do the opposite. "This perceived lack of leadership from the centre has meant that teachers are often not sure what they are supposed to do" (Muijs & Harris, 2007, p.127). For example, at a large, urban elementary school a third-grade teacher was eager to pursue an interest in designing and using rubrics for grade-level wide projects. Even with her background knowledge and intense enthusiasm for the topic, she could not convince her grade level colleagues to jump on board. As she continued to suggest and nudge, her peers began to push back, resulting in strained professional relationships and a series of extremely unproductive team meetings. Aware of the situation, the principal took deliberate and strategic action.

His purpose was twofold: to preserve and honor the interests of the veteran teacher in pursuing a worthwhile instructional endeavor while also allowing a team of teachers not to be rushed into an innovation for which they clearly lacked readiness. Over the summer months, the principal approached the teacher about moving to another grade level to join a team of teachers who would benefit from and respond to her leadership efforts. The teacher agreed, resulting in a more productive situation for both teacher teams.

The Inclusive Administrator's Role in Promoting Collaboration and Trust

A local university representative approached the principal of an intermediate campus about becoming part of a multi-year school improvement network project. Participation included funding to support a campus-wide initiative, providing for release time, needed materials, supplies and stipends for those who participated on the core planning team. Although the principal had great interest in the project and what it would mean in the way of support for the campus, she had previously promised the faculty that any major school-wide initiative would be made collaboratively, requiring the approval of at least 80% of the faculty.

Gathered in the cafeteria for an all-school faculty meeting, the university representative presented the offer to the teachers and administrative team. After addressing a number of questions from faculty the university person left the meeting and returned to campus. Discussion continued with individuals offering comments and thoughts about the presentation. Faculty members cast secret ballots as they exited the room. When the votes were tallied, the proposal was defeated, falling only a few votes short of the 80%

mark. The principal, although disappointed in the outcome, contacted the university to report the results and say that they would not be taking part in the school improvement opportunity.

This anecdote offers an interesting lesson in inclusive leadership and culture shaping—an example of *building trust*. Clearly the principal was interested in the opportunity made available to her campus. She knew the funding and resources that accompanied participation in the network would allow the school to undertake an improvement course she desperately wanted to pursue. But here, the principal did something important—she kept her word. Following through with a professional promise reinforces and enhances trust. In this instance, the principal modeled trustworthiness by making good on her commitment to the faculty regarding collaborative decision-making about potential school-wide initiatives. Although it was not the answer she had hoped for, when the faculty spoke, she listened.

Providing Resources, Time, and Training

Some principals may believe that teachers who appear to be natural leaders and seem to possess prowess for working with others are best left alone. "A review of the available literature on teacher leadership and evidence from teacher leaders themselves suggest that this line of reasoning is false" (Lattimer, 2007, p. 70) and principals can do more to shape school structures so that teacher leadership will flourish. One-way administrators can enhance school leadership is to provide resources to promote the efforts of teacher leaders. A relatively small investment may pay large dividends as teacher leadership begins to take hold across campus. The gift of time is another way principals and assistant principals can encourage and promote leadership across the teaching ranks. Offering to take a teacher's classroom for a day or providing a substitute will allow time for planning without disrupting the instructional life of students.

Gordon (2004) suggests that teachers need both knowledge and skill development to appropriately prepare for leadership roles. He notes that training and development areas may differ depending on the type of leadership capacity being considered (i.e., lead teacher, mentor). Knowledge topics include adult development or the change process. While skills areas can include themes like trust building, planning, problem solving, and program evaluation. Additionally, Gordon suggests that sustained support is necessary for teacher leadership to take hold. The factors that reinforce teacher leadership include the following:

- Incentives and rewards
- Coordinated support

- Clear descriptions of roles and functions
- Time for leadership
- Structures for continuous assistance

In many districts, a central office department can provide assistance in offering training for teacher leaders. In more remote areas, regional educational centers, service districts, or cooperatives assist educators in getting the help they need to assume leadership roles and tasks. An additional alternative is to establish study groups within a school where small cadres of staff can assemble periodically to study various knowledge and skills topics contained in books, excerpts, and educational articles. "Teacher leadership is one of the most exciting frameworks in professional development... But to flourish, it must receive genuine, ongoing support from policymakers, administrators, and staff developers" (Gordon, 2004, p. 106).

In Lambert's 2005 seminal discussion on teacher leadership, she makes clear the distinction between low and high leadership capacity schools. *Low-capacity* organizations are principal-dependent where only the principal holds the leadership reins. Decisions tend to be hierarchical in nature and a spirit of professionalism and collegiality is largely absent. High leadership capacity schools, on the other hand, are markedly different places to work. *High-capacity* learning communities hold fast to and exemplify leadership, learning, and success for all. "The principal is only one of the leaders in the school community and models collaboration, listening, and engagement" (p. 40). While the author readily admits there is no ironclad guarantee of sustainability in the higher capacity environment, the chances of widespread success are much greater in collaborative settings where learning and leadership are shared, practiced values.

Lambert's six critical factors of high leadership capacity schools include the following:

1. The school community's core values must focus its priorities (equity, democracy and accepting responsibility for all students' learning).
2. As teacher leadership grows, principals must let go of some authority and responsibility (lines of leader-followership become blurred and roles blend).
3. Educators must define themselves as learners, teachers, and leaders (sharing and distributing leadership and understanding that all adults can lead and learn).
4. We must invest in each other's learning to create reciprocity (engaging teachers as problem solvers and working as a learning community).

5. The first tenet of leadership capacity is "broad-based participation" (creating school structures that promote and encourage participation).
6. Districts must negotiate the political landscape to provide professional time and development, a conceptual framework for improvement, and tailored succession practices (fitting the principal to the school and building capacity for lasting school improvement). (p. 40)

BEING A PRODUCTIVE AND EFFECTIVE PARTICIPANT: INCLUSIVE LEADER AS FOLLOWER

Sometimes inclusive leadership is most effectively practiced at the participant level. When a middle school began to explore technology applications using innovative hardware and software, the principal sat beside his teachers and participated in the training as a group member. He was steadfast in his attendance and attention as the library media specialist led hands-on professional development sessions targeting the integration of instructional technology across the curriculum. "I had a lot to learn, just like everyone else," the principal remarked. "The only way for me to keep up with what was happening in classrooms was to learn alongside the teachers. It just made good sense," he said. Rather than sitting in the back of the room or peering over teachers' shoulders as they participated in the sessions or—even worse—staying in the front office during an after-school workshop, this principal assumed the role of adult learner *and* participant. "It was wonderful to have him learning with us," a teacher noted. "His presence in the workshops let us all know that these professional learning opportunities were important!"

"Leaders who are able to successfully take a place inside the team or alongside the group serve as powerful models for their professional peers" (McGhee & Boone, 2008, p. 96). Part of developing capable leaders comes from giving others the chance to practice leadership in public and tangible ways. Practicing inclusive leadership sometimes requires formal leaders to step inside a group as someone else assumes the leadership or facilitation function. As noted earlier in the chapter, this does not mean nonchalantly stepping aside in hopes that someone will assume leadership responsibility. Rather, the formal leader is thoughtful and purposeful in knowing when it is time to let others take the helm and has established the infrastructure and environment needed for teacher leadership to prosper. The wise leader knows that sharing leadership duties means sharing accountability and responsibility for accomplishments and outcomes.

Another fertile area for leader followership and teacher leadership is in the arena of professional growth and development. In some schools, a teacher leadership team is completely responsible for planning and facilitating professional learning; they understand how to cultivate and capitalize on relationships and promote professional growth among their school-based peers (McLester, 2018; Smith, 2017). Such approaches can be especially powerful when engaging in diversity and equity initiatives and unconscious bias training (Safir, 2018). "The nature of cultural competency work does not lend itself to a top-down approach regardless of the school environment. People must see the value for themselves, which often starts with a trusted colleague leading the way" (Poplack & Dlesk, 2018, p. 110).

In Sergiovanni and Green's (2015) influential discussion of distributed and reciprocal leadership, they note that the lines between followers and leaders can become hazy and ill-defined. When shared values or dedication to the completion of a project becomes the driving force rather than mandates or authority, followership is key. In such instances, followership *is* an act of leadership.

Practicing followership is sometimes a challenge for principals and assistant principals who are constantly looked to for opinions and decisions in school organizations. When practicing effective followership, administrators must be aware of their attitudes and actions as they can easily enable others to lead or instantly derail their attempts to provide leadership.

Key considerations for followership:

1. In group settings, sit alongside other participants and actively engage in the task at hand. Do not distinguish yourself from others by cherry picking what you will and will not be involved in.
2. Do not constantly leave the room to tend to other duties or tasks. Dedicate the necessary time and "be present."
3. Model appropriate group behavior, including being willing to struggle with tasks that challenge you or are unfamiliar.
4. Resist the temptation to take charge, even if there are minor miscues or if business is conducted differently than if you were leading.
5. If problems or difficulties occur, address them in private at another time. Problem solving behind closed doors will bolster the confidence of and support the individual taking the lead and help to avoid possible embarrassment in front of others.

THE IMPORTANCE OF AND ROLE OF ADMINISTRATORS IN TEACHER LEADERSHIP: LESSONS FROM A TEACHER LEADERSHIP NETWORK

Dr. Lee Rutledge, a former middle school teacher and teacher leader, was the director of a long running teacher leadership initiative at a regional education center. Well-versed on the body of work, Lee accessed and used the teacher leadership literature constantly with teachers and campus teams. Lee began to conduct her own research targeting issues related to teacher leadership as she looked for more effective ways to create and maintain a vibrant network program. In the interview that follows, you see many of the themes explored in this chapter playing out in practical ways as Dr. Rutledge describes some of the most critical lessons she learned throughout her involvement with the initiative, especially what she has come to understand about inclusive campus administrators and teacher leadership.

> **MM:** I want to start by asking you to share a bit about your teacher leadership program to frame our discussion.
>
> **LR:** The program we currently have has evolved over time. The initial teacher leadership initiative was cohort-based and accessed by invitation only. When we encountered skilled, talented teachers, we invited them to become part of our network. At that time, they practiced teacher leadership primarily by planning and leading training sessions for others. At first the training focused only on issues related to the implementation of content mastery and inclusive practices. As time passed, though, we began to expand our outreach to general education. About four years ago the focus changed from an invitation format to a registration process. We weren't completely satisfied with that either because although we would get a whole team from maybe 3 or 4 campuses, we would also get a teacher from here and another from there... This past year we shifted to an application process, which involved administrators *nominating* teachers to be a part of the program.
>
> **MM:** Had administrators been involved up to that point?
>
> **LR:** They were, but not as intentionally. The year before last I actually had a principal sign up with her team. She came to the first meeting and then I never saw her again.
>
> **MM:** Okay, so what was the purpose of pulling administrators into the program in a more meaningful way?
>
> **LR:** To get better buy-in into the process. Teachers were coming to the network meetings but then having trouble going back and connecting their learning to what was happening at the campus. While principals seemed to support the idea of their teachers participating, we often didn't see the follow-through. There was a disconnect. What we wanted was for principals to recognize lead teachers on their campus in a more meaningful way, so we established criteria for them to

nominate someone for participation. First, the teacher had to be exhibiting some form of leadership skills. Second, we made it clear that the teacher participants would be involved in an action research project throughout the year that would connect back to the CIP [campus improvement plan]. We made some specific criteria that would require a principal to truly understand why they were sending the teacher...

MM: Some of it, then, was the follow-through and the long-term support. I mean, you saw the administrators being interested in teacher leadership, but you didn't see it playing out in a long-term way?

LR: Right. But there were other hurdles we had to overcome. For some teachers, even though their principal was there for the first meeting, and they had an understanding of what we were doing, they [the teachers] continued to talk about frustrations they were experiencing. They struggled a bit with going back to their campuses and having time to actually spend with their principal to discuss the things they were doing and would like to implement. What we came to understand was these were newer teachers trying to get into what was already an established leadership network on the campus. These were younger teachers trying to break through the organizational barriers at their schools. Often, the campus administrators were essential to navigating these stumbling blocks.

MM: What I'm hearing you say is that you believe that principals being involved in the process and in the program was vital to success.

LR: Absolutely. What happened differently this time was as teachers were determining their action research question, they went back and shared the information with their principal and two other colleagues at the site. There were some components built into the process that required them to meet and work with their principal. It built that relationship up more than we had done in the past.

MM: Can you talk about what you've learned about the role of the principal in teacher leadership as this program has evolved over time? You've already mentioned that teachers had a hard time if their principals didn't understand what they were doing... What roles have principals played in teachers being able to successfully exhibit and practice leadership?

LR: Probably the thing that stands out most for me are administrators who really understand the notion of *shared leadership*—the idea that they don't have to rely on themselves alone to do everything. They can share leadership duties with teachers and trust that they can do the work. I think the barriers come when principals, even though they try to share leadership, basically keep control of it. Keep boundaries around what the teachers can and can't do. The difference I saw in principals were those who grasped the idea of teacher leadership and those who said they did on the surface, but really didn't.

MM: Do you think it's a matter of trust, or did you just see an array of reasons why you thought principals wouldn't release the leadership duties to teachers?

LR: Sometimes, it was based on fear. Principals have to sit in front of their superintendent and say, "this is what's happening on my campus." It's tough when they are the accountable person for the performance of a campus. It's tough to let go. The fear that, if I don't stay on top of what everybody's doing and have the final say, it's going to backfire. But I'm reminded of how well it can work as I think about a principal who didn't have that fear. This principal trusted the person who was leading the initiatives around early childhood and had confidence that this individual could run the program. In fact, she was looked upon by the staff as a leader on the campus, so she [the principal] had no problem letting her do what she needed to do to make decisions and recommendations. But she never came to the principal with a recommendation that didn't have all the research to support her proposal.

MM: Was that situation common? Do most of the teacher leaders you work with have such skills?

LR: I've worked with teachers who've had to learn that piece. That's what was holding this one teacher back—rushing forward with ideas and things he *might* want to implement in classrooms, but he hadn't done the background work to say, "this is why we need to do this; this is why it will work."

MM: In other words, it's not simply a matter of principals just cutting teachers loose. It's helping teachers who have the prerequisite skills to be a leader identify and practice those skills.

LR: Right. I think about my own experience in the middle school classroom. My principal had confidence that I would not go off on a tangent. I did my background work; I did what I needed to do to sell the program or strategy I wanted to implement, and he trusted that I would follow through. He knew that I could take the reins.

MM: We're not just talking about administrators abdicating power or abdicating responsibility. We are talking about purposefully making sure that someone has the ability and the skills and the confidence to lead. And then stepping back and being a member of the team... I'm interested in this idea, principal as follower. The principal doesn't always have to be the leader. There are times when a principal's skills are best utilized as a member of the group rather than being the person out front leading the initiative.

LR: I couldn't agree more. I met and worked with a principal who told me that one of his jobs was to *part the waters*. His role was to not get in the way of the teachers but to open doors for them; to be the front-line team member clearing the way so they could try new things. That really resonated with me when he explained it that way.

MM: That is very interesting because a lot of times teachers who may well have the skill and the confidence to be a leader, because they have not been in a leadership role in an organization setting, may not understand where or what the barriers are. And if you've got a partner to help with that, maybe that *is* the essence of shared leadership. I'll [principal] run interference over here and open things up, you [teacher] help to lead the initiative back here and together we'll make things happen.

LR: I agree. I think it is a partnership. It's not one giving up something for somebody else. It's, how can we each do our part for the ultimate goal of assisting students?

MM: In your research of teacher leaders and the principalship, was there something that surprised you? Anything that was reinforced?

LR: Many principals I work with articulate their support for teacher leadership. And teachers, in varying degrees, feel like they are supported as teacher leaders, but not all in the same way. Administrators talk about it being an important component of their work—they know it's the right thing to say—but they conceptualize teacher leadership differently. Some place a great deal of trust in the expertise of the members of the faculty who are implementing certain things. One principal I remember in particular jumped on whatever this teacher said they wanted to do and would say, "Yes, that sounds good. Let's do it!" There wasn't a whole lot of shared understanding about what choices were being made for implementing different programs. If the teacher came in and sold it well enough, they could do whatever they wanted.

MM: And that may not be a good idea.

LR: No. Not a good idea at all. This is where I see a lack of leadership on the part of some principals.

MM: When, in fact, there may be questions or concerns about a program or initiative.

LR: Right. I'm not sure some principals understand what they're saying yes to. MM: That's interesting and makes me think about the changing literature on leadership types. Sounds like the "responder principal" who is quick to give over responsibilities to others. They're also concerned with people feeling good about themselves and their work environment. And, not from a professional satisfaction standpoint.

LR: It was very much like that.

MM: That literature describes a superficial or surface orientation. It wasn't that we're going to feel good together because we've struggled through this and asked each other hard questions to get to a new place. It was, "You want to do something? Well, let me tell you yes so that you can feel happy and be pleased with me."

LR: Yes. I'll say whatever you want me to say so that you'll say good things about me when you're asked those questions. It was about pleasing the crowd.

MM: Sounds like there are some interesting parallels. Can you talk more about your experience with principals?

LR: Other principals, again, talk a lot about believing in teacher leadership, but are much more selective about who actually gets to lead. Such principals seem to favor seasoned teachers. Where teachers who have limited experience find it difficult to get their foot in the door to have a conversation with the principal.

MM: Okay.

LR: I knew a teacher who was team lead for the grade level. He was feeling frustrated that some of the things he wanted to bring forward to the principal were often negated by others who had more seniority on campus.

MM: Did you see the teacher as being every bit as able as more seasoned teachers?

LR: Yes. His personality, though, was different in that he was quiet. His ideas and intentions were good, but he didn't know how to approach the principal or rally his colleagues around efforts in a positive way.

MM: I see.

LR: And, if things didn't work out, it wasn't a matter of reflecting back for this person "how could I have done that better? What could I have prepared differently? If I felt there was a lack of follow through, what could I have done to make a change?" It was more than other people were blocking. To me that was a lack of experience and perhaps maturity.

MM: And perhaps something that could have been learned over time...

LR: And then there was the 30-year veteran who had been at her school through a number of principals. Because she'd been on this campus for such a long time, she'd built strong relationships with many colleagues, including her current principal.

MM: Okay.

LR: There was a high level of trust between this teacher and administrator. The way they worked together and approached each other was a true shared relationship.

MM: Through your years of work in this area you've seen lots of principal/teacher relationships, both successful and not so successful. If you were going to talk to principals about what they could do to nurture quality teacher leadership experiences on a campus, are there overarching suggestions you could make? If principals want to nurture and pursue teacher leadership, what would you say to them?

LR: I hope administrators will lookout for leadership opportunities.

MM: Can you say more about that?

LR: There's a tendency to get so engrossed in our work and the management of the school that you miss an opportunity to give a teacher a leadership task, to initiate something that they could do well. And then to follow through and do what the principal we discussed earlier did, open doors for the teacher. It's being aware that there are people out there whether they're quiet, or strong, or whether they're perceived as positive or negative—everybody has the ability to lead. But it's up to the administrator to channel that leadership in a way that's accessible for faculty.

MM: You know, in this chapter I've talked about my own professional experiences as I've worked with a variety of teacher leader styles. Some are out in front while others are more effective behind-the-scenes or in smaller groups. Have you seen these leader types?

LR: Absolutely. In one of our network meetings, we were talking about the four hats of leadership Garmston [2016] identifies—the consultant, the facilitator, the coach, and the presenter. Those are four areas where you can be a leader. And obviously presenting is one that puts you up in front of people, and is the most obvious form of leadership. I mean, if you're asked to do those things, you're clearly leading something.

MM: Sure.

LR: I think coaching has really started to take hold, and at some point, we do coach or consult. Facilitating might be another one that puts you out in front as a leader. But something happened recently in our teacher leadership network that reminded me not everyone is a front and center leader. I asked everyone for our final meeting to think about a way to present the results of their action research. One fabulous teacher pulled me aside and said, "I can't do it. I cannot stand up in front of people. It takes every ounce of energy I have to respond to some of the questions in our group." It's painful for her to speak in front of others. It dawned on me that I'd asked people to do something that's not necessary for everyone to do. I know she can lead, but it's going to be behind-the-scenes. She can work one-on-one with people and be a team player, but she's not going to be the one to stand up and say, "Here's what we've learned." So, I agree totally. That's why I hope administrators will recognize it's not always department heads who can or should lead. On a campus, there are many places and ways that teachers can lead.

MM: Exactly.

LR: Administrators should also realize that faculty members who are resisting change, when embraced in a leadership way, can turn the tide. Not only will they change, but the confidence that they build in themselves will lead them down a more positive path. The people who appear the most negative are individuals who probably fear something.

MM: That's true. And sometimes people who are healthy skeptics in a school community—who ask the hard questions—help us to clarify our own thinking and whether we're going down the right path.

LR: Absolutely. Even those people, who seem not on board, if we listen to the questions they're asking and what it is that they're concerned about, might elevate the discussion to a new level.

MM: I'm intrigued by this idea we discussed earlier, this role of a principal in shared leadership as a background person who, while somebody else is clearly taking the lead, is helping to navigate the pieces of the organization that the teacher leader might not even be aware of. For instance, you may know somebody in the central office who's going to be difficult to manage, or who's support you must secure before an initiative can move forward. By knowing and understanding that and being willing to handle that piece of it, possibilities open up.

LR: Or even on a campus where a teacher who is younger or newer to the school is working with a strong group of more experienced faculty. Trying to support and recognize that younger teacher as a leader on an initiative will help break down walls and barriers. That's something administrators can also do.

MM: That's a good point. Is there anything else about principals and their relationship to teacher leaders you would like to go on record about? Do you think principals *need* teacher leaders?

LR: Absolutely. That's part of the reason so many schools are struggling right now. On some of these campuses, teacher turnover is extremely high. I believe that when teachers feel they're part of the process, feel honored and respected as part of the leadership to change a campus, then you're going to be able to sustain some good things happening at that school. If a teacher is constantly being badgered and fussed at because the principal's being badgered and fussed at, then you just perpetuate the same thing, and teachers aren't going to stay very long. Teacher leadership is one way to recognize that everyone has a role to play and can help campuses turn around. We've got to embrace everybody. It can't be just the principal or the leadership team or the executive cabinet or whatever they want to call themselves. It needs to be everybody.

Lee's success with the regional teacher leadership initiative offers important practical lessons for those interested in pursuing similar projects. Like most long-term programs, adjustments over time have yielded improved results for those involved. When it comes to administrators and teacher leadership, here are several take-away points gleaned from the conversation with Dr. Rutledge. Principals and assistant principals should:

- Understand that they do not have to *go it alone*—there are plenty of able and willing leaders among the teaching faculty;
- Constantly lookout for potential leaders, especially among teachers who might otherwise be overlooked or marginalized;
- Assist younger or new-to-the-school faculty members to be recognized for the leaders they are and can be;
- Understand that leadership takes a variety of forms;
- Deliberately assist teachers in developing and practicing necessary leadership skills;
- Help teachers navigate organizational barriers and stumbling blocks;
- Be mindful that teachers who appear to be *negative* might offer valuable insight regarding possible problems associated with a program, innovation, or change;
- Nurturing leadership among those who seem resistant can make them part of the team and change their attitudes and practices within the school;
- Remember that successful teacher leadership can help reduce teacher turnover and attrition.

TAKING ACTION

As Diamond and Spillane (2016) remind us, the actual practice of on-the-ground leadership is "stretched over people" (p. 148) and empirical evidence suggests that a number of individuals carry out the leadership work in schools. Inclusive school leaders know this to be true and intentionally work to broaden their leadership circle.

Practitioners can check themselves to determine if they are taking appropriate, meaningful action to seek out and develop leaders among their colleagues. By becoming more knowledgeable and well-informed on the teacher leadership literature, principals and assistant principals can develop a richer understanding of the inclusive power of expanded leadership. Teacher leadership networks or initiatives offer structured and supported ways to learn more about establishing opportunities on your campus. Lastly and quite simply—leaders can carefully examine their campus roster and think specifically about each individual; are there potential leaders whose skills have yet to be tapped?

REFERENCES

Cunliffe, A. L., & Eriksen, M. (2011). Relational leadership. *Human relations, 64*(11), 1425–1449.

Diamond, J. D., & Spillane, J. P. (2016). School leadership and management from a distributed perspective: A 2016 retrospective and prospective. *Management in Education, 30*(4), 147–154. https://doi.org/10.1177/0892020616665938

Donaldson, G. A. Jr. (2007). What do teachers bring to leadership? *Educational Leadership, 65*(1), 26–29.

Garmston, R. J., & Wellman, B. M. (2016). *The adaptive school: A sourcebook for developing collaborative groups (3rd ed.).* Rowman & Littlefield.

Gordon, S. P. (2004). *Professional development for school improvement: Empowering learning communities.* Pearson-Allyn and Bacon.

Lambert, L. (2005). What does leadership capacity really mean? *Journal of Staff Development, 26*(2), 38–40.

Lattimer, H. (2012). Agents of change: Teacher leaders strengthen learning for their students, their colleagues, and themselves. *Australian Educational Leader, 34*(4), 15–19. https://search.informit.org/doi/10.3316/aeipt.197395

Lattimer, H. (2007). To help and not hinder. *Educational Leadership, 65*(1), 70–73.

McLester, S. (2018). Share the spotlight. *Principal,* supplement, May/June. 16–21.

McGhee, M. W., & Boone, M. (2008). *Collaborative action research: Developing professional learning communities,* Stephen P. Gordon (Ed.), Teachers College Press.

Muijs, D., & Harris, A. (2007). Teacher leadership in (In)action. *Educational Management Administration & Leadership, 35*(1), 111–134.

Poplack, S, & Dlesk, K. (2018). Hand and hand: Building cultural competency with teacher-leaders and the entire faculty. *Independent School,* Fall/2018, 110–115.

Printy, S. M., & Marks, H. M. (2006). Shared leadership for teacher and student learning. *Theory into practice, 45*(2), 125–132.

Safir, S. (2018). The emergent power of teacher leaders. *Educational Leadership, 75*(6), 69–73.

Sergiovanni, T., & Green, R. L. (2015). *The principalship: A reflective practice perspective,* (7th ed.), Pearson.

Smith, C. (2017). The unsuspecting teacher leader. *Delta Kappa Gamma Bulletin, 84*(2), 19–22.

CHAPTER 7

DISRUPTING THE STATUS QUO

A Call for True Equity in Special Education

Toni Barton
Spelligent

According to the most recent data from the National Assessment of Educational Progress, students with disabilities continue to perform significantly below their general education peers (National Center for Education Statistics, 2019). Over the past ten years, data show their outcomes have remained stagnant, at least 20% below their peers (2019). It is past time for school leaders to make a proactive and intentional decision to disrupt this status quo. This will require school leaders to recognize systemic oppression toward marginalized populations, including students with disabilities (McLeskey et al., 2014a; Khalifa, 2016). Throughout this chapter, we use the phrase exceptional learners to refer to students with identified learning needs using asset-based language.

There has been a growing movement of practitioners across the special education sector working to identify where special education is broken and to identify aligned solutions. The Council for Chief State School Officers

(CCSSO), the National Center for Special Education in Charter Schools, the National Center for Learning Disabilities (NCLD), and Understood are a few organizations representing policymakers, researchers, and practitioners in the field collaborating to identify meaningful solutions.

The CCSSO leads the National Collaborative on Inclusive Principal Leadership (NCIPL) which includes key stakeholders from principal associations, member organizations, technical assistance centers, researchers, educator preparation programs, and nonprofits. This group has outlined guidance to support states in advancing inclusive principal leadership efforts, including eight core strategies (Council of Chief State School Officers, 2018). This chapter aligns to Strategy 4: Promote Principal Development on Inclusive Practices. As a working group leader and state coach for the NCIPL, and as a contributor to NCLD & Understood's guide for school leaders (National Center for Learning Disabilities, 2019), I argue that there is no equity for students with disabilities without disruption: disruption of existing practices, existing systems, and existing structures. This chapter will outline what steps leaders can take toward that end.

Disrupting the status quo to build authentically inclusive schools requires a focus on leading with inclusive mindsets, creating aligned expectations, and aligning systems and structures to those mindsets (Billingsley et al., 2014). Research consistently finds outcomes for students in effective inclusive classrooms are just as good as, if not better than, separate classrooms (Hehir, 2012; Ceedar, n.d.; McLeskey et al., 2012; Doyle & Giangreco, 2013; McLeskey et al., 2014b; Kurth et al., 2015). To that end, recommendations in this chapter are based upon the assumption that inclusive classrooms are the ideal placement for students with disabilities.

In this chapter, we will use the phrase 'authentic inclusion' and 'authentically inclusive' to describe schools where all learners feel safe, supported, and valued; the individual needs of students are met; educators hold high expectations; and educators provide appropriate supports so students, regardless of difference or identity, excel, academically, socially, and emotionally. In my current work with school leaders, I constantly push them to interrogate school-wide systems focusing on authentic inclusion while engaging them in an ongoing cycle of reflection on values, beliefs, knowledge building, and planning. Leaders evaluate the big three systems in their schools, data, instruction, and culture, with the goal of committing to positive change, setting aligned expectations, and identifying key actions needed to lead schools where exceptional learners thrive.

A growing body of best practice supports the four-step process I have outlined to serve as a guide for how leaders can build authentically inclusive schools (Billingsley et al., 2014; CEEDAR, n.d.; Council for Exceptional Children, 2019; Hehir and Katzman, 2012; Jorgensen et al., 2010; McLeskey et al., 2014b; Villa and Thousand, 2003). These steps include:

1. Set an Inclusive Vision: *Leading with Mindset*
2. Set Ambitious Goals: *Goal Setting for Students with Disabilities*
3. Blow Up Existing Systems: *Designing Intentionally Inclusive Systems*
    a. Rethink Discipline: *Build Affirming Classroom Communities*
    b. Urgently Respond to Data: *Use Data Daily to Drive Decision-Making*
    c. Focus on Great General Education Instruction: *Use Student-Centered Instructional Practices*
4. Be a Warm Agitator: *Key Leadership Skills & Competencies*

As we explore the four steps, we will see how setting an inclusive vision grounded in shared values is foundational for building authentically inclusive schools. In these schools, every learner, regardless of classification or need, thrives academically, socially, and emotionally. Inclusion is not inclusive without positive outcomes. With a set of shared values in mind, leaders can explore what it means to set and monitor ambitious goals for exceptional learners by courageously rethinking existing systems for culture, data, and instruction.

STEP 1: SET AN AUTHENTICALLY INCLUSIVE VISION: BELIEFS DRIVE ACTION

The first step toward building schools designed to serve all learners "is simply a decision" (Ben Marcovitz, Collegiate Academies, 2018). Ben Marcovitz is the founder of Collegiate Academies, a charter network in southern Louisiana, who pushes leaders to simply decide that their school is going to be the place that serves every student who walks through the door, no matter their level of need. In a 2019 interview, Jerel Bryant, a Collegiate Principal and the 2021 Louisiana High School Principal of the Year, shared with me his belief that some practices and systems we developed for kids who are in most need of support work beautifully for the rest of our population. Jerel exemplifies an equity-centered leader who decided to invest in his students who need the most support, his exceptional learners, because he believes that their progress represents the progress of all.

Authentically inclusive education works when educators commit to integrating exceptional learners into their schools and work strategically to ensure they make appropriate progress (McLeskey & Waldron, 2000). Exceptional learners deserve leaders who are committed to that goal. Students with disabilities have been among the most impacted student populations deemed likely to have regressed academically, socially, and/or emotionally due to the COVID pandemic (Mitchell, 2020; Stein & Strauss, 2020; Villano, 2020). The pandemic spurred an opportunity for educators to make a renewed commitment to equity with the goal of closing the learning and opportunity gaps for exceptional learners.

Leading researchers on inclusive schools encourage educators to put a core set of beliefs at the foundation of their work to build. Tabvle 7.1 provides an example.

Over the past eleven years, I have conducted countless school visits and trained and coached hundreds of leaders nationwide. I have seen the beliefs in Table 7.1 manifest through a set of common mindsets in inclusive schools where they drive academic and/or social-emotional outcomes for exceptional learners.

When these mindsets are present in a school, exceptional learners actively engage with rigorous curriculum, feel affirmed and valued in an inclusive setting, and demonstrate both academic and social-emotional growth. In an effective inclusive school, these mindsets inform every system, structure, and practice every day.

When these mindsets are not evidenced in name or practice, deficits in knowledge, skills, and self-efficacy are usually to blame. In fact, educator apprehension and failure to implement inclusive practices generally stems from lacking the knowledge and skills to do so (Galiatsos et al., 2019; McLeskey & Waldron, 2000). This lack of knowledge can be misinterpreted as a mindset or belief issue when it's really a knowledge issue. Building an inclusive school, where all learners are thriving, begins with aligned mindsets, a shared definition of inclusion, aligned expectations, and a plan for building educator capacity (McLeskey et al., 2014a).

TABLE 7.1 Comparison of Works on Core Beliefs in Inclusive Education

McLeskey & Waldron (2000)	McLeskey et al., 2014	Brownell et al., 2012
• Students should have meaningful access to the general education classroom • Services should be provided in the general education setting to the greatest degree possible • Instructional systems should be designed to support the needs of students • Learner variability exists in a classroom and teachers must be prepared to meet a variety of needs	• Presumption of competence • Students deserve to be in general education • All teachers must collaborate to support students with special needs	• Progress of students with disabilities is responsibility of GE and SE • All students deserve access to GE • Students with disabilities should feel acceptance, belonging and a sense of community

TABLE 7.2　Inclusive Vision Checklist

Set an Inclusive Vision

Self-Reflection

- [ ] Identify a research-based definition of inclusion
- [ ] Identify your beliefs around inclusive education
- [ ] Ask yourself—Are my beliefs in alignment with the inclusive values? (See Table 7.3)
- [ ] Ask yourself—What steps do I need to take to move toward a more inclusive mindset?

Staff Reflection

- [ ] Share a research-based definition of inclusion with your staff
- [ ] Reflect with your staff—What are their beliefs around inclusive education?
- [ ] Unpack with your staff—Are their beliefs in alignment with the inclusive values listed above?
- [ ] Have staff members to identify—What steps do they need to take to move toward a more inclusive mindset?

Vision Setting

- [ ] Examine an example of inclusive beliefs in action
- [ ] Adopt a research-based definition of inclusive education
- [ ] Develop a vision for inclusion and craft a set of inclusive values

Belief work includes three core components: critical self-reflection (McLeskey et al., 2014a; Khaliffa, 2018), staff self-reflection, and collective vision setting. The checklist in Table 7.2 can be used to help leaders examine their own and their staff's beliefs around inclusive education and make a shared commitment to building an authentically inclusive school.

STEP 2 : BE AMBITIOUS: GOAL SETTING | FOR STUDENTS WITH DISABILITIES

Exceptional learners can meet grade level targets when appropriate services and supports are in place (Yudin and Musgrove, 2015). Once educators have interrogated their beliefs around teaching and learning for exceptional learners, they must work to identify targeted goals for their students. Educators should think beyond short-term IEP goals and think about what they want for their students at the post-secondary level (McLeskey & Waldron, 2000). Traditional standardized measures of accountability are often seen as insensitive to the growth of students with disabilities (Carnine, 2001; McLeskey et al., 2014a). To support achievement for exceptional learners, educators must implement comprehensive practices focusing on ambitious goal-setting (Jung, 2018; Jenkins & Terjeson, 2011), use of growth-sensitive measures to monitor growth (Carnine, 2001; Fuchs, 2017), frequent (daily) assessment of academic progress (Brownell et al., 2012; Carnine, McLeskey et al., 2014a), and analysis of student errors to identify instructional next steps (Brownell et al., 2012; McLeskey et al., 2014a) .

Goal Setting and Growth Monitoring

Each student should have goals that inform instruction. Whether the goals are mandated by a student's IEP or another formal plan, they must be rigorous and aligned to grade level expectations (Jung, 2018; McLeskey et al., 2014a). It is also important to align goals with evidence-based instructional practices. Traditional standardized assessments are not sensitive to the learning of SWDs; therefore, educators must utilize tools that will help support frequent data-based decision making. Curriculum based measurement is essential to setting goals for exceptional learners and monitoring their progress; use of such tools (DibelsNext, AIMSWeb, Wilson) allows educators to set ambitious goals that can be frequently tracked to determine progress.

In my second year as a school leader, we utilized AIMSWeb to set goals for every student in grades 2–7. We used the ambitious growth formula and tracked student progress toward those goals every week. With over 50% of our students having IEPs, over 80% of all students met those goals. Curriculum-based assessments such as AIMSWeb provide formulas that can be used to support ambitious goal setting. As Deno (2001) shared, to make sufficient progress, growth targets for students with disabilities should be the same as those for general education students. Growth targets should be used to monitor the effectiveness of interventions. When students are provided effective intervention, they can achieve growth rates relative to their peers.

STEP 3: BLOW UP EXISTING SYSTEMS: DESIGNING INTENTIONALLY INCLUSIVE SYSTEMS

Once leaders have identified and committed to disrupting the status quo, they must work to strategically implement changes to shift existing systems towards their newly identified goals. Actualizing a vision for an inclusive culture requires intentionally aligning expectations to the vision, designing or adapting a system aligned to the vision, ensuring staff has knowledge and skills to meet those expectations, developing of a system for monitoring expectations, celebrating wins, and allocating resources to meet expectations (Gupta, 2011; Hehir, 2012; McLeskey et al., 2014a; McLeskey et al., 2014b). In my work with leaders, I leverage the principles of improvement science

(Grunrow, 2015) to teach them how to blow up existing systems and bring their vision to life across each element of the core systems within a school (Grunrow, 2015).

What Systems?

Multi-Tiered System of Supports, also known as MTSS, is the go-to framework for transformation of school-wide systems to improve outcomes for exceptional learners, if a school's systems are not designed in a way that allows varied support required by MTSS, schools need to "blow up" those systems. Again, our collective goal is equity for exceptional learners; to accomplish this, leaders must identify how existing systems are promoting the status quo and make a plan to tinker with the system or trash three major systems in a school: culture, data, and instruction.

System 1: Culture (behavior).

Strategy: Rethink Discipline–Build Affirming and Proactive Support Systems
"School is for all students, not just the good ones."
—Curwin et al., 2018

A school's culture is defined by the systems, protocols, policies, and practices that support and respond to student behavior. Curwin et al. remind leaders that their values should come to life in their school's social-emotional support systems, otherwise known as discipline systems (2018). If a school's mission and values include terms such as "equity," "inclusion," "all learners," or other similar language, leaders are responsible to ensure discipline systems are aligned to that mission and values. This means that all protocols, policies, and practices within those systems are grounded in the inclusive mindset that school is for all students, not just the good ones.

It is widely accepted across the field that when students demonstrate challenging behavior, it is a representation of a need or lagging skill that must be identified and addressed. To that end, in my work with leaders, I intentionally reframe what is traditionally called management or behavior systems as 'social-emotional support systems' or 'culture systems.' We then categorize the components of traditional management or behavior systems as a culture system focused on providing social-emotional support in both a proactive and responsive manner. This intentional use of language is foundational in supporting an asset-based and inclusive approach to designing culture systems.

There are several widely accepted criteria for an inclusive and supportive culture system. The system should be data-driven, relationship-centered, have an affirming classroom environment, incorporate social-emotional learning, and utilize responsive intervention. An equity-centered approach to supporting student social-emotional needs through a school's culture systems requires educators to acknowledge that many students come to school with unmet basic needs. Knowing this, leaders must design systems that strategically work to respond to a variety of needs. Curwin proffers that if a school intentionally incorporates the strategies into its culture, the school can proactively support students whose unmet needs may manifest in misbehavior at school (2018). These systems must be monitored and adapted using a strategic approach to data collection. Specifically, schools should use data to identify students in need of social-emotional support, evaluate the effectiveness of the social-emotional support system, and examine individual supports. Targeted support must prioritize explicit instruction to teach desired behavior to students with the greatest needs (IRIS Center, 2005a; IRIS Center 2005b; McLeskey et al., 2017). For long-lasting impact, this work must be a collaborative effort between general and specialized teachers across settings. It requires a plan for specific coaching and feedback.

While the use of data should inform the design of impactful culture systems, a relationship-centered approach is paramount. This approach prioritizes relationship-building between students and staff to proactively support the whole child and set the conditions for learning (Curwin et al., 2018). According to Curwin, leaders should prioritize individual identity, a growth mindset, connections, listening to student voices, and creating a joyful classroom community to foster a relationship-centered approach.

Traditionally, classroom culture systems are designed with management and discipline as the focus. In an affirming classroom environment, classroom practices prioritize student dignity, a positive-approach to behavior and a solution-oriented environment. In an affirming classroom, students across identity markers are intentionally supported by one another, the environment, and their teacher (Rodriguez & Sprick, n.d.; IRIS Center, 2005a; IRIS Center 2005b; Metropolitan Center for Urban Education, 2008; IRIS Center, 2012; Curwin et al., 2018).

Van Ness Elementary School in Washington, D.C, a school featured by WestEd for their work around social-emotional learning, is an example of a school where students are thriving in an affirming, positive, and solution-oriented classroom environment. I became familiar with Van Ness through my work with Transcend Education, an organization focused on supporting schools in building equitable school environments. Van Ness Elementary School has partnered with Transcend to build a school model to support the whole child (WestEd, 2021). At Van Ness, every classroom community prioritizes compassion, collaboration, empathy, and affirmation of identity (2021). Achieving this culture has been a strategic journey and a collaborative effort between families, school leadership, and teachers. The school community came together and made a collective agreement to build a community that would support their priorities. This started with setting a vision, aligning expectations to that vision, designing systems and structures to support the vision, and implementing a core set of practices needed to bring that vision to life.

However, vision setting and identification of aligned practices are not enough. An affirming community is achievable when both students and staff have the skills needed to exhibit compassion and empathy, affirm the identity of others, and collaborate. This skill building can be accomplished through a targeted, school-wide focus on social-emotional learning. This focus emphasizes building and implementing systems that foster strong, respectful, and lasting relationships (Payton et al., 2018). In addition, schools must also commit to interrogating traditional systems of schooling and examining how they might have fostered oppressive practices within schools and communities (2018). This has been a key ingredient of Van Ness' success in supporting the whole child (Whole Child Model, n.d.). Equity-driven leaders intentionally disrupt existing classroom management systems that are enforcing the status quo and not driving positive outcomes for students.

System 2: Data

Strategy: Urgently Respond to Data—Use Data Daily to Drive Decision-Making

In conjunction with an MTSS system, schools must have processes in place to respond to formative and summative assessment data. In the Inclusive Schools Leadership Institute at Relay, we teach a series called Equitably Responding to Data which focuses on how to use data to drive improved performance for exceptional learners. In this series, we built upon Paul Bambrick-Santoyo's work on data-driven instruction to outline a more targeted approach to data analysis for exceptional learners (2019). We encourage leaders to prioritize high-leverage actions to strengthen data analysis and response before, during and after instruction (Bambrick-Santoyo, 2019; Moeller et al., 2018; McLeskey et al., 2014a) . Before instruction, teachers should plan for potential misconceptions based upon the learning profiles of exceptional learners (Fuchs et al., 2008). During instruction, teachers should leverage their understanding of student learning needs to strategically plan whose data to monitor and respond to during targeted instructional moments (Bambrick-Santoyo, 2019). That feedback should be immediate and corrective to promote immediate student growth (McLeskey et al., 2014a).

We can neither wait for nor rely on formal assessments (interim, standardized, screeners) to make instructional changes in support of exceptional learners. Schools must have regular processes in place to respond to the data and instruction informed by the three steps listed above. In such structured and systematic data analysis processes (e.g., weekly or daily data analysis protocol), teachers analyze data from formative classroom assessments and strategically plan responsive instruction for students who did not meet expectations, (McLeskey et al., 2014a; Moeller et al., 2018). Leaders should leverage collaborative problem-solving meetings to answer the following questions around student performance:

- Were there barriers within the classroom environment or instructional design that prevented students from accessing or demonstrating understanding of the content?
- What are the common errors and how did they manifest for exceptional learners?
- How might specific learning needs have caused misconceptions?
- How will we strategically reteach to support mastery of critical standards?
- What interventions are needed in addition to the reteach plan? (e.g., remediating skill gaps, shift in schedule)
- How will we align specialized instruction?
- What teacher gaps need to be addressed? (e.g., quality of planning or instruction; ability to respond to data)

Each structured meeting should include a plan for follow up to support implementation and a continued cycle of using data to be responsive to instruction (McLeskey et al., 2014a; Bambrick-Santoyo, 2019). This meeting should take place in a predictable recurring cycle to support building a data savvy school culture, a necessary ingredient for improving achievement outcomes (Hamilton et al., 2019).Leaders should implement formal progress monitoring measures that measure how instruction and intervention are impacting student growth targets (McLeskey, 2014a). According to McLeskey, effective progress monitoring tools are reliable, meaningful, efficient, can be repeatedly administered, are sensitive to improvement, and link to external accountability measures. Progress monitoring data should be supplemented by other assessments as a part of a comprehensive MTSS data process (2014a). Leaders should consider how to integrate an analysis of progress monitoring data into existing collaboration systems or into their system for weekly data analysis.

Leaders who prioritize strategic data analysis and response to instruction for exceptional learners are one step closer to achieving their vision for equity. Such equity-driven leaders intentionally disrupt existing data systems that are supporting the status quo and hindering positive academic outcomes for students.

System 3: Instruction.
> *Strategy: Focus on Great General Education Instruction—Implement Student-Centered Instructional Practices*

Without effective instruction, ambitious goals and strong data analysis practices will not provide significantly increased growth for exceptional learners. Over the past five years, I've had the opportunity to work with leaders across 13 states and Washington, D.C. My observations and conversations with leaders support the conclusion that effective instructional methods are not broadly evident in teaching students with disabilities. In fact, recent data show that only seventeen percent of teachers believe they have the skills needed to support students with mild and moderate disabilities and fifty percent of these teachers don't believe that students with disabilities can meet grade level standards (Galiatsos et al., 2019). If we are to shift the status quo, this data must change. This data can only change if leaders are willing to "blow up" existing instructional systems.

There are several high-leverage practices for instruction that are known to drive improved outcomes for exceptional learners within and outside of the general education setting These include universal design of lessons, explicit instruction, evidence-based instruction, effective scaffolding, supplemental intervention, strategy instruction, and flexible grouping (Fuchs et al., 2008; Brownell, 2014; McLeskey et al., 2014a; McLeskey et al., 2018; Galiatsos, 2019). If teachers and leaders are not implementing these high-leverage practices they should stop and immediately disrupt their instructional systems.

Teachers can use high leverage practices to remove barriers during lesson planning and instruction. Universally designed instruction asks teachers to proactively identify and then to remove barriers to learning in curricula, instructional goals, methods, and materials (Brownell, 2012; Hehir, 2012; McLeskey et al., 2014a; McLeskey et al., 2018; Galiatsos, 2019). When teachers design flexible lessons and learning environments, student learning is fostered. As a part of my work with *All Means All*, a leadership development program designed to support principals with building inclusive environments, I designed a lesson planning protocol that supports leaders with this process. The planning tool incorporates a series of reflective questions, informed by the work of Understood (2019), Alison Posey (n.d.), a UDL researcher at CAST, and national technical assistance provider, the Ties Center (n.d.). This tool helps leaders to identify and respond to potential barriers to learning. Table 7.3 outlines the planning process in that tool that can support planning for designing accessible lessons.

There are three opportunities leaders can leverage to make grade-level instruction accessible for a wide range of learners: provide scaffolds during planning, plan for teacher "talk-moves" that support scaffolding and provide tools to support scaffolding. In addition to providing scaffolded materials

TABLE 7.3 UDL Planning Tool

Planning Task	UDL Focus Questions
Analyze the Lesson Goal	• Identify what students need to be able to know and do • Identify the big ideas of the lesson or text and what needs to be prioritized for students who have skill gaps

Consider prerequisite skills	• Identify and create a plan for developing
	  – essential background knowledge
	  – key vocabulary/language and symbols essential to understanding

Consider core activities	• Identify each core activity needed to achieve lesson goals
	• For each core activity,
	  – options for progressing through lesson
	  – consider how information is being presented and whether another method is necessary to support meeting lesson goals; identify additional method of presentation
	  – ensure strategies support interest, effort, and/or self-regulation

Identify Misconceptions	• Identify potential misconceptions and design scaffolds to mitigate potential misconceptions • Identify where to provide reinforcement through pre-teaching or re-teaching • Plan for individual conferencing to support students with specific learning needs
Check for Understanding and Formative Assessment	• Identify where you will check for understanding during the lesson, design your CFU questions • Identify how you can provide options for how students are asked to demonstrate understanding while maintaining the objective of the lesson

(e.g., graphic organizers, sentence stems), while planning, teachers should specifically identify when and how they will model, think aloud, prompt, and cue (McLeskey et al., 2018). Doing this in advance empowers teachers to be prepared to respond in the moment, strengthening student understanding. The ultimate goal is to use scaffolds until students have reached a suitable level of independence (Staehr & Snyder, 2017; McLeskey, 2018).

Explicit instruction enables students to make sense of instruction. NCLD outlines four key elements of explicit instruction in their Guide to Creating Inclusive Schools (2019). These are modeling with clear explanations, verbalizing the thinking process, providing practice opportunities, and providing targeted feedback. With explicit instruction, teachers select targeted skills to be taught in a sequential manner and chunk the skills taught to support mastery (McLeskey, 2018). Teachers should then provide practice opportunities that include cumulative review and feedback until students reach mastery (McLeskey, 2018; Galiatsos, 2019). These practices can be leveraged to support both literacy and math instruction (McLeskey et al., 2014a; Galiatsos, 2019).

Effective intervention leverages research-based resources that incorporate explicit instruction as a tool to intensify overall instruction (Galiatsos, 2019; McLeskey, 2018). Instructional needs for exceptional learners with skill gaps in reading or math should be identified using a variety of data sources and that information should be used to develop a plan for delivering intensive intervention. Intervention should not replace grade level instruction; increasing the achievement of exceptional learners requires supplemental intervention. Upon implementation, educators must track progress within the intervention and collect at least three data points before adjusting the intervention (Fuchs et al., 2008).

Once leaders have set expectations and created systems for supporting effective instruction, they must support implementation through targeted development and feedback to both general and special education teachers, a critical step to interrupting the status quo. Delivery of high-quality instruction is the collective responsibility of both general and special educators (Brownell, 2012; McLeskey et al., 2014a; McLeskey et al., 2018; Galiatsos, 2019). One common area of concern, as I have observed in my work with leaders, is relegating responsibility around the performance of exceptional learners in general education to specialist teachers. This often occurs with those specialist educators being left unsupervised and under supported, which sometimes leads to low expectations and minimal monitoring for effectiveness. Leaders who want to improve the effectiveness of their systems for data, culture, and instruction can do so. With a laser focus on prioritizing a core set of practices, as outlined above, and a system for ongoing reflection on and refinement of systems, leaders can be one step closer to disrupting the status quo.

STEP 4 : BE A WARM AGITATOR: KEY LEADERSHIP SKILLS AND COMPETENCIES

There has been limited systemic change in schools suggesting a lack of widespread and substantive progress toward authentic inclusion of exceptional learners in the general education setting (Kurth et al., 2015). Exceptional learners deserve courageous leaders who are willing to "inspire and guide collective action" (Battilana & Kimsey, 2017) toward systemic change. Meeting this call for change requires leaders to rally a team that consists of individuals who are agitators, innovators, and orchestrators (2017). The agitator articulates a grievance with the status quo, creates a common purpose, and initiates action against the status quo. The innovator identifies and creates new or builds on existing proven solutions, organizes and engages stakeholders, and cultivates allegiances. These two roles require support from the orchestrator who coordinates action to bring about change. Effective leadership for change requires the work of all three roles, and it should not be expected that all three of these roles will exist within one individual. I encourage leaders to consider how they will pilot targeted improvements through a strategic process. Through that process leaders should agitate while engaging other *agitators* (like-minded teammates), create teams of *innovators*, and collaboratively *orchestrate* and plan for change. This strategic process, grounded in a core set of inclusive values and vision for effective cultural, data, and instructional systems, will go a long way towards improving outcomes for exceptional learners.

Being a warm agitator requires educators to establish and hold high expectations and create a systematic approach for accountability. To disrupt the status quo in service of improved outcomes for students with disabilities, educators must have high expectations with a clearly articulated set of aligned behavioral standards relating to both adult behaviors and student outcomes. Those standards must be reinforced consistently through a warm approach that communicates a commitment and care for students. Consistent collaborative structures (e.g., staff development, team meetings, etc.) must include established norms that allow team members to ask one another tough questions in service of inclusive values and to hold one another accountable to those values each and every day.

There are several questions teams can ask themselves during these structures to support building a culture of "warm agitation." Some sample questions are:

- Are we living up to our values in the way we are implementing this system?
- How did our actions support the status quo or promote high levels of achievement for exceptional learners?
- How was everyone held accountable for supporting exceptional learners in this system?
- How might student needs be leveraged as an opportunity to innovate within this system?
- How might we rethink resource allocation to drive toward ambitious goals for exceptional learners?

CONCLUSION

Disrupting the status quo for exceptional learners requires school leaders to embody and model inclusive mindsets, understand effective inclusive practices, support teacher development in inclusive practices across both general and special education, set clear and high expectations, and hold themselves and teachers accountable for aligning actions to expectations. This work requires leaders to commit to engage in an ongoing cycle of reflection, goal setting, and rethinking systems when they are not driving toward improved academic and social-emotional outcomes for exceptional learners. Leading systemic change in this way requires courage, expertise, strategy, and commitment. Success in schools should be measured by how well we support our most marginalized and underserved learners. When we commit to this, we can finally meet the call for equity. What will you do to commit to disrupting the status quo?

REFERENCES

Bambrick-Santoyo, P. (2019). *Driven by data 2.0: A practical guide to improve instruction* (2nd ed.). Jossey-Bass.

Battilana, J., & M. Kimsey (2017). Should you agitate, innovate, or orchestrate? A framework for understanding the roles you can play in a movement for social change. *Stanford Social Innovation Review.* https://ssir.org/articles/entry/should_you_agitate_innovate_or_orchestrate#

Billingsley, B., McLeskey, J., & Crockett, J. B. (2014). *Principal leadership: Moving toward inclusive and high-achieving schools for students with disabilities* (Document No. IC-8). University of Florida, Collaboration for Effective Educator, Development, Accountability, and Reform Center https://ceedar.org

Brownell, M. T., Smith, S. J., Crockett, J. B., Griffin, C. C., & Smith, S. J. (2012). *Inclusive instruction: Evidence-based practices for teaching students with disabilities.* ProQuest Ebook Central https://ebookcentral.proquest.com .

Carnine, D., & Granzin, A. (2001). Setting learning expectations for students with disabilities. *School Psychology Review, 30*(4), 466–472. https://doi.org/10.1080/02796015.2001.12086128

CEEDAR Center. (n.d.). *Inclusive education.* http://ceedar.education.ufl.edu/cems/inclusive-education/

Council of Chief State School Officers. (2018). *Supporting inclusive schools for the success of each child: a guide for states on principal leadership.* https://ccssoinclusiveprincipalsguide.org/state-strategies/

Council for Exceptional Children & CEEDAR Center. (2019). *Introducing high-leverage practices in special education: A professional development guide for school leaders.* https://highleveragepractices.org/wp-content/uploads/2019/02/A-Look-at-Instruction.pdf

Curwin, R. L., Mendler, A. N., & Mendler, B. D. (2018). *Discipline with dignity: How to build responsibility, relationships, and respect in your classroom.* ProQuest Ebook Central https://ebookcentral.proquest.com

Deno, S. L., Fuchs, L. S., Marston, D., & Shin, J. (2001). Using curriculum-based measurement to establish growth standards for students with learning disabilities. *School Psychology Review, 30*(4), 507–524. https://doi.org/10.1080/02796015.2001.12086131

Doyle, M. B., & Giangreco, M. (2013). Guiding principles for including high school students with intellectual disabilities in general education classes. *American Secondary Education, 42*(1), 57. https://doi.orgi:10.1177/004005990904100303

Fuchs, L., Fuchs, D., Powell, S., Seethaler, P., Cirino, P., & Fletcher, J. (2008). Intensive intervention for students with mathematics disabilities: seven principles of effective practice. *Learning Disability Quarterly, 31*(2), 79–92. https://doi.org.10.2307/20528819

Fuchs, L. S. (2017). Curriculum-based measurement as the emerging alternative: three decades later. *Learning Disabilities Research & Practice* (Wiley-Blackwell), *32*(1), 5–7. https://doi-org.library.relay.edu:444/10.1111/ldrp.12127

Galiatsos, S., Kruse, L., & Whittaker, M. (2019). *Forward together*. National Center for Learning Disabilities. https://www.ncld.org/research/forward-together/

Grunrow, A. (2015). *Improvement discipline in practice*. Carnegie Foundation for the Advancement of Teaching.https://www.carnegiefoundation.org/blog/improvement-discipline-in-practice/

Gupta, P. (2011). Leading innovation change—The Kotter way. *International Journal of Innovation Science, 3*(3), 141–150. https://doi.org/10.1260/1757-2223.3.3.141

Hamilton, L., Halverson, R., Jackson, S., Mandinach, E., Supovitz, J., & Wayman, J. (2009). *Using student achievement data to support instructional decision making* (ED506645). https://files.eric.gov/fulltext/ED506645

Heath, C., & Heath, D. (2010). *Switch: How to change things when change is hard* (1st ed.). Broadway Books.

Hehir, T., & Katzman, L. I. (2012). *Effective inclusive schools: Designing successful school-wide programs*. https://ebookcentral.proquest.com/lib/relay/detail.action?docID=817348.

Khalifa, M. A., Gooden, M. A., & Davis, J. E. (2016). Culturally responsive school leadership: A synthesis of the literature. *Review of Educational Research, 86*(4), 1272–1311. https://doi.org/10.3102/0034654316630383

The IRIS Center. (2012). *Classroom management (Part 1): Learning the components of a comprehensive behavior management plan*. https://iris.peabody.vanderbilt.edu/module/beh1/

The IRIS Center. (2005a). *Addressing disruptive and noncompliant behaviors (part 1): Understanding the acting-out cycle*. https://iris.peabody.vanderbilt.edu/module/bi1/

The IRIS Center. (2005b). *Addressing disruptive and noncompliant behaviors (part 2): Behavioral interventions*. https://iris.peabody.vanderbilt.edu/module/bi2/

Jenkins, J., & Terjeson, K. J. (2011). Monitoring reading growth: Goal setting, measurement frequency, and methods of evaluation. *Learning Disabilities Research & Practice* (Wiley-Blackwell), *26*(1), 28–35. https://doi-org.library.relay.edu:444/10.1111/j.1540-5826.2010.00322

Jorgensen, C. M., McSheehan, M., & Sonnenmeier, R. M. (2010). *The beyond access model: Promoting membership, participation, and learning for students with disabilities in the general education classroom*. Paul H. Brookes.

Jung, L. A. (2018). *From goals to growth: Intervention and support in every classroom*. ProQuest Ebook Central https://ebookcentral.proquest.com

Khalifa, M. (2018). *Culturally responsive school leadership*. Harvard Education Publishing Group.

Kotter, J. P. (2012). *Leading change.* ProQuest Ebook Central https://ebookcentral.proquest.com

Kurth, J. A., Lyon, K. J., & Shogren, K. A. (2015). Supporting students with severe disabilities in inclusive schools: A descriptive account from schools implementing inclusive practices. *Research and Practice for Persons with Severe Disabilities, 40*(4), 261–274.

McLeskey, J., & Waldron, N. (2000). *Inclusive schools in action: Making differences ordinary.* ProQuest Ebook Central. https://ebookcentral.proquest.com/lib/relay/detail.action?docID=3002075

McLeskey, J., Landers, E., Williamson, P., & Hoppey, D. (2012). Are we moving toward educating students with disabilities in less restrictive settings? *The Journal of Special Education, 46*(3), 131–140. https://doi.org/10.1177/0022466910376670

McLeskey, J., Waldron, N. L., Spooner, F., & Algozzine, B. (Eds.). (2014a). *Handbook of effective inclusive schools: Research and practice.* ProQuest Ebook Central https://ebookcentral.proquest.com/lib/relay/detail.action?docID=1691388

McLeskey, J., Waldron, N. L., & Redd, L. (2014b). A case study of a highly effective, inclusive elementary school. *Journal of Special Education, 48*(1), 59–70. https://journals-sagepub-com.library.relay.edu:444/doi/pdf/10.1177/0022466912440455

McLeskey, J., Barringer, M-D., Billingsley, B., Brownell, M., Jackson, D., Kennedy, M., Lewis, T., Maheady, L., Rodriguez, J., Scheeler, M. C., Winn, J., & Ziegler, D. (2017). *High-leverage practices in special education.* Council for Exceptional Children & CEEDAR Center. https://ceedar.org

Metropolitan Center for Urban Education (2008). *Culturally responsive classroom management* strategies.https://steinhardt.nyu.edu/scmsAdmin/uploads/005/121/Culturally%20Responsive%20Classroom%20Mgmt%20Strat2.pdf

Mitchell C. (2020). Bridging distance for learners with special needs. *Education Week.* https://www.edweek.org/teaching-learning/bridging-distance-for-learners-with-special-needs/2020/09

Moeller, E., Seeskin, A., & Nagaoka, J. (2018). *Practice-driven data: Lessons from Chicago's approach to research, data, and practice in education.* UChicago Consortium on School Research. https://consortium.uchicago.edu

National Center for Education Statistics. (2019). *NAEP report card: Math* https://www.nationsreportcard.gov/mathematics

National Center for Education Statistics. (2019). *NAEP report card: Reading.* https://www.nationsreportcard.gov/reading

Payton, J., et al. (2008). The positive impact of social and emotional learning for kindergarten to eighth-grade students. *Collaborative for Academic, Emotional, and Social Learning.* https://www.casel.org/wp-content/uploads/2016/08/PDF-4-the-positive-impact-of-social-and-emotional-learning-for-kindergarten-to-eighth-grade-students-executive-summary.pdf

Posey, A. (n.d.) *UDL lesson planner.* Understood. https://www.understood.org/en/school-learning/for-educators/universal-design-for-learning/lesson-planning-with-universal-design-for-learning-udl

Rodriguez, B.J., Sprick, R. (n.d.). Why a positive approach to discipline: a research summary). Safe and Civil Schools https://www.safeandcivilschools.com/research/references/positive-approach-to-behavior.pdf

Staehr Fenner, D., & Snyder, S. (2017). *Unlocking English learners' potential: Strategies for making content accessible.* Corwin.

Stein, P. & Strauss, V. (2019, August 7). Special education students are not just falling behind in the pandemic: They're losing key skills, parents say. *The Washington Post.* https://www.washingtonpost.com/local/education/special-education-students-are-not-just-falling-behind—theyre-losing-key-skills-parents-say/2020/08/05/ec1b91ca-cffd-11ea-9038-af089b63ac21_story.html

Ties Center. (n.d.). *The 5–15–45 tool.* https://tiescenter.org/inclusive-instruction/overview

Whole Child Model. (n.d). *Whole child model.* https://www.wholechildmodel.org/our-vision

Villa, R. A., & Thousand, J. S. (2003). *Making inclusive education work educational leadership, 61*(2), 19–23. Association for Supervision and Curriculum Development. http://www.ascd.org/publications/educational-leadership/oct03/vol61/num02/Making-Inclusive-Education-Work.aspx

Villano, M. (2020). *Students with special needs face virtual learning challenges.* CNN https://www.cnn.com/2020/09/24/health/special-needs-students-online-learning-wellness/index.html

WestEd. (2021). *Social Emotional Learning in action: Van Ness Elementary School.* Center to Improve Social Emotional Learning and School Safety. https://selcenter.wested.org/resource/social-emotional-learning-in-action-van-ness-elementary-school/#.

Yudin, M., & Musgrove, M. (2015). *Dear colleague letter.* U.S. Department of Education, Office of Special Education and Rehabilitation Services. OSEP DEAR COLLEAGUE LETTER on Speech and Language Services for Students with Autism Spectrum Disorder (July 6, 2015)–Individuals with Disabilities Education Act

CHAPTER 8

EQUITY LABS—CAN THEY INCREASE TEACHER AND LEADER EFFECTIVENESS?

Georgia Evans
The University of West Georgia

EQUITY SCENARIO: A PARENT'S DILEMMA:

My children and I just moved back in with my father to help care for him. His health has declined, and he can't afford to hire someone to assist him with his care. My name is Monica Adams, I'm 28 years old, and I have two children, ages 7 and 5.

Dad's apartment has two bedrooms and one bathroom, so the kids and I share a bedroom. The neighborhood isn't very safe, so I don't want my kids to play outside here.

Yesterday, I went to enroll my kids at the district-assigned elementary school. The school has graffiti outside the building and a fence around it. The principal, Dr. Smith, is new this year. While polite, she seemed stressed and did not have the time to talk with me. The secretary, Ms. Thornton, gave me a tour of the school. I met the Assistant Principal, an older gentleman whose office had stacked papers and piles everywhere. The Assistant Principal told me he had been in charge of discipline at the school for 26 years. While he and I talked, the kids waiting outside of his office were loud, using foul language, and playing around.

Ms. Thornton took me to meet the children's teachers. My son, Ricky, is in second grade. His teacher, Ms. Brown, told me she was new to teaching and trying to get used to elementary school. She said she was a history major and planned to teach at the high school, but there were no high school history jobs if you weren't a coach. Ricky has a hard time reading, so I'm hoping he will get extra help this year. When I told Ms. Brown about Ricky's reading issues, she said most of her students were behind in reading. There was a substitute in Mia's teacher's room, so I didn't meet her.

The next day, at the bus stop, there were lots of kids playing around and rough-housing. I was worried about putting the kids on the bus because it was so crowded. The older kids pushed Ricky and Mia out of the way to get on first. I was anxious all day about the kid's first day.

Ricky told me he did worksheets all day, and Ms. Brown couldn't find any of the school's paperwork he was supposed to bring home today. Ricky seems to like the other kids in his class. He told me he played with other boys at recess; Samuel and Juan. Ricky liked both boys but had to get Samuel to tell him what Juan said. Ricky said, "Ms. Brown didn't understand what Juan was saying either, but she must not have known to ask Samuel to explain it to her."

My daughter, Mia, is shy and small for her age. She doesn't talk much and has difficulty with some of her words. It takes her a long time to get comfortable with someone. Mia said her teacher, Ms. Green, is really pretty. She said there were lots of kids in her class, and they had to bring in a seat for her. While Mia was telling me about her day, she said, "Ms. Green told the class she was absent yesterday because she had an interview at a big office downtown."

After hearing about their first day, I'm more concerned. I was a good student in school. I graduated high school with honors and finished two semesters of college. Then I met the kid's dad, got married, and moved out of town. I was going to finish school, but Ricky came along. I want my kids to have a good education, so they can have better options than I have now. What can I do to make sure Ricky and Mia have a good school year and get a good education?

Reflecting on the Scenario

In schools across our country, parents like Monica have children with similar inequities: inexperienced, out-of-field, and ineffective teachers and leaders (Garcia & Weiss, 2019). In the Parent's Dilemma scenario, there are multiple equity issues in Ricky and Mia's urban elementary school. One of the first issues is the school's leadership. Dr. Smith, the school principal, was new and appeared overwhelmed. As a new and inexperienced leader, she may struggle to manage the multiple tasks associated with effectively leading a school, have limited knowledge of her role, and lack the confidence that comes with experience. The Assistant Principal (AP), the disciplinarian of the school for 26 years, is likely ineffective, evidenced by the absence of student respect, organizational skills, and lack of career advancement.

Ms. Brown, the 2nd-grade teacher, is certified in high school history. She is a new teacher, teaching out of field. Both factors imply she does not have the skills to work with elementary students, struggling readers, or English learners. Ms. Green, the kindergarten teacher, is looking for a job outside of education. The "interview at a big office downtown" suggests Ms. Green may have a degree in business. If so, she is teaching on a provisional or emergency certificate and out of field. While we are unsure if she is inexperienced or ineffective, we know she does not want to continue to teach. Other inequities include inadequate housing, unsafe neighborhoods, overcrowded buses and classrooms, discipline problems, and limited English learners' support.

This story could easily occur in a rural area. District locations do influence the availability of teachers. Research reveals students attending high-poverty, high minority schools are more likely to encounter teachers and leaders lacking the skills, experience, certification, knowledge, and commitment to work with children (Goldhaber et al., 2015; Goldhaber et al., 2016; Isenberg et al., 2016; Sass et al., 2012). In these schools and classrooms inequities of poverty, language, disability, ethnicity, homelessness, and foster care are prevalent; thus, inequity increases when teachers and leaders lack the skills to effectively serve marginalized students. Finding and retaining effective educators for high-poverty and minority schools is challenging, especially for low-performing ones. Research indicates these schools face the greatest issues of student achievement, teacher shortages, and effectiveness (Darling-Hammond, 2003; Tucker & Stronge, 2005). High-poverty districts are often located in areas with declining industry, lower home values, depressed property taxes, lack of social opportunities, and more minimum wage incomes (Erickson et al., 2008). These districts often have less money to supplement state allotments, which reduces teacher salaries, educational resources, and the overall quality of education (Adamson & Darling-Hammond, 2012). In other cases, schools and districts with high poverty and minority populations are concentrated in areas with increased crime, joblessness, overcrowded housing, student mobility rates, large numbers of English language learners, and discipline issues (Erickson et al., 2008). Regardless of the variations in poverty, there is one common factor, schools that serve low-income students struggle to fill teacher vacancies and have more inexperienced, uncertified, out-of-field teachers (Dee & Goldhaber, 2017; Garcia & Weiss, 2019; Sutcher et al., 2016). Equity labs help to put the spotlight on educator inequities.

WHY EQUITY LABS?

Every student deserves a quality education. Data on achievement, discipline, funding, and teacher effectiveness indicates students of color, low income, disability, and English Learners often do not receive the same quality of education and may lack college and career readiness (Akin & Neumann, 2013; Goldhaber et al., 2016, Sass et al., 2012). The educational disparities our most marginalized students face are not new, and we see little positive change. "Equity labs can kick off crucial conversations about how Local Education Agencies (LEAs), State Education Agencies (SEAs), and other partners can join forces to overcome racial and socioeconomic injustices that may have limited student access to the teachers and education they deserve" (Equitable Access Support Network, 2017, p.4).

An Equity Lab, sometimes called an Inclusion Lab, seeks to disrupt inequities by providing a structured process for drawing attention to inequity in schools, districts, and organizations. Equity Labs engage groups in a deep analysis of their data, identifying educational inequities, and developing a plan of action to improve issues related to race, equity, diversity, and inclusion. Equity Lab participants include district and school leaders, representatives from higher education, and members from various state agencies. The labs serve as a professional development experience for these educational leaders. Inclusive leadership is crucial in efforts to improve education at local, regional, and national levels. students face classroom and school discrepancies without strong, inclusive leaders committed to equitable access and opportunity for each student,

While public education has been scrutinized for decades, the focus on achievement gaps in education intensified in January 2002 with No Child Left Behind (Klein, 2015). This focus continued, along with an emphasis on equity, with the 2015 reauthorization of the Elementary and Secondary Education Act (ESEA) of 1965, referred to as Every Student Succeeds Act (ESSA) (Lee, n.d.). This law mandated that states and districts develop and submit new equity plans to outline "how low-income and minority children...are served at disproportionate rates by ineffective, out-of-field, or inexperienced educators." (Battelle for Kids, 2016). Equity labs became a resource offered by state education departments to support local LEA equity plans. According to the Equitable Access Support Network (2017),

> An equity lab is a convening of districts and other local stakeholders focused on advancing equitable access to excellent educators locally, in alignment

with a state's educator equity plan. An equity lab can be a catalytic force to help close State equity gaps. It is a start of a crucial conversation about how districts, SEAs, and other partners can join forces to overcome racial and socioeconomic injustices that may have limited student access to the teachers and education they deserve regardless of background or zip code (p. 4).

The format, focus, and process for Equity Labs vary across states, The anticipated outcome is the same: increased awareness, deep conversation, a focus on inclusive leaders, and an urgency to act on one or more educational inequities. Following is a description of how one state developed, implemented, and used Equity Labs.

ONE STATE'S EQUITY LABS:

As noted, the Every Student Succeeds Act (ESSA) required a state Educator Equity Plan. In one state, the response involved assembling a committee of stakeholders from various educational groups. The state committee convened to review data, conduct a root cause analysis, and identify state equity gaps. Through this work, the state committee identified the most critical equity gaps: inexperienced educators, out-of-field teachers, the number of classes taught by teachers deemed to be not highly qualified, teacher salary, and turnover of both teachers and principals. Common themes, such as recruitment, teacher preparation, retention, professional growth, and teacher and principal effectiveness, emerged, becoming targets for the state's Equity Plan (USDOE, 2015).

While Equity Labs were not explicitly identified as a strategy in the state's Educator Equity Plan, the committee agreed the labs were worthwhile tools to increase the urgency of emphasis on equity. The Equity Lab process was developed and vetted through a partnership between the State Department of Education, the higher education agencies represented by the Board of Regents, and the Professional Standards Commission for educator certification. Upon approval of the process, the state utilized existing regional groups made up of school districts, higher education institutions, and representatives from regional and state agencies as venues for the equity labs (Warner & Duncan, 2018). Using the regional rollout of the Equity Lab, participants examined local data on district teacher and leader effectiveness, experience, and out-of-field certification, which led to the identification of equity issues, rich discussions related to the data, root cause analysis, and identification of potential local solutions. Because one goal of the Equity Lab was replicating this work in districts and other organizations, the sessions also provided a "train the trainer" component.

The Equity Lab Process

The Equity Lab process included a team structure, where school districts, higher education entities, and others from their various institutions would attend together. The data focused on LEAs, and the district teams became the focus groups for the activity. A higher education representative and attendees from various state agencies participated in each district group to increase understanding and collaboration. Equity Labs were completed in approximately three hours and were structured to include stakeholder engagement, regional and district data analysis, equity gap identification, root cause determination, and strategies and solution development.

Data Preparation

Since session attendees examined state, regional, and district data, it was important to have accurate data. State agencies provided raw data on ineffective, out-of-field, and inexperienced teachers and leaders. Once received, the data were analyzed to obtain overall state percentages and sorted by region. We developed charts with the percentages and numbers of ineffective teachers and the percentages and numbers of students taught by these teachers, as shown in Figure 8.1. Other charts displayed the percentages of out-of-field teachers by certification areas, as displayed in Figure 8.2.

State P-20 Regions P-20 NAME	% of Teachers at Level I & II*	% of Students Taught by Level I & II*	# of Students Taught by Level I & II*	% of Students (by course) Taught by Level I & II*	# of Students (by course) Taught by Level I & II*
State	1.87	8.89	157655	1.87	268578
Region 1 (13 districts)	0.76	3.24	3384	0.64	5057
Region 2 (11 districts)	1.16	8.80	10230	1.69	16349
Region 3 (20 districts)	1.62	8.20	87500	1.70	149857
Region 4 (14 districts)	1.72	6.52	9276	1.58	17113
Region 5 (13 districts)	0.64	2.92	2388	0.48	3084
Region 6 (22 districts)	0.47	1.76	4531	0.40	8028
Region 7 (37 districts)	0.85	3.16	1063	0.54	1276
Region 8 (41 districts)	2.90	10.98	9743	2.80	16756
Region 9 (7 districts)	2.17	8.35	4112	2.41	7535

*Levels I & II indicate teachers receiving a less than satisfactory/proficient summative evaluation on the state effectiveness measure.

Figure 8.1 Ineffective teacher data for state and regions.

Equity Labs—Can They Increase Teacher and Leader Effectiveness? • 145

SYSTEM NAME	FTE FY18 Total Student Count	FY18 Total Teachers Count	2018 Percent of Out of Field Areas										
			Special Educ.	ESOL	Gifted	ELA	World Lang.	Fine Arts	Math	Science	Social Studies	PE/ Health	Pre-K	CTAE/ JROTC
District 1	42,309	2718	26.0%	11.2%	2.5%	9.5%	18.8%	6.1%	10.1%	13.8%	11.3%	9.5%	0.9%	11.0%
District 2	4,131	273	24.4%	0.0%	3.2%	6.1%	0.0%	3.4%	8.0%	12.2%	4.1%	7.5%	10.5%	2.6%
District 3	7,440	462	44.7%	10.6%	3.7%	13.6%	0.0%	8.0%	16.8%	19.1%	8.7%	14.7%	0.0%	5.9%
District 4	4,391	292	17.9%	0.0%	31.3%	19.6%	0.0%	9.3%	15.2%	19.4%	16.5%	17.6%	0.0%	27.1%
District 5	13,073	883	29.6%	0.7%	7.8%	7.1%	0.0%	1.8%	10.4%	11.0%	6.8%	3.1%	0.0%	12.8%
District 6	32,078	2060	41.2%	10.3%	20.1%	9.5%	3.4%	5.5%	11.0%	13.8%	11.3%	9.5%	2.2%	9.9%
District 7	18,443	1022	33.7%	0.5%	3.1%	5.9%	0.2%	4.3%	9.6%	18.6%	4.6%	7.5%	5.4%	6.6%

Figure 8.2 Out of field teacher data for state and regions.

146 ▪ G. EVANS

Additional tables, graphs, and charts presented the percentages of inexperienced teachers and leaders, subgroup demographics, per-pupil expenditures, and teacher production numbers.

INTRODUCTION TO THE EQUITY LAB

The first part of the Equity Lab was the Parent's Dilemma scenario, which was used as an activator and a way to create engagement. After listening to the scenario, small groups reviewed the data in Figure 8.3 for Ricky and Mia's school and identified inequities from both the scenario description and the school data charts.

In Figure 8.3 for Sample Elementary, the small groups noted increasing enrollment, decreasing student achievement, and demographic shifts, such as increases in economically disadvantaged and Hispanic students. When looking at the Teacher and Leaders Data for the school, participants were alarmed at the percent of inexperienced (36.5%), out-of-field (22.5%), and emergency/provisional (11.2%) certified teachers. While participants noted the educational issues associated with those percentages for this fictitious school, most had no idea that the percentages reflected many school districts in the state.

Sample Elementary School:

Demographics:

Enrollment	# of Students	Black (%)	Hispanic (%)	White (%)	Multiracial (%)	F/R %
2018-19	436	55.9	26.8	6.9	10.4	91.4
2017-18	397	58.5	22.7	7.2	11.6	87.9
2016-17	374	60.1	19.5	7.5	9.7	85.0

Academics:

State Accountability Score	2018--19	2017-18	2016-17
	50.2	58.6	63.4

Teacher / Leader Data:

System	School	Ineffective TE (Levels 1 & 2)		Emer. & Prov.		Out of Field (All Courses)		Inexperienced TE	
		FY 19	FY 18	FY 19	FY 18	FY 19	FY 18	FY 19	FY 18
Example Co.	Sample ES	2.76%	2.30%	11.2%	10.6%		22.5%	36.5%	35.2%

Figure 8.3 Data for Sample Elementary (parent scenario).

Equity Lab Data Analysis Activity

Before receiving their actual data, participants analyzed the chart containing overall state data on ineffective teachers (Figure 8.1). By beginning with the state data, participants became familiar with the format of the charts, visualized the state as a whole, compared each region, and identified some of the state's equity issues.

Once the state data had been analyzed, regional and district data packets composed of various charts were provided to small group participants. After familiarizing themselves with the data handouts, the groups began to note data concerns. To ensure all groups considered specific data points, guiding questions were used to focus the participant's attention and conversation points.

As the groups examined the data and answered the guided questions, they identified their district's top three equity concerns. A prioritized list of top concerns was developed for the whole group. The session attendees selected one of the identified needs from the list as their focus for the next activity, the Root Cause Analysis.

Root Cause Analysis

With data concerns identified, the next step was determining the causes of the prioritized equity issues. Selecting the root cause process most appropriate for the group was a major consideration. During the author's years of experience working with schools and districts, she has observed educator frustration and limited success with root cause analysis (RCA). Educators who have participated in root cause analysis tend to hold a negative view of the process, considering it time-consuming, complicated, or ineffective. One reason for this frustration is found in the name, which implies there is a single root cause (Peerally et al., 2016).

When considering the typical root system of a plant, there is a structure of roots working together to support, nourish, and sustain the organism (see Figure 8.4). The concept of having only one cause for a complex problem is most likely why educators grapple with the root cause analysis process (Groopman, 2007). Schools are complex social systems working with human beings; thus, they tend to have multiple causal factors rather than one specific root cause (Clark County School District, n.d.). Some root cause methods can be flawed because potential causes are discarded to identify one final cause. Groopman (2007) also notes educators have limited knowledge and no training in the root cause analysis. For the Equity Lab, it was

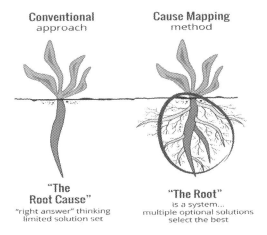

Figure 8.4 Root cause comparison.

essential to use a simple process with a system of causes that would create engagement, be time effective, and provide worthwhile causes.

The affinity diagram process, sometimes called the KJ process, after the creator, Jiro Kawakita, provided the method for generating, organizing, and consolidating the participants' ideas (Savina, n.d.). The affinity diagram process begins as most root cause methods by turning the identified problem into a Why question. Then participants use notes or index cards, work independently to write the numerous possible reasons/causes to the Why question, with each response placed on a separate card. At the end of the allotted work time, session attendees, with their responses, move into a larger group with others who considered their identified topic. The larger group reads, discusses, and assembles individual responses into common or related categories.

Usually, with a root cause analysis process, categories or items focusing on something out of a group's control, such as parents or students, are discarded. Due to the complexity of the identified concerns, we wanted all factors to be considered, so this step was omitted. For example, "retirement of current leaders" could easily be a cause for the question, "Why is there a high percentage of inexperienced leaders?" This answer would typically be discarded. However, if not every educational leader leaves the field at the 30-year mark, one must consider why some leaders delay retirement and extend their careers. The answers to this more complicated question could lead to possible solutions like district support, commitment to the school, desire to see an initiative come to fruition, or feeling valued by the superintendent. Answers, such as these, can lead to actions and possible strategies and deep discussions focused on solutions.

Once all responses are sorted into categories, the participants name each collection of related responses. Participants count the number of cards in each category to determine the three largest categories, considering the root causes of each identified concern. As a spokesperson for group explains the three root causes to all session attendees, each identified root cause becomes a chart heading

Solutions Walk for Root Causes

With the identified root causes listed as chart headings, session attendees divide into small groups again to do a "solutions walk." As the groups move from chart to chart, they discuss the root cause heading and list possible solutions. After groups rotate through all charts, the groups return to their assigned first chart, where they read and discuss all solutions added to the chart by other participants, determining which solutions are most viable. At the end of the activity, the solution charts are collected, typed, and recorded ideas are emailed to the participants for further consideration and use in their continued equity work.

Concluding the Equity Lab

Since one purpose of the session was to prepare participants as trainers back in their districts and organizations, the steps used for the Equity Lab's process are provided and reviewed with the attendees. To plan for the continuation of the equity work, like-groups determine the next steps for their organization and for the regional group (Warner & Duncan, 2018). The next steps are shared within the whole group, charted, and included in the day's minutes to increase accountability for continuing the work. During the final part of the Equity Lab, participants, regardless of their organizational affiliation, were reminded of their role and responsibility in ensuring the process, data, and identified inequities were acted upon. Inclusive educational leaders owe it to our students to promote equity and address inequities.

A SUCCESSFUL EQUITY LAB SCENARIO

It is always a good sign when the room is set up, coffee is brewing, and someone meets me at the door with a smile. As I arrive early in the southeastern part of the state for an Equity Lab, this is what I find. The preparation before the Equity Labs is a sure indicator of success.

As I walk into the room, I note the ample space available and ask how many people were expected. My co-leads say eight teams are coming from the 23 districts in the region. I am thrilled to hear the word teams, as all too often, only one person from an LEA attends. The first three people arrive, and I am surprised to find all three are from the regional public library. I ask about their interest in the session; they explain they are there because they were invited to attend and want to find ways to support the schools and students. By 8:45, the room is filling up, and the LEA teams are claiming their tables. The largest school district in the region has sent a team of 11 people, and other LEAs have teams of 3 or 4 district office staff.

After the welcome by the regional team leads, the Equity Lab begins. My first step is to reassign the institutions of higher education (IHE) and regional and state representatives to the various LEA tables. In one of my first labs, I left teams at the table of their choice. When we got to the data analysis part of the lab, those not associated with an LEA found little reason to "dig" deep into the data, connect the information to their organization, and quickly disengaged from the work. By sitting with a related LEA, the higher education team members, regional support agency representatives, and the Department of Education colleagues listen to the LEA discuss the issues associated with the data, ask clarifying questions, and consider how to support the district with its equity issues.

Once everyone has met their new table mates, I ask participants to listen to the Parent's Dilemma Scenario, review the data for Ricky and Mia's school, and identify the inequities faced by the two children. We do an open discussion of the inequities we identified, as I want people to feel free to talk and interact both with their table colleagues and with me. Opening this discussion to everyone helps to "break the ice."

We discuss the state data as we prepare to look at the regional and district data (Figure 8.1). The table groups receive their data packets and begin to review their district data. During this early part of the analysis, the discussion and engagement are intense as participants begin to look at their specific information. There are often questions about how the data is calculated or what a term means. For example, an "inexperienced" teacher is defined as someone with three years or less experience in a school district. Currently there is no way to identify teacher experience in other districts; thus, it is possible to have a veteran teacher of 20 years counted as "inexperienced" because they moved to another school district.

Another question that often comes up is, "where did you get the data?" I explain that the Department of Education and other state agencies provide the data. In some cases, the LEA representatives want their own "raw data" to review, and in other cases, the LEA representatives question the validity of the data. This is the case with the largest school district in attendance at this Equity Lab.

One of the eleven group members immediately tells her table that the data is incorrect, causing table participants to stop their analysis. To reassure the group, I quickly locate the excel data file from the state and let her compare the data on the handout to the excel spreadsheet. The data in the spreadsheet matches the handout. Work at the other tables is going beautifully. After about 15 minutes, I remind each table to use the guiding questions to narrow their discussion. Without the reminder, most participants get so deep into the analysis and discussion that they do not look at the entire packet. At 10:30, all groups must identify their top three areas of concern. Responses include ineffective teachers, out-of-field teachers, inexperienced teachers, emergency-provisional certificates, specific out-of-field content areas (e.g., special education, gifted, science), or inexperienced leaders. We collect and prioritize the top concerns based on the number of times they were identified.

As the groups come back together, they review the prioritized list and discuss the top two concerns: (1) ineffective teachers and (2) a high percentage of out-of-field Special Education teachers. I ask each participant to decide which of the two concerns they will choose and explain the steps of the Root Cause Analysis process. I remind the groups to work independently, write as many reasons as possible for the Why question, and not focus on solutions. As each participant takes a pack of post-it notes, each concern becomes a Why question. For example, "Why do we have such a large percentage of out-of-field Special Education teachers?" For four to five minutes, participants work on the causes. When time is called, each person takes their post-it notes to a table designated for their area of concern. Once the post-it notes are grouped into common categories, We count and rank order the post-it notes. The special education group identifies (1) state certification requirements for special education teachers, (2) special education teachers moving into general education fields, and (3) school leadership. The ineffective teacher table notes three causes: (1) lack of fidelity in applying the state effectiveness rubric; (2) lack of preparation during internships; (3) difficulty in replacing ineffective teachers. Each of these six topics becomes the heading for a new chart. Participants are assigned six new groups for the "solutions gallery walk." Each small group is assigned a chart and given at least five minutes to brainstorm and record their ideas. Groups then rotate to the next chart, where they read what has been listed and add to the solutions. Group reassignments for this activity are intentional. Groups from the same district are more likely to hinder the brainstorming with comments like, "that won't work, because...," "we've tried that before, and it didn't work," or "if we knew the solution, we would have already fixed the problem." A mixed group from various LEAs, higher education, and support agencies are less likely to focus on what will not work and think creatively. As the small groups rotate back to their initial chart, they read and discuss any additional solutions and identify two or three viable solutions to present.

After the solutions are presented, participants return to their job-alike

> groups. LEA participants work with their colleagues, higher education personnel form a group, and all support agency representatives partner. In these job-alike groups, the participants identify the next steps for two groups: (1) their specific representative group and the (2) Regional Group. The next steps are charted, presented to the entire group, and included in the minutes.
>
> At the end of the session, I debrief with the regional co-leads and the state liaison. As I roll up the charts to take home to type, I reflect on the morning. This was a good day, not because of anything I did, but because of the commitment and work of the co-leads and the state representative. This is a region that will continue to explore and address equity.

Outcomes and Results

As noted in the successful Equity Lab scenario, the success of the Equity Lab work varied by region. The regional groups have embraced and continued the work in the areas with strong leadership from state agency liaisons. Subsequent regional meetings have included clarifying certification rules for Special Education Teachers, professional learning on inclusive leadership, and collaborative discussions on improving and strengthening teacher intern placements. Within these regions, districts replicated the Equity Labs, started "Grow our Own: Teacher Intern Programs," and strengthened options for high school students interested in a career in education. Schools and universities partnered to create "future teacher" graduation ribbons and sashes and started "future teacher" signing days for seniors.

However, not every region was ready for the conversation about equity. In areas with less guidance and involvement by the state liaison, attendance for the Equity Labs was limited. Participants attended individually, not as a district team, and sufficient time for the Equity Lab was not always provided. Since it was the state liaison's job to work with the regional co-leads to develop the agenda, advertise the session, and communicate the goal of the Equity Lab, the level of commitment and involvement of the liaison was critical to the success of the lab. When the preparation and communication were lacking, the labs were less successful. In these cases, districts waylaid conversations with excuses, challenged the Equity Lab process and/or data and had limited participant engagement. One region felt the state had forced the Equity Lab on them, so they were disconnected throughout the lab. In another Equity lab, the only attendees were from higher education, limiting conversational depth.

Overall, the positive outcomes outweigh the negative. Equity conversations, data analysis, and proactive solutions by LEAs, higher education institutions, and regional groups have increased following the Equity Labs.

Teachers across the state are participating in professional learning on equity, social-emotional learning, and diversity, and inclusive leadership. In most regional meetings, the LEAs and higher education entities continue the focus on equity, inclusive schools, and ways to increase access to effective teachers and leaders. Participating LEA and IHE personnel have stepped up to become leaders and champions for equity. They have conducted equity labs, joined state groups, presented at conferences, and, most importantly, taken stands within their organization.

ONE DISTRICT'S SUCCESS STORY

While there were numerous success stories, the Central County School District story is worth examining. Central County Schools is a large district in the middle of the state. Approximately 60% of their students are economically disadvantaged, 12% are students with disabilities, and 10% have limited English proficiency. When examining ethnicity, 36% of the students are Black or African American, 37% are White, and 17% are Hispanic. Traditionally, the district has been plagued with poor leadership, frequent educator turnover, a lack of collaboration among schools, low test scores, poor graduation rates, and an overall reputation as a mediocre district.

A few months prior to the Equity Lab, Central County Schools hired new district leadership with a strong commitment to improvement for students. After the Equity Lab experience, the district representatives who attended met with the district leaders. They shared the data packet, discussed the process, reviewed the results, and were asked to replicate the Equity Lab with a larger group of district and school leaders. However, the superintendent had one requirement. He wanted more district data analyzed during the Equity Lab; thus, student achievement, attendance, discipline, and graduation data were collected. In addition, the district data packet added stakeholder engagement and satisfaction data, poverty levels, annual income, crime rate statistics, and even data on mortality rates and health issues in the different school zones. The superintendent invited members of the Board of Education and representatives from business, industry, government entities, and parents to participate in the lab. As the data were reviewed, analyzed, and considered, participants made notes on a huge map of the district. Graduation rates and test scores were recorded beside each school in the district. Ineffective, inexperienced teacher percentages were displayed by school zone on the map. Crime, mortality, and income levels were color-coded by the different regions of the district. The results were alarming when all the data was analyzed and displayed on the district map. There were clear pockets throughout the district where student achievement was low, ineffective teachers were high, and community income, health, and mortality were noticeably lower.

While stakeholders in the region always knew there were affluence and

> poverty areas in the district, this level of analysis had never been considered. Because of this Equity Lab, the district has completely restructured funding and allocations. The neediest schools and students are now provided greater resources, better teachers, lower teacher-student ratios, extra support for at-risk students, and more wrap-around services for parents and the community. The more affluent schools still receive adequate funding, but the allocations are based on need rather than "treat everyone the same." The district has contracted with the Hanover Institute to provide professional learning and support, and they are beginning to see positive results in several areas. The transition and change have not been easy, and there has been resistance from many individuals and groups. However, the map of "inequities" created during the district Equity Lab continues to be displayed in the Boardroom as a reminder of the reason and purpose behind the change.

RECOMMENDATIONS AND NEXT STEPS

Follow-up is needed if the positive effects of Equity Labs are to continue. All three partnering state agencies who started the equity lab work have new leadership, so the initial urgency of the work seems to have shifted. We need a meeting of state agencies to discuss the initial equity labs' outcomes and "next steps." State agencies need to conduct a needs assessment in each region to identify the work status and determine regional concerns. The momentum and energy for the work among the regional groups are still high, but if follow-up training, conversations, and sessions are not planned, they will soon wane.

The equity work is essential, and timing is critical. Along with identifying the next steps, it will be important to schedule new Equity Labs., particularly in regions and school districts where attendance for the first labs was low. Continuing the focus on Equity Labs will increase involvement across the state and strengthen the emphasis on the equity gaps identified in the state and local LEA Educator Equity plans.

The Equity Labs should be expanded to consider other areas of inequity, such as educator bias, discipline disproportionalities, subgroup achievement gaps, and school class and program assignments. Working with educational preparation programs to examine data on teacher retention, ineffective teachers, and certification needs can provide a different view of equity. The first equity labs offered in this state were a good start, but there is a need to extend the focus to different data and groups.

Leaders are an essential group for equitable schools; thus, they need training, support, and guidance on equity and inclusive leadership. If educational leaders do not understand and practice inclusive leadership, then districts, schools, and students will continue to deal with the current inequities. The work of helping leaders recognize inequity can start with Equity Labs. (OESD, 2012).

CONCLUSION

Inequities in education are numerous, long lasting, and show little to no improvement. Creating equitable schools is essential for students, especially our most marginalized populations (Darling-Hammond, 2003; Goldhaber 2016; Kane & Staiger 2008; Marzano et al., 2001; Sander & Rivers, 1996; Schmoker, 2006; Tucker & Stronge, 2005). Challenging, addressing, and eliminating inequities can be overwhelming for educators, leaving many unsure where to start. Equity labs provide a mechanism for starting the process. Equity labs are based on the following problem-solving steps; begin with the data, identify the concern, find the root cause(s), research and brainstorm solutions, and determine the next steps for applying the solutions.

Commitment to achieving equity and inclusive schools requires inclusive leaders at all levels, state, district, and school. Educational leaders must take the lead in removing barriers to learning, addressing systemic racism, and providing the supportive learning environments quality education for each student; the process must start with educational leaders (Blankstein & Noguera, 2015; Linton, 2011). Addressing inequities within school organizations begins with recognizing the "gaps" arising from discrimination patterns, implicit bias, and inequality. Achieving educational equity will require changing mindsets from viewing differences as problematic to developing a proactive perspective (Fraser, 2008; GLEC, 2012, 2016a; Lindsey et al., 2009). To change the Parent's Dilemma Scenario, there has to be an unwavering commitment, courageous conversations, and an impetus to start the process. Equity Labs can provide that momentum.

James Baldwin notes, "*Not everything that is faced can be changed, but nothing can be changed until it is faced.*" Equity labs help educators identify and face the problem. The equity lab process can be a critical component in assisting educators in recognizing the reality and the needs of schools and districts. If nothing else, equity labs start the conversation.

REFERENCES

Akin, L., & Neumann, C. (2013). Identifying proactive collaborative strategies for teacher readiness for marginalized students. *Journal of College Teaching & Learning, 10*(4), 235–244.

Battelle for Kids. (2016). *Building the talent pipeline: Three steps to attract and retain educators.* https://battelleforkids.org/docs/default-source/publications/bfk buildingtalentpipeline_threesteps_final.pdf?sfvrsn=2

Bowers, A. J. (2017, July). Quantitative research methods training in education leadership and administration preparation programs as disciplined inquiry for building school improvement capacity. *Journal of Research on Leadership Education, 12*(1), 26–50.

Cantrell, St., & Thomas J. K. (2013, January). *Ensuring fair and reliable measures of effective teaching: Culminating findings from the MET Project's three-year study.* Bill & Melinda Gates Foundation.

Chetty, R., Friedman, J.N., & Rockoff, J.E. (2014, May). Measuring the impacts of teachers II: Teacher value-added and student outcomes in adulthood. *American Economic Review, 104*(9), 2633–2679.

Clark County School District (n.d.). *School improvement planning basics: Root cause analysis.* http://ccsd.net/resources/aarsi-school-improvement/pdf/planning/school-improvement-planning-basics-root-cause-analysis.pdf

Crance, R., Bartlett, B., & Dortch, C. (2019, October). *Each child our future.* http://education.ohio.gov/getattachment/Topics/Career-Tech/CTE-Performance-Data-and-Accountability/Perkins-Resources/Carl-D-Perkins-V-State-Plan/Carl-D-Perkins-V-State-Plan-Equity-in-Career-Tec/Equity-Lab-Workbook-11-08-19-DRAFT.pdf.aspx?lang=en-US

Darling-Hammond, L. (2003, May). Keeping good teachers: Why it matters and what can leaders do? *Educational Leadership, 60*(8), 6–13.

Darling-Hammond, L. (2000). *Solving the dilemmas of teacher supply, demand, and standards: How we can ensure a competent, caring, and qualified teacher for every child.* National Commission on Teaching and America's Future. http://nctaf.org/wpcontent/uploads/2012/01/supply-demand-standards.pdf

Equitable Access Support Network. (2017). *How can states ensure equitable access to quality teachers?* https://education-first.com/can-states-ensure-equitable-access-quality-teachers/

Georgia Department of Education. (n.d). *Why inclusion matters: Fact sheet.* https://www.gadoe.org/Curriculum-Instruction-and-Assessment/Special-Education-Services/Pages/InclusiveLeadership.aspx

Goldhaber, D., Lavery, L., & Theobald, R. (2015). Uneven playing field? Assessing the teacher quality gap between advantaged and disadvantaged students. *Educational Researcher, 44*(5), 293–307.

Goldhaber, D., Quince, V., & Theobald, R. (2016). *Reconciling different estimates of teacher quality gaps based on value-added.* National Center for the Analysis of Longitudinal Data in Education Research (CALDER), American Institutes for Research.

Groopman, J. E. (2007). *How doctors think.* Houghton Mifflin.

Isenberg, E., Max, J., Gleason, P., Johnson, M., Deutsch, J., & Hansen, M. (2016). *Do low-income students have equal access to effective teachers? Evidence from 26 districts* (NCEE 2017-4007). U.S. Department of Education, Institute of Education Sciences, National Center for Education Evaluation and Regional Assistance.

Kane, T. J., & Staiger, D. O. (2008, December). Estimating teacher impacts on student achievement: An experimental evaluation. *National Bureau of Economic Research.*

Klein, A. (2015, April 10). No Child Left Behind: An overview. *Education Week.* https://www.edweek.org/policy-politics/no-child-left-behind-an-overview/2015/04

Knips, A. (2019, June 13). *Education equity: 6 steps to equitable data analysis.* https://www.edutopia.org/article/6-steps-equitable-data-analysis

Lee, A. M. I. (n.d.) *Every Student Succeeds Act (ESSA): What you need to know.* https://www.understood.org/en/school-learning/your-childs-rights/basics-about-childs-rights/every-student-succeeds-act-essa-what-you-need-to-know

Leithwood, K., Harris, A., & Hopkins, D. (2008). Seven strong claims about successful school leadership. *School Leadership and Management, 28,* 27–42. http:// https://doi.org/10.1080/13632430701800060

Marzano, R. J., Pickering, D. J., & Pollock, J. E. (2001). *Classroom instruction that works: Research-based strategies for increasing student achievement.* ASCD.

Musu-Gillette, L., Robinson, J. McFarland, J. Kewal-Ramani, A., Zhang, A., & Wilkinson-Flicker, S. (2016). Status and trends in the education of racial and ethnic groups. *National Center for Education Statistics* 2016-007. https://eric.ed.gov/?id=ED567806

OECD. (2012). *Equity and quality in education: Supporting disadvantaged students and schools.* http://dx.doi.org/10.1787/9789264130852-en

Phuong, A. E., Nguyen, J., & Marie, D. (2017b). Evaluating an adaptive equity-oriented pedagogy: A study of its impacts in higher education. *The Journal of Effective Teaching, 17*(2), 5–44.

Rowland, C., Feygin, A., Lee, F., Gomez, S., & Rasmussen, C. (2018, October). Improving the use of information to support teaching and learning through continuous improvement cycles. *American Institutes of Research.* https://eric.ed.gov/?id=ED592098

Sanders, W.L., & Rivers, J.C. (1996). *Cumulative and residual effects of teachers on future academic achievement.* University of Tennessee Value-Added Research and Assessment Center.

Sass, T. R., Hannaway, J., Xu, Z., Figlio, D. N., & Feng, L. (2012). Value-added of teachers in high-poverty schools and lower poverty schools. *Journal of Urban Economics, 72*(2), 104–122.

CHAPTER 9

ACTIONS OF EQUITABLE, SOCIALLY JUST, CULTURALLY RESPONSIVE, AND INCLUSIVE EDUCATIONAL LEADERS

Amie B. Cieminski
University of Northern Colorado

Kristine J. Melloy
Thompson School District

This chapter aims to examine inclusive leaders' actions to ensure equitable, socially just, culturally responsive, and inclusive special education services, as defined by the Individuals with Disabilities Education Act (2004), for students with disabilities (SWD). The chapter is based on current literature and vignettes from the field. The chapter is divided into five reader-friendly sections. In section one, we review literature that supports the civil rights of SWD to receive special education services in inclusive schools and key principal actions for leading staff in special education service delivery. We then introduce social justice school leaders (Theoharis, 2007) and culturally responsive

Inclusive Leadership, pages 159–178
Copyright © 2024 by Information Age Publishing
www.infoagepub.com
All rights of reproduction in any form reserved.

school leaders (Khalifa et al., 2016). Next, we discuss how principals might demonstrate characteristics of equitable, socially just, culturally responsive, and inclusive schools. We describe how these characteristics align with the Professional Standards for Educational Leadership (PSEL; National Policy Board for Educational Administration [NPBEA], 2015b). Finally, we allow the reader to apply what they learned to their own leadership.

CIVIL RIGHT TO DISABILITY SERVICES

The foundation for inclusive schools stems from a history of decisions by influential decision-making groups worldwide and landmark legislation in the United States (Melloy, 2018). The Education for All Handicapped Children Act (1975) and the reauthorizations of that act in the form of the Individuals with Disabilities Education Act in 1990, 1997, and 2004 guarantee the right to a free and appropriate public education in the least restrictive environment for SWD based on their individual education program (IEP).

Despite the strong foundation that supports inclusive school communities, many students continue to be marginalized and excluded from their civil right to an equitable, socially just, culturally responsive, and inclusive education (Kozleski et al., 2020; National Center for Education Statistics, 2022; U.S. Commission on Civil Rights, 2019). Billingsley et al. (2017) and others (Billingsley et al., 2018; DeMatthews, Billingsley et al., 2019; DeMatthews, Kotok et al., 2019; Melloy et al., 2021) posited that inadequate preparation of principals to lead inclusive schools continues to perpetuate inequitable education for SWD. Fortunately, there is guidance available for leaders in educational leadership preparation programs and school districts to address the need for initial preparation and ongoing professional development of school leaders (Bateman & Bateman, 2014; Bateman & Cline, 2019; McLeskey et al., 2014, 2019; Pazey & Lashley, 2018). We offer the Council of Chief State School Officers (CCSSO, 2020) definition of inclusive principal leadership developed by the National Collaborative on Inclusive Principal Leadership adopted as the common definition of inclusive leadership for this book series:

> Inclusive principals create strong school cultures and distribute leadership across staff to serve all learners well and ensure students feel safe, supported, and valued in school. In promoting equity for "all," inclusive principals must respond effectively to each student's potential and needs. Inclusive principals ensure high expectations and appropriate support so that each student can excel in school across race, gender, ethnicity, language, disability, sexual orientation, family background, and family income. ("What is Inclusive Principal Leadership?" section)

Pazey and Lashley (2018) described nine concepts that are "foundational to understanding and implementing the special education process" (p. 124) that results in free and appropriate public education for SWD in the least restrictive environment based on their IEP. Further, Bateman and Bateman (2014) provided nine themes related to the primary special education responsibilities principals must know and do to lead inclusive schools.

Crucial to effective leadership is preparing educational leaders with a deep understanding of and the ability to implement the special education process. Given that 15% of all students in U.S. schools are eligible for special education services (National Center for Education Statistics, 2022), principals and other educational leaders must be prepared to lead inclusive schools. Guidance for preparing these leaders is available from standards geared toward that end. This guidance is in the guise of the National Educational Leadership Preparation Standards (NPBEA, 2015a), the PSEL (NPBEA, 2015b), and the Special Education Administration Specialist (SEAS) Standards for Professional Preparation (Council for Exceptional Children, 2015). Table 9.1 provides a crosswalk between (1) Bateman and Bateman's (2014) principal's primary special education-related responsibility themes, (2) Pazey and Lashley's (2018) nine concepts of the special education process, (3) the SEAS Standards for Professional Practice (Council for Exceptional Children, 2015), and (4) resources for a deeper dive into topics. Although PSEL standards are not included in Table 9.1, we explore them in depth later in the chapter. Vignette #1 describes an example of an educational leadership preparation program based on school leader and special education administration standards.

VIGNETTE #1
Leadership Preparation Program With a Mission for Promoting Civil Rights to Disability Services

A few years ago, a department of educational leadership and policy studies working with a school of special education in a public university developed an Interdisciplinary Educational Leadership and Special Education Administration Degree Program. The mission includes preparing school and district-level administrators to lead equitable, socially just, culturally responsive, and inclusive schools. Candidates in the program earn a master's degree or education specialist degree and apply for both a building-level principal license and district-level special education director endorsement. Students take coursework in both educational leadership and special education administration in addition to completing field-based internships in the principalship and special education directorship. Coursework is based on the National Educational Leadership Preparation Standards (NPBEA, 2015a), the PSEL

TABLE 9.1 Crosswalk for Principal Responsibilities for Inclusive Leadership: Responsibility Themes, Special Education Process Concepts, Standards, and Resources

Themes: Principal's Primary Special Education Related Responsibilities (Bateman & Bateman, 2014)	Concepts: Special Education Process (Pazey & Lashley, 2018)	SEAS Standards for Professional Practice (Council for Exceptional Children, 2015)	Resources For a Deeper Dive into the Topic
Student Focus • Ensure education of all students in the school • Know all students in the building and can talk about them	• Child with a disability	• Programs, Services, and Outcomes • Leadership and Policy • Collaboration	Special Education Law and Regulations • U.S. Supreme Court http://www.supremecourt.gov • U.S. Department of Education Office of Civil Rights http://www2.ed.gov/ocr • U.S. Department of Education Office of Special Education Programs http://www2.ed.gov/about/offices/list/osers/osep
Laws & Procedures • Know the concept and practice of special education • Lead efforts for data collection and interpretation • Lead meetings for services related to SWD • Ensure staff members are aware of the process for identifying SWD and provide special education services	• FAPE • Identification and Referral • Individual Evaluation • Eligibility • IEP • LRE • Parental Involvement • Due Process of Law	• Assessment • Programs, Services, and Outcomes • Research and Inquiry • Leadership and Policy • Professional and Ethical Practice • Collaboration	Special Education Law and Regulations • Individuals with Disabilities Education Act http://idea.ed.gov/ Principal Leadership & Development • The Wallace Foundation on school leadership http://www.wallacefoundation.org/

(continued)

Actions of Equitable, Socially Just, Culturally Responsive, and Inclusive Leaders • 163

TABLE 9.1 Crosswalk for Principal Responsibilities for Inclusive Leadership: Responsibility Themes, Special Education Process Concepts, Standards, and Resources (continued)

Themes: Principal's Primary Special Education Related Responsibilities (Bateman & Bateman, 2014)	Concepts: Special Education Process (Pazey & Lashley, 2018)	SEAS Standards for Professional Practice (Council for Exceptional Children, 2015)	Resources For a Deeper Dive into the Topic
Staff Practices • Verify that staff members are appropriately implementing services for SWD • Promote positive behavior and school culture to prevent discipline problems	• FAPE • IEP • LRE	• Assessment • Curricular content knowledge • Programs, Services, and Outcomes • Leadership and Policy • Professional and Ethical Practice • Collaboration	Evidence-based practices • What Works Clearinghouse http://ies.ed.gov/ncee/wwc/ • High Leverage Practices for Inclusive Classrooms/SWD https://highleveragepractices.org/ Positive Behavioral Intervention and Supports • Center on PBIS https://www.pbis.org/ • Key Elements of Policies to Address Discipline Disproportionality • Embedding Culturally Responsive Practices in Tier 1 Cultural Responsiveness • Culturally Responsive Instruction ies.ed.gov/ncee/edlabs/regions/midwest/blogs/culturally-responsive-instruction-best-practices.aspx

Note: FAPE = Free and Appropriate Public Education, IEP = Individual Education Program, and LRE = Least Restrictive Environment.

(NPBEA, 2015b), and the Special Education Administration Specialist (SEAS) Standards for Professional Preparation (Council for Exceptional Children, 2015). Graduates gain employment as building-level administrators or district-level special education administrators. The graduates have reported that preparation in educational leadership and special education administration resulted in the ability to implement the special education process and perform their primary responsibilities related to serving all students.

CHARACTERISTICS OF SOCIAL JUSTICE SCHOOL LEADERS

Social justice leaders make "issues of race, class, gender, disability, sexual orientation, and other historically and currently marginalizing conditions in the United States central to their advocacy, leadership practice, and vision" (Theoharis, 2007, p. 223). Social justice leaders begin with a mindset that values and respects diversity. They promote inclusion by ending segregated and pull-out programs. They align their instructional leadership practices (e.g., hiring, teacher evaluation, shared decision-making) to ensure that each student has access to core instruction, high-quality teaching in general education, and a culturally relevant curriculum. To ensure high-quality teaching based on students' IEPs, these leaders support teachers through professional development on topics such as culturally responsive pedagogy, universal design for learning, multi-tiered systems of support, differentiated learning, data-driven instruction through the lens of equity, and high leverage practices for inclusive schools (McLeskey et al., 2019). Inclusive leaders support SWD so that each student's IEP is developed with a team of social justice-minded, collaborative professionals and family members. Vignette #2 describes a socially just leader in action.

VIGNETTE #2
Socially Just Leader in Action

Dr. Maple was an experienced elementary principal in a diverse school district with several lower-performing schools. When the superintendent asked Dr. Maple to serve as the principal of a newly formed elementary school, the principal could hire teachers from two other schools in the district. The priority was to hire teachers with experience working with diverse populations that would embrace high expectations for every learner. During the first year, Dr. Maple assembled parent, student, and staff groups to develop a mission statement and shared value statements to guide the daily work. The groups reached a consensus, posted these belief statements in English and Spanish on the school's website, and revisited them before making any decisions. These belief statements included:

- embracing diversity
- ensuring academic success through high expectations, clear goals, accountability, and effective instruction;
- supporting responsible decision-making through example, guidance, and a variety of opportunities; and
- providing a safe and nurturing child-centered environment.

Dr. Maple carefully built collaborative grade-level teams and assigned special educators, interventionists, and teachers for English learners to each team. Additionally, the principal integrated the classrooms and offices of specialists and itinerant staff rather than physically separating SWD services from their grade-level peers. The staff crafted norms of collaboration and emphasized shared responsibility for the success of every student. The leadership team designed professional development opportunities for the staff focused on promoting high-quality instruction in literacy and using data to plan instruction and monitor the success of each student. As they finished year one, they surveyed parents about the school climate and support for their children. After listening to the voices of stakeholders, the leadership team made establishing and maintaining positive student-family-school relationships and creating a safe school environment a priority for the second year.

CHARACTERISTICS OF CULTURALLY RESPONSIVE SCHOOL LEADERS

While there are many approaches to understanding leadership through a lens of advocacy and cultural proficiency, we choose the term culturally responsive leadership since it implies continuous reflection and action, which is necessary to promote inclusion for all students. Khalifa et al. (2016), in their synthesis of the literature on culturally responsive leadership, identified four behaviors that signify culturally responsive leadership: critically self-reflecting, developing culturally responsive teachers, creating and maintaining culturally responsive inclusive environments, and engaging students and parents in community contexts.

Culturally responsive leaders practice critical self-awareness regarding values, beliefs, and practices (see Vignette #3). They develop culturally responsive teachers by securing resources, providing professional learning, mentoring, modeling, and challenging beliefs and practices in the school.

While teachers are responsible for their classroom climate, school leaders create a culturally responsive and inclusive schoolwide climate (Tracy-Bronson, 2020), beginning with a vision for inclusive practices. These leaders resist exclusionary practices, challenge the status quo, and have courageous conversations (Singleton, 2013). They engage students, parents, and the community through developing positive relationships, resisting deficit thinking about students and families, and advocating for families within their community context.

> **VIGNETTE #3**
> **Culturally Responsive Leader in Action**
>
> When Mrs. Conrad became the principal of Marisol Ramirez School, the school was categorized as underperforming. The school served 90% of students who qualified for free and reduced lunch, 80% whose home language was not English, and a high number of SWD receiving instruction in reading and math in resource settings. The school had the lowest test scores in the school district and was in danger of being shut down due to low ratings on the state's accountability report card. When older siblings came to school for a performance or family night, several reported that they had dropped out of high school. To learn about the community, Mrs. Conrad met with teachers, families, and students. She made home visits and interviewed the family of Marisol Ramirez, for whom the school was named. She learned that Marisol was a staunch advocate for family and education.
>
> When the school year started, Mrs. Conrad worked collaboratively to create the Ramirez Family Values: attend school every day, demonstrate positive behavior, and graduate high school (at a minimum). Today, students at Ramirez are identified by their high school graduation year (e.g., "The Class of 2030"), and the school mascot wears a graduation cap. In addition, each year, the principal and staff visit former Ramirez "family members" in their secondary schools to check on their attendance, behavior, and academic success by bringing pizza and a familiar face. The staff also attends every high school graduation to congratulate former Ramirez students. They believe in the power of the school-home partnership and work hard to build and maintain authentic connections with each family.
>
> When Mrs. Conrad became the leader, over 50% of the staff had under three years of experience, and the school had a high turnover rate. Today, educators from around the area want to be a part of the exciting work at Ramirez. Each year, the staff revisits the vision of helping each child achieve their dreams and makes plans so that every student has access and opportunity to high-quality, culturally relevant instruction. The school is a leader in inclusive approaches for SWD and students learning English. The staff worked with city officials to subsidize low-cost broadband for families, and each child receives a technology device. Each year, more and more students from Ramirez

> achieve grade-level standards and graduate. Through her unwavering commitment to the idea that the school would help every student achieve their dreams, Mrs. Conrad made what others said was impossible possible.

ACTIONS ALIGNED TO THE PRINCIPAL STANDARDS

In this section, we expand the notion of what building-level principals and other educational leaders need to know and do to serve all learners well across race, gender, ethnicity, language, disability, sexual orientation, family background, and family income. First, although it is not always clear that 'all' learners mean SWD, we emphasize what leaders need to do to include SWD in their descriptions of all learners. Then, using the PSEL (NPBEA, 2015b) and ideas from the chapter, we describe the critical actions of principals for leading inclusive schools.

The CCSSO, in collaboration with the Collaboration for Effective Educator Development, Accountability, and Reform Center (CEEDAR; CCSSO & CEEDAR, 2017), offered guidance for leaders by identifying aspects of the PSEL important for supporting SWD. They posited that principals should build upon their existing skills and practices to address the needs of SWD. Principals also need to acknowledge the systemic racism and discrimination built into the public school system since many of the practices in school leadership are color-evasive (Diem & Welton, 2021). In 2015, Carpenter and Diem examined the language of several standards and policy documents for educational leaders. They noted the lack of equity-related policy vocabularies and the need to address race, social justice, English learners, migrant students, and SWD issues. While there were implicit references to equity and diversity, these authors advocated for more explicit guidance for leaders since these policy documents influence educational leadership programs' approach to curricula, pedagogy, and licensure standards. Thus, we delineate the characteristics and actions needed for principals to be equitable, socially just, culturally responsive, and inclusive leaders aligned to the PSEL standards.

PSEL and Key Actions for Principals

Standard 1. Mission, Vision, and Core Values
Standard 1 of PSEL 2015 requires principals to collaboratively develop a mission, vision, and core values to improve students' achievement and outcomes. Mission statements often describe what organizations do (i.e., their

purpose), while vision statements may be aspirational or describe the preferred future of the school. In addition, many mission statements ascribe to the notion of serving "all" students. Unfortunately, "all" may not include SWD, students of color, or students from marginalized populations.

Khalifa et al. (2016) highlighted critical self-awareness or critical consciousness of values, beliefs, and dispositions as a characteristic of culturally responsive principals. Principals begin by interrogating their personal beliefs, assumptions, and implicit biases about race, class, gender, ethnicity, and ability. Next, principals use this understanding to promote and envision a restructured school environment that produces more equitable outcomes. Finally, principals are encouraged to collaborate with teachers, parents, and other stakeholders to review and revise the mission, vision, and core values to ensure the success of every student, regardless of their background or experiences. For example, principals may promote a more welcoming and inclusive environment where each student and their family feel included by explicitly drawing attention to various groups that may have been invisible or underserved. Principals then have the responsibility to promote a mutual commitment to this mission and vision and shape their practice and the practice of others accordingly (CEEDAR, 2017).

Standard 2. Ethics and Professional Norms

Standard 2 calls on principals to adhere to and promote ethical norms. At times, it can be challenging for principals to embody the values of justice and care, equality and equity, and community in service of each student due to the unique needs of students and the systemic oppression that educational systems have reproduced. Leaders use different ethical lenses to make decisions, such as the ethic of justice, care, or critique (Shapiro et al., 2014). Ethical leaders acknowledge the inherent systemic injustices that have resulted in discrimination and opportunity gaps for students from diverse backgrounds. While school leaders might typically function using an ethic of justice in which they follow rules and due process, this may inadvertently reinforce the unfair norms, especially for students from traditionally marginalized groups. For example, Black students receive more exclusionary discipline consequences, such as suspensions and expulsions for subjective offenses such as defiance, disruption, or disrespect creating a pattern of disparities (Girvan et al., 2017). Students may be suspended for hairstyles, clothing, and behaviors that the school system deems inappropriate but follow a particular group's cultural patterns. These disparities in exclusionary discipline practices and reasons for suspensions related to cultural patterns are particularly apparent for Black SWD (Kozleski et al., 2020; U.S. Commission on Civil Rights, 2019). Using the ethic of care, leaders may choose restorative approaches to discipline, which strengthen relationships between students, school personnel, and families, rather than exclusionary practices, which can lead to disengagement and dropout (Evanovich et al., 2020).

Also, using the ethic of critique, leaders realize that the traditional or current rules and procedures unfairly advantage or disadvantage certain individuals and groups. For example, a principal may notice a student arriving late due to transportation issues. Following the ethic of justice, tardies would result in detention which, if missed, would result in suspension and missing more school, further exacerbating possible achievement gaps. Socially just leaders work with community organizations, families, and district officials to resolve the root cause of the transportation issues rather than punish a student for an unfair or out-of-control situation.

Standard 3. Equity and Cultural Responsiveness

Standard 3 focuses on leaders' responsibility to strive for equity and employ culturally responsive practices. Effective school leaders understand that equality does not mean equity. Principals work with teachers and other community members to move beyond technical fixes to understand the institutional barriers that impede the success of all students. While equity must be called out specifically in standards, inclusive leaders avoid equity traps and tropes such as siloing, blanketing, and tokenizing equity (Safir & Dugan, 2021). Equity requires ongoing work on the part of school principals to continually ensure each student's academic, social, and emotional welfare. Student well-being happens through effective, culturally responsive instruction.

Equity-minded principals hold asset-based views of students rather than allow deficit thinking to invade their school's culture. They create school communities in which social, political, and cultural capital is enhanced to provide equity of opportunity for students (Shields, 2010). They often ask what students can do rather than make assumptions and label students. They understand the liabilities of labeling and the power of expectations that may set off a chain of life-altering events that advantages or disadvantages specific individuals and groups of students (Avelar La Salle & Johnson, 2019).

Standard 4. Curriculum, Instruction, and Assessment

Standard 4 begins with principals communicating high academic expectations for all students regardless of background, language, circumstance, or ability level, including access to grade-level instruction with the appropriate supports and scaffolds. While some schools have moved to de-track coursework or include SWD in the general education classroom, principals ensure teachers are supported to provide high-quality, differentiated instruction that meets the needs of all students (Bateman & Bateman, 2014).

Principals work to level the playing field concerning access and outcomes (Shields, 2010), as it is not enough to allow open access to advanced coursework. Principals need to support teachers using culturally responsive pedagogies and provide appropriate support so traditionally marginalized students can succeed in rigorous coursework.

Principals can leverage multi-tiered systems of support (MTSS) to provide universal, targeted, and individualized supports. Well-crafted MTSS systems begin with a focus on quality first instruction. Rather than separate tracks for remediation or advancement, MTSS offers layered support so that all students receive universal instruction AND additional support using small group or individual instruction. This approach allows students to be included in the general education classroom to the maximum extent while meeting their individual needs. Educators meet various needs such as language development, objectives related to their IEP, and social-emotional or behavioral goals in the general education classroom based on the MTSS framework.

In addition, principals can consider co-teaching (Bateman & Bateman, 2014; McLeskey et al., 2019; Theoharis, 2007) to support SWD, in which content or grade-level teachers partner with special educators. This way, students receive the appropriate accommodations, modifications, and scaffolds with their grade-level and neurotypical peers. Robust MTSS promotes educational equity by ensuring every student gets what they need.

Standard 5. Community of Care and Support for Students

Standard 5 asks principals to build safe, caring, and healthy environments that embrace racial, cultural, and socioeconomic diversity. Given the diversity in student demographics, school environments either engage students through validation and affirmation of their cultural and learning identities or disengage them by enacting implicit biases, systems, or exclusionary practices (Leverson et al., 2021). Schools around the United States utilize schoolwide positive behavioral interventions and supports (SWPBIS) focused on promoting prosocial behavior through defining, teaching, and reinforcing expectations for behavior (Leverson et al., 2021). Educators using SWPBIS seek to create and refine systems of behavioral support that are culturally responsive rather than fix and punish students for not conforming. School leaders use SWPBIS to engage diverse students, families, staff, and community in determining expectations and positive and negative consequences and then monitoring the student data to watch for disparities in the outcomes. They ask themselves if the system needs adjusting rather than blaming students and families.

Another aspect of student support is to include SWD in the general education classroom. For most students, this means pushing resources and scaffolds into the general education classroom instead of pulling out, sorting, and remediating students separate from their peers without disabilities. Recent data indicate that the least restrictive environment for 66% of SWD is the general education classroom, where they spend 80% or more of their school day (National Center for Education Statistics, 2022).

Principals are more aware of the need to support students academically, socially, and emotionally. Social-emotional learning (SEL) has myriad benefits for all students and improves student achievement, engagement, motivation, behavior, and well-being (Durlak et al., 2011). However, it is essential for principals to analyze and adjust their approach to SEL to ensure that it is culturally responsive or transformative (Jagers et al., 2019) and does not reinforce deficit thinking, devalue local cultures, or further marginalize students and their families. Transformative SEL is a newer approach to SEL that leverages cultural assets and promotes the well-being of students of color and those from under-resourced backgrounds (Jagers et al., 2018). In addition, community-building practices and structures such as morning meetings, advisory classes, or homeroom periods may be important for building communities of care.

One aspect of transformative SEL is identity development which may be particularly important for ethnic-racial or disability/ability identity development. Identity development involves developing a unique sense of oneself and intersecting identities such as ability, race, gender, or ethnicity. While identity development is individual, it is also communal since an individual's sense of self depends on their interactions with others and how various identities are valued within the larger socio-cultural contexts, including schools (Forber-Pratt et al., 2017). As such, principals are influential decision-makers and shape school contexts and cultures to promote positive identity development for students.

Standard 6. Professional Capacity of School Personnel

In Standard 6, principals are called on to increase the professional capacity of school personnel through the recruitment, hiring, development, and retention of quality general education staff members and the staff to support students with specific needs (e.g., SWD). However, hiring and retaining qualified and experienced educators continues to be challenging, especially in areas such as mathematics, special education, and bilingual education/English language development and in high-poverty schools (Sutcher et al., 2016). Besides, teacher attrition rates are higher for teachers of color, teachers in high-poverty schools, teachers in high-minority schools, and under-prepared teachers (i.e., have not completed comprehensive preparation) (Sutcher et al., 2016). Additionally, there is growing evidence that teachers of color can improve the outcomes for all students, especially students of color (Carver-Thomas, 2018). Therefore, principals examine hiring practices, support systems such as mentoring and induction, professional development, and educator evaluation systems with an eye on retaining a diverse teaching staff that can meet the unique needs of students.

Principals also develop current staff. Staff may need particular professional development to become highly effective when working in more inclusive environments so that SWD have access to high-quality instruction and grade-level content. Just as principals engage in critical self-awareness, they work with teachers to examine race, culture, bias, power, and privilege so that all staff members can fulfill the vision of providing an excellent and equitable education for every student.

Standard 7. Professional Community for Teachers and Staff

Standard 7 begins with principals promoting collaborative cultures. Professional collaboration takes many forms, including "professional learning communities, collaborative planning, learning walks, instructional rounds, collaborative inquiry, lesson study, school networks, data teams, self-evaluation processes, and peer review" (Hargreaves, 2019, p. 618). Principals distribute responsibility, so all staff members have mutual responsibility for student success and fulfilling the mission and vision of the school. Principals create positive working conditions that promote a just and democratic workplace that provides teachers and other staff a voice in decision-making. Principals promote collaborative cultures by setting clear expectations, creating structures, and providing resources for collaboration that can enable and empower staff members. By empowering teachers and promoting collaboration, principals increase student achievement and reduce teacher resistance to change.

Standard 8. Meaningful Engagement of Families and Community

Standard 8 charges principals with partnering with families and communities that go beyond traditional parent involvement, such as attending parent-teacher conferences or volunteering. Inclusive principals partner with families to meet the unique needs of their children. Safir and Dugan (2021) implored school leaders to engage with students and families; use their voices to "build classrooms and schools and systems around students' brilliance, cultural wealth, and intellectual potential" (p. 4); and move past fixing students and achievement gaps. Principals stop having a token parent from underserved groups attempt to learn about "how school is done here" to engage families purposefully and productively.

Standard 9. Operations and Management

Standard 9 implores principals to use all resources effectively and efficiently. These resources include time, finances, and human resources. To promote culturally responsive teaching, principals are responsible for securing culturally responsive resources and curriculum (Khalifa et al., 2016). When moving toward more inclusive environments, principals restructure schedules, expertise, and basic structures to promote equity of resources (Theoharis, 2007).

Standard 10. School Improvement

Standard 10 stipulates that principals are change agents who support teachers' work to achieve the school's mission and produce better outcomes for all students. Continuous improvement requires principals to engage staff in ongoing data analysis, progress monitoring of student outcomes, and adjusting strategies to better serve student needs.

When looking at school ratings and performance indicators, principals avoid being lulled by averages or rating systems that hide the disparities in outcomes for certain students and groups. Instead, equity-minded leaders are called to "peel back the wallpaper" (Avelar La Salle & Johnson, 2019, p. 33). By peeling back the wallpaper, leaders analyze the data layer by layer to make the invisible visible and reveal hidden inequities. In conjunction with their leadership team, principals also conduct equity audits (Skrla et al., 2009) that allow educators to examine inequities in teacher quality, programmatic placement and support, and student academic achievement. By examining how these elements intersect, principals can see the systems that may be creating the inequities (e.g., novice educators teaching struggling students; the overidentification of students of color in special education). To get a complete picture of what is impacting improvement efforts, leaders examine the intersections of data from multiple measures: student learning (i.e., state, local, and classroom summative and formative assessment); student demographics (gender, disability, race); school process (implementation of instruction and initiatives); and perception (student, parent, and staff surveys) before making plans for improvement (Bernhardt, 2013). Through a more expansive view of data, the disaggregation of data, and collaborative data dialogue, principals answer questions such as: Who is doing well? What adult actions and school-level systems are contributing to that success? Who needs additional support? What are the systemic barriers to their success? What improvement efforts are most aligned with the needs of the school's particular context and population?

By examining the PSEL with a focus on equity, social justice, cultural responsiveness, and inclusive leadership, principals begin to integrate support for each student and their success. In the next section, we provide suggestions for action planning.

ACTION PLANNING

This last section allows readers to apply what they learned about inclusive leadership. After reading the chapter, readers are invited to examine their practices around each PSEL standard. Table 9.2 provides the reader with prompts to begin to analyze their learning and leadership by creating an action plan related to equitable, socially just, culturally responsive, and

TABLE 9.2 Action Planning Tool

PSEL 2015 Standard	Key Questions to Ask	Current Status (not started, in progress, in place, needs refinement)	Next Steps
1. Mission, Vision, and Core Values	How do our school's mission and vision statement reflect our students and their unique needs?		
2. Ethics and Professional Norms	How is the ethic of care and ethic of critique reflected in decision-making?		
3. Equity and Culturally Responsiveness	How does our school community define equity and live out our commitment to cultural responsiveness?		
4. Curriculum, Instruction, and Assessment	How are all students afforded high expectations, quality curriculum, and excellent teaching?		
5. Community of Care and Support for Students	How do tiered systems of support address the needs of students with diverse needs?		
6. Professional Capacity of School Personnel	How are hiring, development, and retention systems supporting staff in high-need areas, from diverse backgrounds, and with equity mindsets?		
7. Professional Community for Teachers and Staff	How is the school culture inclusive, welcoming, and supportive for teachers and staff? How do we model collaboration?		
8. Meaningful Engagement of Families and Community	How do we define and promote meaningful engagement of families? How are student, family, and community voices represented in our work and decisions?		
9. Operations and Management	How does our approach to resource allocation and management reflect our values of inclusion and educational equity?		
10. School Improvement	How do our data analysis and plans for ongoing improvement reflect our goals for equitable outcomes for every student?		

inclusive leadership that ensures free and appropriate public education in the least restrictive environment for SWD based on their IEP. Column 1 of the tool includes the PSEL 2015 Standards. Column 2 presents key questions to ask. Column 3 provides a space to rate the school's current status of the practice. Finally, column 4 of the action planning tool contains space to write the next steps for planning.

The tool prompts readers to reflect on their preparation and practice as equitable, socially just, culturally responsive, and inclusive leaders. We recommend that school leaders work collaboratively with diverse stakeholders to examine how their school's practices support inclusive schools. For deeper introspection and planning, school leaders and their teams might consider the following resources: digital simulations to develop prospective leaders' contextual knowledge and skill (see Dexter et al., 2020) or the "Quality Standards for Inclusive Schools Self-Assessment Instrument" (Inclusive Schools Network, 2017).

Today's students are more diverse than ever, and school leaders are called to provide an excellent and equitable, socially just, culturally responsive, and inclusive education for each one. Although researchers and practitioners are more aware of the intersecting identities of students and the need to address their unique needs, much of the literature continues to silo the topics of inclusive schools, social justice leadership, and culturally responsive leadership. This chapter included numerous examples of what principals should know and be able to do to ensure equitable, socially just, and culturally responsive services for SWD in hopes that aspiring and practicing principals and school leaders weave these areas of leadership together in service to children.

REFERENCES

Avelar La Salle, R., & Johnson, R. (2019). *Shattering inequities: Real-world wisdom for school and district leaders*. Rowman & Littlefield.

Bateman, D. F., & Bateman, C. F. (2014). *A principal's guide to special education* (3rd ed). Council for Exceptional Children.

Bateman, D., & Cline, J. (2019). *Special education leadership: Building effective leadership in schools*. Routledge.

Bernhardt, V. (2013). *Data analysis for continuous school improvement* (3rd ed). Taylor & Francis.

Billingsley, B., DeMatthews, D., Connally, K., & McLeskey, J. (2018). Leadership for effective inclusive schools: Considerations for preparation and reform. *Australasian Journal of Special and Inclusive Education, 42*, 65–81.

Billingsley, B., McLeskey, J., & Crockett, J. B. (2017). *Principal leadership: Moving toward inclusive and high-achieving schools for students with disabilities* (Document No. IC-8). Collaboration for Effective Educator Development, Accountability, and Reform Center. http://ccedar.education.ufl.edu/tools/innovation-configurations/

Carpenter, B. W., & Diem, S. (2015). Guidance matters: A critical discourse analysis of the race-related policy vocabularies shaping leadership preparation. *Urban Education, 50*(5), 515–534. https://doi-org.unco.idm.oclc.org/10.1177/0042085914528719

Carver-Thomas, D. (2018). *Diversifying the teaching profession: How to recruit and retain teachers of color*. Learning Policy Institute. https://learningpolicyinstitute.org/product/diversifying-teaching-profession-report

Council for Exceptional Children. (2015). *What every special educator must know: Professional ethics and standards* (7th ed.).

Council of Chief State School Officers. (2020). *Supporting inclusive schools for the success of each child*. https://ccssoinclusiveprincipalsguide.org/

Council of Chief State School Officers & Collaboration for Effective Educator Development, Accountability, and Reform Center. (2017). *PSEL 2015 and promoting principal leadership for the success of students with disabilities*. https://www.ccsso.org/sites/default/files/2017-10/PSELforSWDs01252017_0.pdf

DeMatthews, D. E., Billingsley, B., McLeskey, J., & Sharma, U. (2019). Principal leadership for students with disabilities in effective inclusive schools. *Journal of Educational Administration, 58*(5), 539–554. https://doi.org/10.1108/JEA-10-2019-0177

DeMatthews, D. E., Kotok, S., & Serafini, A. (2019). Leadership preparation for special education and inclusive schools: Beliefs and recommendations from successful principals. *Journal of Research on Leadership Education*. Advance online publication. https://doi.org/10.1177/1942775119838308

Dexter, S., Clement, D., Moraguez, D., & Watson, G. S. (2020). (Inter) active learning tools and pedagogical strategies in educational leadership preparation. *Journal of Research on Leadership Education, 15*(3), 173–191. https://doi.org/10.1177/1942775120936299

Diem, S., & Welton, A. J. (2021). *Anti-racist educational leadership and policy: Addressing racism in public education*. Routledge.

Durlak, J. A., Dymnicki, A. B., Taylor, R. D., Weissberg, R. P., & Schellinger, K. B. (2011). The impact of enhancing students' social and emotional learning: A meta-analysis of school-based universal interventions. *Child Development, 82*(1), 405–432. https://doi.org/10.1111/j.1467-8624.2010.01564.x

Education for All Handicapped Children Act, 20 USC § 1401 et seq. (1975).

Evanovich, L. L., Martinez, S., Kern, L., & Haynes Jr., R.D. (2020). Proactive circles: A practical guide to the implementation of a restorative practice. *Preventing School Failure: Alternative Education for Children and Youth, 64*(1), 28–36. https://doi.org/10.1080/1045988X.2019.1639128

Forber-Pratt, A. J., Lyew, D. A., Mueller, C., & Samples, L. B. (2017). Disability identity development: A systematic review of the literature. *Rehabilitation Psychology, 62*(2), 198–207. http://dx.doi.org.unco.idm.oclc.org/10.1037/rep0000134

Girvan, E. J., Gion, C., McIntosh, K., & Smolkowski, K. (2017). The relative contribution of subjective office referrals to racial disproportionality in school discipline. *School Psychology Quarterly, 32*(3), 392–404. http://dx.doi.org/10.1037/spq0000178

Hargreaves, A. (2019). Teacher collaboration: 30 years of research on its nature, forms, limitations, and effects, *Teachers and Teaching, 25*(5), 603–621. https://doi.org/10.1080/13540602.2019.1639499

Inclusive Schools Network. (2017). *Quality standards for inclusive schools self-assessment instrument.* https://inclusiveschools.org/inclusion-resources/self-assessment/

Individuals with Disabilities Education Act of 1990, 20 USC § 1401 *et seq.* (1990).

Individuals with Disabilities Education Act Amendments of 1997, Pub. L. No. 105-17, 105th Cong., 1st sess. (1997).

Individuals with Disabilities Education Improvement Act of 2004, 20 USC §1401 *et seq.* (2004).

Jagers, R. J., Rivas-Drake, D., & Borowski, T. (2018). *Equity and social-emotional learning: A cultural analysis.* Collaborative for Academic, Social, and Emotional Learning. https://measuringsel.casel.org/wp-content/uploads/2018/11/Frameworks-Equity.pdf

Jagers, R., Rivas-Drake, D., & Williams, B. (2019). Transformative social and emotional learning (SEL): Toward SEL in service of educational equity and excellence. *Educational Psychologist, 54*(3), 162–184. https://doi.org/10.1080/00461520.2019.1623032

Khalifa, M. A., Gooden, M. A., & Davis, J. E. (2016). Culturally responsive school leadership: A synthesis of the literature. *Review of Educational Research, 86*(4), 1272–1311. https://doi.org/10.3102/0034654316630383

Kozleski, E., Stepaniuk, I., & Proffitt, W. (2020). In the eye of the storm: When retreat is an unacceptable option. *Multiple Voices: Disability, Race, and Language Intersections in Special Education, 20*(1), 16–31.

Leverson, M., Smith, K., McIntosh, K., Rose, J., & Pinkelman, S. (2021, March). *PBIS cultural responsiveness field guide: Resources for trainers and coaches.* Center on Positive Behavioral Interventions and Supports. www.pbis.org.

McLeskey, J., Maheady, L., Billingsley, B., Brownell, M. T., & Lewis, T. J. (Eds.). (2019). *High leverage practices for inclusive classrooms.* Taylor & Francis.

McLeskey, J., Waldron, N. L., Spooner, F., & Algozzine, B. (2014). *Handbook of effective inclusive schools: Research and practice.* Routledge.

Melloy, K. J. (2018). Preparing educational leaders for 21st-century inclusive school communities: Transforming university preparation programs. *Journal of Transformative Leadership and Policy Studies, 7*(2), 13–24. https://doi.org/10.36851/jtlps.v7i2.504

Melloy, K. J., Cieminski, A. B., & Sundeen, T. (2021). Accepting educational responsibility: Preparing administrators to lead inclusive schools. *Journal of Research in Leadership Education.*

National Center for Education Statistics. (2022). *Students with disabilities. Condition of education.* U.S. Department of Education, Institute of Education Sciences. https://nces.ed.gov/programs/coe/indicator/cgg

National Center for Education Statistics. (2021). *Condition of education: Students with disabilities.* (Annual Reports). https://nces.ed.gov/programs/coe/indicator/cgg

National Policy Board for Educational Administration. (2015a). *National educational leadership program standards.*

National Policy Board for Educational Administration. (2015b). *Professional standards for educational leaders 2015.*
Office of Special Education and Rehabilitative Services. (2019). *41st annual report to Congress on the implementation of the Individuals with Disabilities Education Act, Parts B and C.* https://www2.ed.gov/about/reports/annual/osep/2019/parts-b-c/index.html
Pazey, B. L., & Lashley, C. (2018). Supporting socially just, equitable, and inclusive schools. In L. Bass, W. C. Frick, & M. D. Young (Eds.), *Developing ethical principles for school leadership: PSEL standard two.* Routledge.
Safir, S., & Dugan, J. (2021). *Street data: A next-generation model for equity pedagogy, and school transformation.* Corwin.
Shapiro, J. P., Stefkovich, J. A., & Gutierrez, K. J. (2014). Ethical decision making. In C. Branson, & S. J. Gross (Eds.), *Handbook of ethical educational leadership.* Routledge.
Shields, C. (2010). Transformative leadership: Working for equity in diverse contexts. *Educational Administration Quarterly, 46*(4) 558–589. https://doi.org/10.1177/0013161X10375609
Singleton, G. (2013). *More about courageous conversations about race.* Corwin.
Skrla, L., McKenzie, K. B., & Scheurich, J. J. (2009). *Using equity audits to create equitable and excellent schools.* Corwin.
Sutcher, L., Darling-Hammond, L., & Carver-Thomas, D. (2016). *A coming crisis in teaching? Teacher supply, demand, and shortages in the US.* Learning Policy Institute. https://learningpolicyinstitute.org/product/coming-crisis-teaching
Theoharis, G. (2007). Social justice educational leaders and resistance: Toward a theory of social justice leadership. *Educational Administrative Quarterly, 43*(2), 221–258. https://doi.org/10.1177/0013161X06293717
Tracy-Bronson, C. P. (2020). District-level inclusion special education leaders demonstrate social justice strategies. *Journal of Special Education Leadership, 33*(2), pp. 59–77.
U.S. Commission on Civil Rights. (2019). *Beyond suspensions: Examining school discipline policies and the connection to the school-to-prison pipeline for students with disabilities.* https://www.usccr.gov/pubs/2019/07-23-Beyond-Suspensions.pdf

SECTION III

NARRATIVES—PERSONAL PERSPECTIVES
ON THE FIELD

CHAPTER 10

EXPLORING INCLUSIVE LEADERSHIP THROUGH TONGLEN

A Contemplative Framework for Supervision

Steve Haberlin
University of Central Florida

Ian Mette
University of Buffalo

For far too long society in the United States has put faith in the PK–12 public education system to serve as a progressive mechanism to help the U.S. society move forward in addressing systemic inequities. In reality, the system has done little to harness the social and cultural capital of those in principal positions (Cowart Moss, 2020), almost 80% of whom are White (NCES, 2020a), to create inclusive school cultures that promote equity for all. Since the early 2000s U.S. society has become increasingly divided, specifically

Inclusive Leadership, pages 181–198
Copyright © 2024 by Information Age Publishing
www.infoagepub.com
All rights of reproduction in any form reserved.

along political, racial, and socioeconomic backgrounds (McGhee, 2021) as people try to live with the reality of a society that systemically oppresses people based on various sociocultural identities.

As such, a core challenge for school leaders is to be intentional and hypervigilant in understanding the power they wield and how they signal to an entire community not only the importance of inclusion within a school system, but also how the system seeks to understand the implicit biases that it perpetuates (Arnold, 2019; Willey & Magee, 2018). As educators, we know that since the foundation of the United States as a country, various systems, including economic, social, political, legal, and education, have been built and maintained for the betterment of White people (Mills, 1997). Increasingly, however, there are social and political battles about the ways in which U.S. society marginalizes and minoritizes people based on a variety of sociocultural identities, including but not limited to race, ethnicity, gender, sexuality/orientation, ability, and other lived experiences (Khalifa, 2018). As such it is critical for school leaders to not only develop inclusive practices to better lead their schools into the 21st century, but also to truly attempt to address the suffering of stakeholders who are marginalized, those who feel unsafe and unsupported, and those who are pushed to the fringes because of the preferential treatment supported by various privileged identities.

One of the most direct ways instructional leaders might support and promote greater equity and inclusive practices throughout the U.S. P–12 education system is through the lens of supervision. Supervision is included as a required course in almost any masters-level educational leadership program, and teacher supervision and evaluation systems are implemented in all fifty states in varying fashions and degrees (Mette et al., 2020), giving a legal framework for supervision to exist, be implemented, and address structural inequities perpetuated in society and school systems. Traditionally, supervision practices are generally defined as formative feedback structures that help create reflective conversations around instructional practices between a supervisor (usually a principal or field supervisor) and a teacher. Supervision practices typically focus on issues of pedagogy (Glickman et al., 2018; Zepeda, 2019) and help provide roadmaps for effective instructional leadership. However, we found little literature on how supervision might be used to address issues of social justice to help educators move past inequitable and exclusive practices (Cormier, 2018; Mette, 2020). Scholars have long pointed out that centralizing race, among other identities, is necessary to understand the inequities that exist and are experienced by various historically marginalized and otherized communities within the U.S. education system (Brooks & Watson, 2018; Khalifa, 2018; Milner IV, 2008). This argument is often ignored in supervision, providing a gap in the literature. As such, there is an opportunity for principals and university-based supervisors to address social justice and systemic inequities to better understand how instructional practices can become more culturally responsive and value the students and parents who come from less privileged sociocultural identities.

In this chapter we hope to provide a synopsis of what we think supervision could be by merging concepts that can be used in teacher preparation by teacher supervisors, as well as in leadership preparation, and certainly by practitioners in the field. That said, supervision has for far too long largely ignored issues of race, culture, ethnicity, gender, and diversity more broadly in conceptualizing and theorizing supervision practices (Cormier, 2020; Guerra et al., 2013; Jacobs & Casciola, 2015; Lynch, 2018; Mette, 2020). When diversity is addressed, it is often as an add-on, something that is tangentially addressed through one chapter of a book, one section of a paper, or somehow as secondary side-items (Guerra et al., 2022).

Since the 1990s there have been a plethora of scholars who have produced critical literature on the role of race and other sociocultural identities on the United States and U.S. P–12 public school system (Dixson & Rousseau, 2005; Khalifa, 2018; Ladson-Billings, 1995; Mills, 1997; Milner IV, 2008; Solorzano, 1997). As society in the United States continues to experience divisiveness along sociocultural lines, it falls squarely on the shoulders of supervisors, 80% whom are White principals (NCES, 2020a), supervising teachers who are comprised of nearly 80% White educators (NCES, 2020b), and nearly 75% of full-time professors whom are White (NCES, 2020c), to critically examine their role in perpetuating issues of race and other privileged identities that help contribute to systems of oppression and deconstruct them to produce more equitable outcomes for students. To make this shift in supervision, educators must not only reconceptualize accepted supervision frameworks, but must also borrow from other paradigms to expand the understanding of what supervision could be.

One of the conduits for this type of inclusive practice is for educational leaders to engage in contemplative studies and mindfulness about the experiences of others. If educators, particularly White educators, are to ever contribute to addressing racial inequities in the United States that are perpetuated and continued through various systems of oppression, then educational supervisors must be able to possess the skills to a) first contemplate and feel the lack of belonging experienced by students from historically marginalized communities when there is a lack of representative curriculum and when instruction lacks cultural responsiveness, to then b) address injustices and help instructors create more inclusive learning communities that are able to see racial and culturally diverse identities as an asset. As such, White educators have much work to do to help contribute to a re-envisioned education system that loves all children for who they are culturally, as well as helping liberate them from the oppressive U.S. education system more broadly.

While White educators can never fully understand what it means to experience racial discrimination in the United States, they can contribute to anti-racist practices by acknowledging the psychological wounds that exist due to white supremacy and systematic oppression. Additionally, by acknowledging how other sociocultural identities also contribute to a society that marginalizes, minoritizes, and otherizes people in the United States, including but not limited to ethnicity, gender, socioeconomic status, sexuality/orientation, ability, and other lived experiences, White educators can begin the process of acknowledging how those racialized as Black experience the historic conceptualization of race (Williams, 2019). As such, teacher and leadership preparation programs alike need to develop scholarly practitioners who can connect with the students, families, and communities they serve, and to approach instruction as an interactive activity where the teacher sees the culture of each student as an asset and adjusts instructional practices to empower students to address the inequities they experience in their day-to-day existence. Educators who are able to reflect on social constructs (e.g., race, ethnicity, gender, sexual orientation) will be more likely to create learning environments that are able to acknowledge and address systemic prejudices and biases as a social construct.

The journey all educators (not just supervisors) must take is one that is intrapersonal (internal reflection) and interpersonal (exchange of ideas with students, parents, and teachers) in order to lead to a better understanding of self and of others. Doing so helps establish more inclusive learning environments that supervisors must establish and support in order to a) acknowledge privileged identities, b) examine and accept the discomfort of perpetuating a system of oppression through the U.S. P–12 education system, and c) transition towards helping change instructional practices that produce culturally responsive outcomes. Supervisors of instruction therefore function as vehicles—they help provide feedback and engage in conversation that supports teachers in their own exploration of self and how this translates into pedagogical practices. To accomplish this goal a supervisor must develop contemplative inquiry stances to meet teachers where they are, help them become more aware of their place in the school, the community, the state, and the country more broadly, and to help reduce the pain and suffering students in the U.S. PK–12 public school system that have historically been marginalized and otherized. Thus, the contemplative supervisor helps empower educators to emancipate their teaching by becoming "interested in the welfare of other beings" (Moacanin, 1986).

POSITIONALITY

Below we offer our own positionalities in more detail. In doing so we offer insight into the professional spaces we inhabit, the methodological approaches to supervision we connect with, and the theories we hope to use to help reenvision the field of supervision. While our own experiences and backgrounds limit us in fully understanding our racialized world, we also hope to offer insight to others how they might better practice acknowledging privilege and how these reflections can be used as contributions for reconstructing an education system that is more culturally responsive (Gay, 2018) to all children.

Steve

As an educator I, Steve, am a White male. While raised as a Catholic, I do not identify with any particular religion or ideology, though I lean towards Buddhist beliefs and have spent a quarter of my life studying meditation and Eastern thought. I was raised in a small, Italian American community, where family, friends, and adults (i.e., teachers, coaches) expressed racist views at times. As I matured and befriended and worked in jobs with those of color and other races and cultures, I began to reflect on my inherited beliefs and question them. Rather than act defensively (which I think was my first reaction when learning of social justice/anti-racial justice movements and notions of White privilege), I try to better understand all sides and respond with compassion, openness, and kindness. Through study and reflection, I acknowledge I enjoy privileges that are provided to me simply because I am a White person living in the United States. I do believe those with privileges and in positions of power must carefully consider their circumstances and what can be done to help others. I do not agree with all racial justice scholars, and I think my interest in Buddhism and Eastern views has shaded my perspectives on the situation.

Specifically, I believe all human beings suffer to different degrees. For example, everyone will suffer from aging, illness, and death (including those around them and their own). However, I believe that societal structures and greed, power, hate, bias, and "wrong views," create situations, systems, and a society that causes others to suffer more intensely, and in many cases, unnecessarily. Indigenous groups, African Americans, and Asian Americans have suffered what Magee (2019) calls a "surplus of suffering" at the hands of White people. They have been subjected to discrimination, bias, prejudice, hate, physical abuse, extreme violence, and death. At times, I think and feel the work is overwhelming in terms of how to help White people move away from angst and towards allyship. However, I see great value in contemplative practices, such as meditation and mindfulness, as possible methods to help bridge difficult racial/equity discussions and help expand feelings of compassion and altruism, and ultimately lead to calls to action as well as strategies that can help result in an awakened mind.

Ian

As a White male educator who has experience as a teacher, administrator, and as a professor, I have learned of the importance of ongoing conversations with others and reflections with myself about better understanding how whiteness has benefited me throughout my life. While I identify as a Taoist and non-Christian, I also understand the privilege my race, skin tone, and cultural background have given me, which I was not required to deeply think about for the first 21 years of my life until I entered an alternative education program and started teaching students from different racial and ethnic backgrounds than mine, shows just how privileged one can be and not have to think deeply about the power afforded to race in the United States. I am an educator who is on a never-ending journey to better understand how I can translate my own privilege afforded by Whiteness by learning firsthand from the students, parents, and community members schools serve.

Informed by Bourdieu (1984), I look at my identity of being White as shaped by three things: 1) growing up rural (*field*); 2) my socioeconomic status as a child (*capital*); and 3) both parents coming from recent immigrant families (*habitus*). First and foremost, a central part of my identity is centered around growing up in a rural space and developing a spatial identity through countless exchanges, experiences, and messages that communicated perspectives about the inferiority of ruralites. Second, I have a deep seeded fear of living in poverty as I grew up working poor in a family that made me eligible to receive free and reduced lunch. While over time I have become what is considered upper-middle class, I have embedded trauma of not having enough resources from my childhood, which impacts how I attempt to avoid the punishment of an economic system that neglects those living in poverty in the United States. Third, I have a deep connection to both sides of my family that immigrated to the United States within the last several generations, and over the course of my life I have literally observed how my own family has exchanged language, food, and culture for acceptance into U.S. society and Whiteness broadly.

None of these experiences prevent me from benefiting from privileged identities. However, these reflections do provide insight into what Whiteness reinforces throughout the United States, including but not limited to how spatial, economic, and social systems communicate messages of superiority and elitism, and how many people in our country (un)consciously pursue privilege to avoid punishment inflicted by various systems. As an educator, I can use my background to help understand that privileged sociocultural identities create messages about belonging and inclusion, specifically in understanding the harm this has done to students and teachers from historically marginalized communities. As such, I use my positionality to not defend my identities, but to better support educators in understanding how they themselves might contemplate the experiences of others who navigate the discriminatory U.S. society.

EMBEDDING CONTEMPLATIVE PRACTICES WITHIN SUPERVISION

In exploring Eastern views as possible pathways to inclusive and equitable supervision frameworks, we gravitated towards Buddhism, particularly Mahayana Buddhism, one of the main branches, which developed in Tibet and has been passed down through some 1,000 years by various teachers and masters. Mahayana's framework includes the *lam rim*, or a gradual path towards awakening. Deeply embedded in Mahayana Buddhism is the notion of compassion, or a mindset that wants to eliminate suffering in other sentient beings. Due to space limitations in this chapter, there is no way to adequately describe a complex religion or mental training such as Mahayana Buddhism. Nevertheless, the ethos that undergirds our work is that of compassion and what is known in Buddhism as *bodhicitta*, or the aspiration to awaken to benefit all sentient beings. We embrace this spirit of compassion and altruism as we explore ways to develop supervision practices that ask teachers and supervisors to continually engage in reflection about instructional practices that allow students to see themselves in the curriculum and feel empowered to address inequities in U.S. society. Before this can happen, however, educators must learn to develop an increased awareness of sociocultural identities and how these identities historically have created educational systems that privileged certain identities over others requires a practical reflection process and method.

One such method that could hold much promise in racial justice supervision is *tonglen*, a form of meditation originating in India in the 10th century. The practice of tonglen is attributed to a Buddhist teacher, Atisha Dipankara Shrinjana, but was later written down by Langri Tangpa, who introduced the meditation to Tibet (Trungpa, 2003). Tonglen involves imagining experiencing the suffering of others and, with that emotional experience, actively focusing on giving happiness, compassion, and relief to others. Within this gradual and ongoing reflective practice, supervision practices that embed contemplation can serve as an important practice to better understand how education systems marginalize and otherize students.

Tonglen's use of radical imagining works to dissolve emotional barriers that keep us feeling separate from others, which in the United States is a myriad of factors, the most visible of which is the delineation of people based on race and skin tone that is used to maintain the racial contract needed to reinforce White supremacy (Mills, 1997). In addition to race, U.S. society also discriminates among a variety of other sociocultural identities (Gay,

2018; Khalifa, 2018). Using tonglen, instructional supervisors can learn how to generate stronger feelings of compassion and altruism by increasing the awareness of students' experiences within the U.S. education system, specifically the ways in which privileged sociocultural identities are expressed through curricula and day-to-day instructional practices. Chödrön (2007) points out, "In tonglen practice, we breathe in what we normally push away and send out what we normally cling to. This dissolves the ego's strategies and reveals the clarity of our mind" (p. 34). As such, training in tonglen could help establish the mindset needed to engage in often uncomfortable, much needed difficult conversations around social injustices and inequities found in U.S. schools and throughout traditional ahistorical and apolitical supervision practices. Tonglen can also serve as a method to deeply explore privileged identities, which is required by both teachers and administrators to create an education system that is more equitable and inclusive for all children (Khalifa et al., 2016).

A CONTEMPLATIVE RACIAL JUSTICE SUPERVISION APPLIED FRAMEWORK

With tonglen at the basis, we present here an applied framework that can help instructional supervisors and educational leaders enhance their ability to reflect on their own privilege, which in turn will help others reflect on theirs. Specifically, our framework provides a paradigm for educators to consider what might be preventing them from critiquing and reimagining an education system that sees racial and cultural identity from a deficit perspective. The framework, seen in Figure 10.1, takes educators through the tonglen stages or psychological points with a focus on inequities in instructional supervision.

To situate this work within the supervision, we believe it is useful to reference existing supervision paradigms but reconsider how it can be used as a guiding framework to address social inequities and biases in instructional practices and reflection on pedagogies. One prominent model is the Development Supervision Model provided by Glickman et al. (2018), which involves supervisors using the paradigm to guide teachers through a directive to non-directive continuum. Using this approach, a supervisor might provide directive actions and/or questions about culturally responsive practices for an educator to consider, then move towards a more collaborative interaction, before eventually encouraging more autonomy through a non-directive approach. We believe this framework coincides well with, and can help provide some contextualization, for the contemplative supervision framework posited in this chapter. For example, educators engaging in the steps of our framework (see Figure 10.1) will certainly need close guidance

	Guiding Questions	Developmental Supervision Model
Point 1: Equalize self and other (within supervision context)	*How do social constructs (e.g. race, ethnicity, gender, sexual orientation) create division and feelings of separateness?*	**Directive Control** Supervisor assigns reflections on how to consider social constructs impacting supervision
Point 2: Contemplate disadvantages of self pre-occupation	*Feeling divided, how does pre-occupation with the self or self-centeredness create conflict, anger, prejudice, bias?*	**Directive Informational** Supervisor suggests reflections on how to consider social constructs impacting supervision
Point 3: Contemplative benefits of compassion and altruism	*On the other hand, how does compassion, altruism, and kindness, result in feelings of joy, connectedness, equity?*	**Collaborative** Supervisor and teacher contemplate interconnectedness and relational aspects of practice together
Point 4: Exchanging self with other: Visualize taking in suffering and giving happiness, compassion, relief	*Are you willing to temporarily exchange self with other, to take on the suffering of another, to develop your capacity for compassion and permanently alter systems of oppression?*	**Non-Directive** Supervisee is more autonomous and on own volition, "volunteers" to exchange self and other
Result		
Increased capacity for compassion, altruism, equalizing self and other as educational leaders working with historically marginalized teachers and students.		

Figure 10.1 Contemplative Racial Justice Supervision Framework Process (adapted from the Supervisory Behavior Continuum; Glickman et al., 2018).

and direction, at least at the early stages, to think more deeply about how and why contemplative practices can contribute to understanding the feeling of not belonging based on sociocultural identities that are privileged through instruction provided within classrooms. As supervisors, educators (supervisors and teachers alike) progress through their own development and growth to address issues of inequity and lack of culturally responsive teaching, their reflections might shift into more collaborative discussions, and eventually might even evolve into more non-directive work and reflection. However, to begin this work, supervisors need a framework to support their own reflective practices, as well as the teachers they serve.

Preliminary Step

Prior to engaging in tonglen, we suggest that supervisors and teachers establish the proper mental platform. Some suggestions include: 1) find a relatively quiet place, 2) sit in a comfortable position either on a floor mat or chair, 3) the back should be straight but not stiff and the chin should be slightly tilted down, eyes either closed or looking downward, 4) place the hands face up, cupped, below the waist or face up, palms resting on the knees, and 5) begin focusing on the breath, simply observing the inhalation and exhalation through the nose. Try to feel the coolness of the in-breath as it enters the nostrils and the warmness as it leaves the nostrils. With each breath, easily notice how the breath starts to deepen. Breathe in this manner for 10 repetitions.

Stage 1: Equalizing Self and Other Within the Context of Supervision

With the mind settled, begin to reflect on how we create mental division and separation. For example, reflect on how various, sociocultural identities, such as race, ethnicity, gender, socio-economic status, sexuality/orientation, ability, and other lived experiences, are privileged within education systems and contribute to a system of oppression. Seeing this within the context of supervision is critical to reflecting on how supervisors and teachers reflect on creating more culturally responsive and inclusive instructional practices. For example, educators should reflect on personal experiences as well as what they have read, discussed, and observed within U.S. society, particularly how U.S. education often perpetuates exclusive practices. For example, educators should ask themselves (and continually be asked) questions such as the following:

1. How were you and/or classmates defined, treated, labeled, or marginalized while progressing through the P–12 education system? How might these scenarios contribute to feelings of separateness?
2. As an educator, how might you reflect on the U.S. political ideologies that reinforce polarizing views and stances that create mental division between citizens?
3. How might privileged sociocultural identities reinforce socially created paradigms, and how might you use your privileged identities to create more inclusive instructional experiences for students? Reflect on how privileged identities create exclusive learning environments and generate a sense of separateness as human beings.

To establish an inclusive environment, instructional leaders need to continuously contemplate how to support teachers and themselves from unconsciously reinforcing these mental divisions for those they supervise and how this might impact their interactions, relationships, and instructional supervision practice. Realizing that fundamentally all beings want happiness and to feel a sense of belonging in the public education system is essential to accomplishing this goal, and to do so educators and supervisors must first be able to accept the exclusion marginalized and otherized students, parents, and community members experience.

Stage 2: Detriments of Self Preoccupation

During this stage, instructional leaders should reflect on the cause of mental states of division and separateness that are socially constructed and underpinned through systems of oppression: the self-centered, preoccupation, self-preservation that whiteness and other privileged identities reinforce. As educational leaders, we are subjected to the same pervading, self-serving, preoccupied mind, the "me, mine, I" principle (Neale, 2013), and as such we must be aware of, and help others to be aware of, the ways in which societal constructions message privilege in what is taught, how it is taught, and who the curriculum serves. Consider how much time is spent thinking about your own interests and identities as a supervisor (or the lack thereof), and how your own goals and beliefs can create pain and suffering from instructional practices because of practices that do not take into account cultural responsiveness. By meditating on the experiences of students, parents, and community members connected with your practice, school administrators, teachers, and teacher candidates can begin the process of developing the ability to reflect on the needs of the students and parents they serve rather than the techno-rational approach of high stakes accountability education that has been reinforced since the inception of No Child Left Behind.

Stage 3: The Benefits of Compassion and Altruism

This stage involves contemplating the advantages of being compassionate and altruistic. For example, recollect a time you have experienced feeling loved, happy, successful, or fulfilled, and how others were likely involved and how they contributed to your sense of belonging. Also, think about the positive feelings you have gained when you have helped another by being supportive, caring, and providing love and support. From this, educators can further realize that human happiness and well-being is deeply reliant and connected to others. For supervision, this could mean meditating how a classroom observation felt when all students were engaged in the lesson and/or when student work represented various sociocultural identities of students in the class. Reflecting on moments where students connected deeply to instruction being provided and were proud of the work being accomplished because they saw themselves in the curriculum is central to this feeling of compassion and altruism.

Stage 4: Exchanging Self and Other

Finally, during this stage, let yourself use radical imagining to experience the suffering of others. As a side note, the inhaling of negativity or suffering in tonglen is often described as black smoke or a dark cloud, however we prefer a description provided by Chödrön (2001), in which the inhaling breath is described more as a "heavy" quality. We prefer the heavy description over the black smoke description due to the negative connotation associated with the color black and the overall attributes associated with anti-Blackness. It is important for educators and supervisors to make the object (the person) of your meditation connected to your supervision practice, particularly a person who has experienced prejudice, racial or social injustice, or who has been marginalized or otherized in some way. You can also focus on groups of people for example, for "black, indigenous, people of color, you can breathe in for the women across the planet that have been dominated, for those of different sexual orientation, for anyone, any being, anywhere, that has been dominated or experienced injustice or violence and open yourself to that pain" (Brach, 2020, n.p.).

DISCUSSION

As two White males writing this chapter, we acknowledge we do not know what it is like to live as a person of color, a woman, or a person who identifies as part of the LGBTQ+ community (as well as other marginalized and otherized socio-cultural identities) who are subjected to the oppressive societal structures and systems in the United States—and we will never know.

That said, we do believe that it is the responsibility of all educators to deeply examine their privileged identities and to increase awareness of them to provide equitable outcomes and learning experiences for all students (Khalifa et al., 2016; Milner IV, 2008). In the context of instructional supervision, this requires educators, 80% of whom are racialized as White in the United States (NCES, 2020a), to develop a greater sense of empathy, urgency, and compassion for students from historically marginalized communities if we are to improve conditions and establish more culturally responsive instruction in educational settings. This involves deep, unabashed, authentic self-reflection, first starting with our own potential bias and limiting beliefs, then moving beyond our own self-encapsulated 'bubble' which we can emerge from using contemplative reflection such as tonglen.

To accomplish more inclusive instructional strategies, supervisors must serve as a thought partner to help teachers reflect on, and engage in, instructional practices that result in curriculum and pedagogy to meet teachers where they are, help them become more aware of their place in the school, the community, the state, and society more broadly, and reduce the pain and suffering experienced by students in the education system that treats whiteness and other privileged sociocultural identities as the norm. The goal, then, of the contemplative supervisor is to support the collective consciousness of a school building to move past ignorance and delusions of what privileged identities in the United States traditionally have perceived the country to be, and instead focus all teaching to be centered on the happiness and wellness of students and parents, seeing their culture and identities as assets, by loving them for who they are and not by attempting to change them through an oppressive education system. The framework introduced in this chapter, with tonglen at its heart, can be a working tool for principals, teachers, and higher education faculty to increase awareness of how the education system historically has valued whiteness, patriarchy, heteronormative, and cisgender identities (among others), and what educators must do to continually reflect on practices, policies, and paradigms to create more inclusive learning environments.

Through radical imagining, educational leaders and teachers can be intentional in learning about the pain and suffering of those who have been historically excluded from the U.S. education system through the instructional practices reinforced by teachers, including those marginalized and otherized, and with enhanced compassion seek out ways to further develop liberation coalitions. However, as noted by hooks (1996), when critically examining the impact of education systems and mass media on racism, "there must exist a paradigm, a practical model for social change that includes an understanding of ways to transform consciousness that are linked to efforts to transform structures" (p. 118). In this spirit, we believe through intentional supervision practices, educators can transform both consciousness and instructional structures, with tonglen as its basis, that will lead to more equitable learning outcomes for students. In short, this type of contemplative reflection should serve as a call to action as a result of an awakened mind, where supervisors and teachers transform ideas into instructional strategies that occur within the schoolhouse.

Transforming Stage 1: Assigning Reflections to Consider Social Constructs

When providing supervision that addresses sociocultural identities that are privileged in the U.S. education system and U.S. society more broadly, many educators will need feedback that is directive in nature and where the supervisor assigns key reflections (Glickman et al., 2018). This type of supervision requires instructional supervisors to not only engage in questions about sociocultural identities and representations in assignments and within the curriculum, but also requires the supervisor direct these reflections with supporting materials that include, but are not limited to:

- Practitioner-friendly articles that provide action steps to address equity in action, including anti-racist and anti-biased teaching practices;
- Podcasts that allow practitioners to wrestle with the difficulties of closing the theory-practice gap, including policies and practices that disproportionately and negatively impact marginalized and minoritized students;
- Social media that provides perspectives on implementing equity work and how to prevent resistance to the implementation of practices that lead to equitable outcomes;
- Books that detail culturally responsive teaching and leadership practices, including literature that describes how to use data to drive equitable improvements.

Therefore, to begin to transform consciousness on how constructs such as race, ethnicity, nationality, socio-economic status, and gender, are embedded within systems of oppression, inclusive supervisors and instructional leaders must engage in direct dialogue *and reflective practices* to help teachers who are unaware of how their instruction is culturally insensitive or culturally unresponsive. Directing reflection and engaging in material that awakens a deeper understanding to social constructs is the first step to making instruction more culturally responsive and inclusive.

Transforming Stage 2: Suggesting Reflections to Move Past Pre-Occupation

Once educators have become aware of their sociocultural identities that are privileged, supervisors can make a subtle shift and transition away from assigning reflection to suggesting reflection (Glickman et al., 2018) that will lead to more inclusive instructional practices. In this stage, supervisors will need to help teachers continue to move forward with reflecting on the inequities perpetuated by the U.S. PK–12 education system. Specifically, supervisors will need to be prepared to support educators to move past feelings of conflict, anger, prejudice, or bias, often times which is referred to as white tears or white angst, as a result of a guilty conscious once there is a realization of pain suffered by students and parents who are marginalized and otherized. During this stage, supervisors must rely on their own contemplative journey and what is continually required to move past the preoccupation of the "me, mine, I" principle (Neale, 2013). Here the work for a supervisor is to continue to suggest reflection about how instructional practices might be seen as culturally insensitive or culturally unresponsive, particularly because of an education system that devalues sociocultural identities and sees cultural differences as deficits. Specifically, the goal of supervision feedback here should be supporting educators to continually circle back to their discomfort and engage in their own development of an awakened mind, one that can help start to more systemically address the issues of instruction that occur through inclusive instructional practices and representative curricula.

Transforming Stage 3: Collaboratively Contemplating Interconnectedness

Once a supervisor has established the importance of creating inclusive instructional practices with a teacher, one that centers the importance of belonging and representation, the supervisor and teacher can contemplate together the interconnectedness and relational aspects of instructional practices. At this point supervisors could hope to switch to a collaborative developmental approach (Glickman et al., 2018), specifically focusing on an interaction and exchange of ideas about how education is a large driving force as a social system to improve equitable outcomes for all. Discussions at this stage could include 1) how the racialized social system more broadly permeates the education system (Meghji, 2022), 2) how whiteness and other privileged sociocultural identities are socially constructed and what this means for educators who want to enact anti-racist and anti-biased practices, and 3) responses to anti-democratic policies that seek to prevent education systems from talking about racial inequities (McGhee, 2021). Once a supervisor has helped a teacher be more aware of the social and structural inequities that exist, they can then in collaborative, compassionate contemplation that leads to action to transform consciousness and structures. When this occurs, educators can work together to recreate an altruistic system that focuses on supporting and loving students and families and that sees their culture as an asset.

Transforming Stage 4: Voluntary Capacity for Compassion That Leads to Change

If and when educators have accepted that equitable school improvement is a never-ending process (Irby, 2021), non-directive feedback can be used to develop their reflective stance about instructional practices if they are willing to use their instruction to alter the oppressive educational system within the United States. During this stage, the exchange of supervisory conversations is more about what is being done, collectively, to alter the education system so that all socio-cultural identities are valued, honored, and represented within instructional practices and the curriculum. As such, the meditative work of the supervisor is ongoing, but the reflections are continually translated into actions to help address how the United States has perpetuated racism, prejudice, or social injustice that has resulted in the marginalizing and otherizing of various peoples.

CONCLUSION

We openly acknowledge that this framework is conceptualized from our own particular worldview and experience, which is situated within a White, heterosexual, cisgender male experience. Despite these limitations, we believe this framework advances the poignant discussion of inequitable practices and beliefs embedded within supervision circles that often do not acknowledge privileged socio-cultural identities as central to an educator's experience or understanding. Tonglen, with its emphasis on embracing the uncomfortable and becoming vulnerable, could help provide this space and a platform to engage in the important work of acknowledging—and addressing—the inequities that exist throughout the U.S. education system. For far too many educators, 80% of whom are racialized as White, it is critical that instructional leaders are able to support the development of viewpoints, ideas, and conceptualizations that create greater representation and inclusion for the students and parents schools are intended to serve. If the U.S. education system is to serve all students and not just those whose sociocultural identities are privileged, educators must learn to see sociocultural identities as assets, and understand that to shift away from a deficit mindset will require reflecting heavily upon the intent of schooling. We hope this writing sparks new thought, new emotion, and new action in the realm of inclusive, just, and compassionate supervision.

REFERENCES

Arnold, N. (2019). Supervisory identity: Cultural shift, critical pedagogy, and the crisis of supervision. In S. Zepeda & J. Ponticell (Eds.), *The Wiley handbook of educational supervision* (pp. 575–600). Wiley-Blackwell.

Bourdieu, P. (1984). *Distinction: A social critique of the judgment of taste*. Routledge.

Brach, T. (2020). *Tonglen meditation with Tara Brach: Discovering the boundless space of compassion* [Video] YouTube. https://www.youtube.com/watch?v=amrGu1oHsvQ

Brooks, J.S., & Watson, T. N. (2018). School leadership and racism: An ecological perspective. *Urban Education, 54*(5), 631–655. https://doi.org/10.1177%2F0042085918783821

Chödrön, P. (2001). *Tonglen: The path of transformation*. Vajradhatu Publications.

Chödrön, P. (2007). *No time to lose: A timely guide to the way of the Bodhisattva*. Shambhala Publications.

Cormier, D. R. (2018). *Culturally responsive supervision: An appropriate epistemology for attending to the demographic transformation within US PK–12 public schools*. Paper presented at the annual meeting of the Council of Professors of Instructional Supervision, Orono, ME.

Cormier, D. R. (2020). Assessing preservice teachers' cultural competence with the Cultural Proficiency Continuum Q-Sort. *Educational Researcher*. https://doi.org/10.3102/0013189X20936670

Cowart Moss, S. (Winter 2020). Infusing inclusive leadership into a program redesign at Georgia State University. *UCEA Review*, 17–19.

Gay, G. (2018). *Culturally responsive teaching: Theory, research, and practice* (3rd ed.). Teachers College Press.

Glickman, C. D., Gordon, S. P., & Ross-Gordon, J. M. (2018). *SuperVision and instructional leadership: A developmental approach* (10th ed.). Pearson.

Guerra, P. L., Baker, A. M., & Cotman, A. M. (2022). Instructional supervision: Is it culturally responsive? A textbook analysis. *Journal of Educational Supervision, 5*(1), 1–26. https://doi.org/10.31045/jes.5.1.1

Guerra, P. L., Nelson, S. W., Jacobs, J., & Yamamura, E. (2013). Developing educational leaders for social justice: Programmatic elements that work and need improvement. *Education Research and Perspectives, 40*, 124–149.

hooks, b. (1996). *Killing rage: Ending racism*. Holt and Company.

Irby, D. (2021). *Stuck improving: Racial equity and school leadership*. Harvard Education Press.

Jacobs, J., & Casciola, V. (2015). A social justice lens in supervision. In J. Glanz & S. Zepeda (Eds.), *Supervision: New perspectives for theory and practice*. (pp. 221–239). Rowan & Littlefield.

Khalifa, M. (2018). *Culturally responsive school leadership*. Harvard Education Press.

Khalifa, M. A., Gooden, M. A., & Davis, J. E. (2016). Culturally responsive school leadership: A synthesis of the literature. *Review of Educational Research, 86*(4), 1272–1311.

Ladson-Billings, G. (1995). Toward a theory of culturally relevant pedagogy. *American Educational Research Journal, 32*(3), 465–491.

Lynch, M. E. (2018). The hidden nature of whiteness in education: Creating active allies in White teachers. *Journal of Educational Supervision, 1*(1), 18–31. https://doi.org/10.31045/jes.1.1.2

Magee, R. V. (2019). *The inner work of racial justice: Healing ourselves and transforming our communities through mindfulness*. TarcherPerigee.

Meghji, A. (2022). *The racialized social system: Critical race theory as social theory*. Polity Press.

Mette, I. M. (2020). Reflections on supervision in the time of COVID-19. *Journal of Educational Supervision, 3*(3), 1–6. https://doi.org/10.31045/jes.3.3.1

Mette, I. M., Aguilar, I., & Wieczorek, D. (April 2020). *A fifty state review of teacher supervision and evaluation systems: The influence of ESSA and implications for policy and practice*. Paper session at the Annual Meeting of the American Educational Research Association, San Francisco, CA.

McGhee, H. (2021). *The sum of us: What racism costs everyone and how we can prosper together*. One World Press.

Milner, IV, H. R. (2008). Critical race theory and interest convergence as analytic tools in teacher education policies and practices. *Journal of Teacher Education, 59*(4), 332–346. https://doi.org/10.1177/0022487108321884

Mills, C. W. (1997). *The racial contract*. Cornell University Press.

Moacanin, R. (1986). *Jung's psychology and Tibetan Buddhism: Western and Eastern paths to the heart*. Dorrance Publishing.

NCES. (2020a). Characteristics of public school principals. https://nces.ed.gov/programs/coe/indicator_cls.asp#:~:text=In%202017%E2%80%9318%2C%20about%2078,and%209%20percent%20were%20Hispanic.

NCES. (2020b). Characteristics of public school teachers. https://nces.ed.gov/programs/coe/indicator_clr.asp

NCES. (2020c). The Condition of Education 2020 (NCES 2020-144), Characteristics of Postsecondary Faculty. https://nces.ed.gov/fastfacts/display.asp?id=61

Neale, M. (2018). *Gradual awakening: The Tibetan Buddhist path of becoming fully human*. Sounds True.

Solorzano, D. G. (1997). Images and words that wound: Critical race theory, racial stereotyping, and teacher education. *Teacher Education Quarterly, 24*(3), 5–19.

Trungpa, C. (2003). *Training the mind and cultivating loving-kindness*. Shambhala Publications.

Willey, C., & Magee, P. A. (2018). Whiteness as a barrier to becoming a culturally relevant teacher: Clinical experiences and the role of supervision. *Journal of Educational Supervision, 1*(2), 33–51. https://doi.org/10.31045/jes.1.2.3

Williams, D. T. (2019). A call to focus on racial domination and oppression: A response to "Racial and ethnic inequality in poverty and affluence, 1959—2015." *Population Research and Policy Review, 38*, 655–663.

Zepeda, S. J. (2019). *Instructional supervision: Applying tools and concepts* (4th ed.). Routledge.

CHAPTER 11

BUILDING A STRONGER LEADER PREPARATION MODEL

Inclusive Practice Grounded in Research and Experience

Karen Caldwell Bryant
The University of Georgia

Jami Royal Berry
The University of Georgia

Robin Christian
Atlanta Public Schools

Niles Davis
Gwinnett County Public Schools

Michele Dugan
Forsyth County Schools

Brian Keefer
Georgia Association of Elementary School Principals

Kristen McRae
Henry County Public Schools

Summer Tuggle Smith
Clarke Central High School

The United States continues to require substantive reforms in leader preparation informed by voices of leaders in the field and scholarly research. This chapter examines how leadership preparation programs must support the development of inclusive leaders for *each* student, emphasizing marginalized populations and students who are differently abled, given the context of schools in the era of COVID-19. Inclusive leaders create strong school cultures and distribute leadership to serve all learners well, ensuring students feel safe, supported, and valued in school. In promoting equity for "all," inclusive leaders must respond effectively to the potential and needs of *each* student. Inclusive leaders ensure high expectations and appropriate support so students, across race, gender, ethnicity, language, disability, sexual orientation, family background, and/or income, can excel in school (Council of Chief State School Officers, 2018).

The chapter begins with an overview of scholarly literature on inclusive leadership and a discussion of current practice in integrating the research base into educational leadership preparation program curricula. Next, it presents voices of inclusive leaders at the building and district levels to explore how preparation programs might approach inclusivity through a practice-informed lens supported by scholarly literature. This chapter seeks to use the voices of leaders to inform the work of preparation program providers as they labor to integrate elements of inclusivity into their course content and clinical practice. The chapter closes with guiding questions for leadership preparation program faculty to consider and suggested initial steps for programmatic enhancement.

REVIEW OF RELATED LITERATURE

Today's leaders face challenges of ensuring that all students have opportunities to fully access a rigorous curriculum and participate in activities that enrich their learning in classroom settings and co-curricular activities. According to the U.S Commission for Civil Rights (2019) and the National Council on Disability (2018), students of color, students from low-income backgrounds, and differently abled students continue to face disproportionate rates of instructional and social segregation compared to their counterparts, leading to adverse educational and social-emotional outcomes. The impact of COVID-19 has further highlighted these inequities, especially in student access to technology, academic and social-emotional services (McLeod & Dulsky, 2021). In order to address issues of equity and inclusion, leaders must be able to transform learning during a crisis and create an inclusive school environment that is culturally responsive and reflective of the racial and cultural diversity of their communities (Annamma & Morrison, 2018; Darling-Hammond et al., 2020; DeMatthews, 2020).

Adaptive and inclusive education requires meaningful relationships with staff, students, and community partners and value-driven leadership practices focused on a social justice-oriented mission (Bagwell, 2020; DeMatthews et al., 2020; Gross et al., 2015; Ravitch, 2020). In the words of Villa and Thousand (2003), "For inclusive education to succeed, administrators must take action to publicly articulate the new vision and lead all stakeholders to active involvement" (p. 21).

Beyond developing and communicating a clear vision of inclusivity, school leaders must understand the tools needed to fulfill that vision, preparing to adapt tools to reflect current challenges (Smith & Riley, 2012). From knowledge of education laws and accommodations to specific asset-based supports, tools, and other resources, school leaders should enable empowerment by connecting students, families, and staff to the best options for support (Khalifa et al., 2016; Taylor, 2011). As school leaders gain knowledge about inclusive practices, they will be able to better support teachers, advance organizational effectiveness, and improve school climate (Council of Chief State School Officers, 2018; DeMatthews et al., 2019). School leaders who commit to and build community trust, organizational resilience, and inclusive decision-making will also support better institutional responses to educational inequities even during challenging times like the pandemic (Bagwell, 2020; Fernandez & Shaw, 2020; Rigby et al., 2020). Theoharis and Causton (2014) outlined essential elements for successful inclusive leadership: (a) setting a vision, (b) developing democratic implementation plans, (c) using staff members (teachers and paraprofessionals) in systematic ways to create inclusive service delivery, (d) creating and developing teams who work collaboratively to meet the range of student needs, (e) providing ongoing learning opportunities for staff members, (f) monitoring and adjusting the service delivery each year, and (g) purposefully working to develop a climate of belonging for students and staff members.

Social-emotional health plays a fundamental role in student success (Reyes et al., 2013; Weiss et al., 2009). Considering recent data highlighting the increased stress and trauma students have faced due to health concerns, lost school relationships, and an uncertain future, school leaders must integrate restorative and inclusive practices in their schools (Darling-Hammond et al., 2020). Attitudes and beliefs of educators and students impact how the school community will be able to move forward as the consequences of the pandemic (and long-standing racial injustices) continue to define students' societal context. Shogren et al. (2015) discovered that students valued belonging to an inclusive school. Students who were members of inclusive classrooms reported that the opportunity to learn alongside peers of various abilities gave them a stronger sense of belonging. Moreover, students continued to interact outside the classroom, with positive effects on their socialization. Shogren et al. (2015) also reported, "students described benefiting from the implementation of evidence-based practices at the classroom level, including classroom monitoring systems, strategies to promote self-determination, frequent re-teaching and assessment, and multiple means of representation, expression, and engagement" (p. 256). Cook-Sather (2002) argues that student perspectives are of primary importance when considering reforms such as inclusion. The impact of inclusion on student academic achievement was explored in a nine-year quantitative study conducted in North Carolina. Finkel (2011) indicated that students with disabilities who participated in an inclusive classroom and were held to higher learning standards increased academic achievement, through improved reading scores and graduation rates.

Preparation programs must systemically emphasize culturally responsive competencies to ensure that new leaders recognize inherent value in all students and are equipped to create inclusive communities in their classrooms and schools (Boser, 2014; Dilworth & Coleman, 2014; Kozleski, 2019). This is especially pertinent when the confines of schools have expanded to include online environments and homes. All students, regardless of ability, sexual orientation, cultural background, or racial and ethnic heritage, will benefit from representative, culturally responsive teachers and school leaders (Grissom, 2015; Albert Shanker Institute, 2015).

VOICES OF EDUCATIONAL LEADERS IN THE FIELD

As the original co-authors and two leadership preparation program faculty members, we felt compelled to include the voices of both school and district-level leaders to provide a comprehensive look at the issues associated with leading for inclusivity during and beyond the COVID-19 pandemic. We felt that having the voices of students enrolled in a leadership preparation program during the pandemic would be effective in crafting relevant recommendations for preparation program providers to equip students with skills to lead for inclusivity in a post COVID-19 educational environment. We placed a call to a cohort of doctoral students in educational leadership asking them to tell their stories and offer recommendations to leadership preparation programs on how they might embed more inclusive models into course content and pedagogy.

Importantly we wanted the student/leaders' own words and experiences to frame the readers' understandings of their recommendations, thus giving them an authentic and inclusive voice in the process. The sections that follow are the inclusive leadership stories of six public school leaders.

Michele's Inclusive Leadership Story—The Many Villages of Inclusive Leadership

If it takes a village to raise a child, then it takes many villages to raise educators. In my district, a suburb of a large metro area, we offer an alternative education preparation program for candidates with bachelor's degrees who wish to transition into education. Unlike traditional preparation programs, there is no gradual release model. This alternative certification route requires candidates to work as full-time classroom teachers while they earn credentials. As an inclusive leader in this work, I must partner with my fellow district and building leaders to assure that candidates engage in culturally responsive practices, research-based instruction, and family engagement. Our villages—composed of schools, community partners, higher education consultants, and district leaders—all work together to ensure quality learning experiences for our candidates.

The vital need for inclusive leadership became undeniable when COVID-19 disrupted our world in March of 2020. As schools moved online, so did our alternative certification pathway. We conducted online seminars and phone calls to support candidates in teaching virtually. Overnight, many of the strategies and procedures we taught our candidates shifted from *best practice* to *obsolete*. We knew we needed to expand our village to meet the needs of our candidates and their students. I collaborated with district technology specialists, school-based mentors, and national experts on virtual instruction. Using the knowledge I gained from the courses and professors in my leadership doctoral program, I designed surveys and interviews to use with parents to ensure we were meeting our community's needs. Together, our team used these reflections to create job-embedded professional learning opportunities and continuous mentoring for candidates.

The professional learning and candidate support was a responsive and impactful start, but we were treating the symptoms of the challenge. I reflected on how education preparation leaders might enhance programming to be more inclusive of the needs and voices highlighted in this crisis. After connecting with state leaders, I had the opportunity to join our statewide digital learning task force. I connected with state leaders to address a need for evolution in the education preparation standards regarding virtual instruction. We proposed clarification to an existing rule enhancing the requirement for virtual learning preparation. While I never imagined that my village would expand to university and state levels, I am thankful for the myriad of opportunities our team had to engage with leaders to improve educator preparation.

Michele's story highlights the importance of monitoring and adjusting service delivery every year (Theoharis & Causton, 2014) and points out that stakeholder engagement is essential (Reyes et al., 2013).

Brian's Inclusive Leadership Story—The Importance of Community Connections

The elementary school where I serve as principal has a long-standing tradition of collaboration with its community. The area lacks grocery stores and healthy food options. In essence, it is a food desert, and many families lack transportation. Our elementary school is known for its Farm to School program, project-based learning, and STEAM connection programs. These three big rocks produced a link to our community and opened our students' lens to dive into authentic, real-world knowledge. Market Day started with a seed, known as the driving question, where the entire student body asked the question: "How can we provide our community with healthy food options?" Every grade level collaborated with our STEAM teacher to actively create innovative ways to provide healthy food for the community aligned to grade-level specific standards.

We found an opportunity to partner with the Metro Community Food Bank (MCFB) to solve this real-world problem. We began a mobile Market Day in November 2019 and opened it to all city residents in January 2020. Many families struggled with food insecurity due to the COVID-19 pandemic, so we expanded the program. We received additional support from our school district, and MCFB increased the food supply order to meet community needs. In March 2020, we began weekly community service at a local park. We quickly realized that we needed a larger venue. A large neighboring racetrack agreed to host our weekly Market Day. In April and May 2020 we fed over 35,000 individuals from across the entire metro region. The program was recognized by the Statewide Association of Elementary School Principals, earning the 2020 School Bell Award.

Brian's main theme is connecting with community partners as stated in the literature review: "Adaptive and inclusive education requires meaningful relationships with staff, students, and community partners and value-driven leadership practices focused on a clear social justice-oriented mission (Bagwell, 2020; DeMatthews et al., 2020; Gross et al., 2015; Ravitch, 2020)."

Niles' Inclusive Leadership Story—Building Community Across the Digital Divide

My story started when I was hired as a special education paraprofessional in a large urban school district in 2010. My assistant principal mentored me and provided multiple learning opportunities, eventually leading to a teaching position with students in the Emotional/Behavioral Disorder (EBD) program. This led to the opportunity to serve as the school's Positive Behavior Interventions and Supports (PBIS) Coach. I worked with a group of staff members to disaggregate data and look for behavior patterns. The analysis uncovered equity issues within the school. This was the beginning of my focus on inclusion and equity, which eventually led me to pursue a position as a district instructional coach. Things came full circle when my mentor, now a principal, hired me as a first-time assistant principal in 2019.

As an educational leader and doctoral student, I was working diligently to support our staff and students when COVID-19 sent everyone home for digital learning in March 2020. This created an immediate need to shift the way we supported our students and communities. My initial memories from spring 2020 were isolation, overwork, mental and physical exhaustion. The isolation led to hope as I met with colleagues and observed digital classes via virtual platforms. Although our administrative team met daily, and weekly as a course team, there was still a great deal of connection missing. One of our goals was to build collaborative teams. We were able to start this during digital learning. Many teachers were previously working in silos under the same roof. Working from home broke down the silos and moved the work forward. Although we saw progress in collaboration, educational inequities were evident. Student isolation, depression, and lack of resources were serious realities. Eventually, we provided digital resources to our students, and delivered Chromebooks to their homes. This connection gave us a way to encourage them and helped all of us to keep moving forward.

Upon returning to our school building in fall 2021, it was vital to continue our support for our community. One strategy was via schoolwide participation in Great Days of Service. For the past 21 years, Great Days of Service has mobilized thousands of individuals, corporations, churches, schools, civic organizations, and government entities in meaningful volunteer service. Both digital and in-person students were extremely generous in their donations of non-perishable goods amongst other things. This was a clear reminder of the importance of community and finding ways to build connections between our learners, school, and the community.

Niles highlights the importance of connecting students, families, and staff to options for support to meet individual student needs (Khalifa et al., 2016; Taylor, 2011).

Summer's Inclusive Leadership Story—
Understanding Your Own Bias

I am a white woman. I have spent almost twenty years in a predominantly minority school district. First as a teacher, instructional coach, and then as an assistant principal. My school serves about 1800 students and is composed of approximately 75% minority students. I was fortunate to have an African American female mentor early in my career. She always shared her perspective about school, our students, and life. Over time I noticed that my perspective shifted because of our honest and frank talks. She encouraged me to be reflective, to seek clarity, and to always think about those left behind.

I am now on a diverse leadership team serving a staff of predominantly white teachers. Our conversations around race started timidly a couple of years ago, mostly driven by district initiatives. We also started a restorative justice program. Teachers facilitated weekly circle talks with students to create meaningful dialog in an informed community. Students repaired harm through restorative circles with other students and teachers. We also used circles as a staff during professional learning as we began to broach subjects like inclusion. Talking and sharing gradually became our norm.

The 2020–2021 school year was a virtual delivery model. Oddly, the physical separation seemed to bring the staff together. COVID-19 and the June 2020 riots laid the issues of race bare. The administrative team knew we had to face these issues with our staff head-on to serve our students. We chose to speak frankly about how our student body was affected by the happenings in our world. We began a book study of *The Racial Healing Handbook* (Singh, 2019) in groups of 5–8 teachers. The book and circle discussions prompted a deep introspection of personal bias. A group of teachers set up a separate open conversation time. Anyone could join and talk about race. Different staff who did not usually interact socially came together virtually to talk about the hurt that many in our country faced and continue to face.

This was the beginning of peeling back the awkwardness and hesitation that shrouds the race conversation. It has not been perfect, and we do not always agree or understand one another, but we are talking, learning, and reflecting on our biases. Open dialogue holds the potential to change perspectives to help us reach each student.

Summer's story affirms the importance of self-reflection and open, respectful dialogue as for creating an inclusive school climate (Shogren et al., 2015).

Kristen's Inclusive Leadership Story—Effective and Inclusive Leadership Strategies

The greatest challenge I have experienced as an elementary school principal is leading a team of 80 staff members and approximately 750 students and families during the time of a pandemic During this time I learned: 1) while change is inevitable and often resisted by adults, it can also foster growth and innovation 2) as humans, we carry our own biases, whether unconscious or conscious, which inform our decision making and planning 3) leading during a pandemic will teach one how to show grace, empathy and understanding toward families and stakeholders.

When planning and preparing for the 2020–2021 school year, my inclusive leadership story began with the development of a *local school playbook* which would guide the way toward opening schools during a pandemic. This playbook outlined daily operational and instructional decisions that would be implemented throughout the school year with respect to equity and inclusion. For events such as a student of the month celebration, end of year class party, or awards day, we determined how to include our remote learning students with in person learners. We made a commitment to invest in remote learners by removing obstacles related to state and district testing, instructional resource acquisition, and daily instruction. Further, as a district, we provided internet hot spots to low-income families, and printed instructional materials to ensure the learning could continue at home. In partnership with our school counselors and social worker, we created a Care Team which met weekly to discuss student attendance, missing assignments, failing students, and family hardships. We made the commitment to connect with families and know each marginalized student by name and need.

Challenges were prevalent in the beginning of the pandemic. Master schedules were drafted, implemented, and then redrafted to support each student in and outside the building. This process became cyclical as students quarantined due to COVID-19, or changed their learning option due to safety, or fear. As educators, we constantly had to consider our own biases and perceptions related to the pandemic and operate as a unified school.

Kristen's story reflects that gaining knowledge about inclusive practices helps equip leaders to provide structural support for teachers to meet the needs of each student (Council of Chief State School Officers, 2018; DeMatthews et al., 2019).

Robin's Inclusive Leadership Story—Self-Awareness and the Importance of Cultural Responsiveness

Inclusive leadership involves commitment to the ideals of creating a school climate where others feel valued, heard, and connected. As a leader during a pandemic, my inclusive leadership lens was broadened to spend time thinking about how new challenges have entered the workspace. Prior to COVID-19, inclusive school leaders led in varied demographics which yielded different needs and foci. With the pandemic, inclusive leaders needed to balance multiple layers of complex issues. As a principal serving an extremely marginalized and poverty-stricken area, inclusive leadership has taken me on a new journey. The ever-present issues of poverty have been exacerbated with many of our students facing large gaps in student achievement. The inclusive leadership lens led me to consider the varied issues facing parents such as loss of income, displacement, or homelessness.

As an inclusive leader, the focus of providing additional support for teachers took on a more layered approach as we expanded wrap-around services.

One inclusive leadership practice I found to be beneficial for virtual instruction to over half of our student population was the implementation of our *N.E.S.T. (Nurturing Every Student Timely)* support team. The team meets weekly to triage and provide timely support for students ranging from health services to financial support for families in need. Each student is assigned a member of the team who is responsible for overseeing the specific support to help that student.

Inclusive school leadership continues to focus on embedding opportunities for teachers and school staff members to have access to environments and a climate where they feel connected with others. During the pandemic, teachers expressed the need for more conversations related to self-care and balancing the new demands of work and home. I needed to increase my time focusing on the mental health of teachers and school staff. I experienced COVID-19 firsthand and became more empathetic toward teachers' mental health and the daily feelings of burnout.

The self-awareness lens of my inclusive leadership entails more reflection on how I am listening and staying connected to how teachers feel supported in a global pandemic. One of the most difficult aspects of my inclusive leadership has involved balancing and prioritizing change management processes during COVID-19. It was critical to find multiple ways to communicate new information with staff, ranging from safety precautions to serving students in face-to-face settings. Hearing different perspectives and creating safe spaces for staff members are two of our most desired inclusive school practices. I have implemented new processes related to creating more time sensitive support structures for teacher voice and input. The creation of two-way communication tools and assigning direct virtual workspace "captains," provided staff members support for the demands of teaching during a pandemic. Contextually, in my urban setting, I have had to introduce and discuss becoming more culturally responsive to the perils facing many of our families. For example, as our families have had to return to work, students are left home to manage being a student and serve as a sitter for younger siblings. Understanding the importance of cultural responsiveness in the urban setting with underlying issues of poverty, led me to exercise inclusive leadership practices to create innovative teaching and learning structures to support students.

Robin's account of leadership during a pandemic affirms assertions in the review of related literature. School leaders who build community trust, organizational resilience, and inclusive decision-making will also support effective institutional responses to educational inequities even during challenging times like the pandemic (Bagwell, 2020; Fernandez & Shaw, 2020; Rigby et al., 2020).

As each of these leaders articulated their journeys to becoming the inclusive leaders they are today, they spoke to processes that were accelerated by the COVID-19 pandemic. Whether they shared stories of newly developed skills due to the overnight shifts in content delivery, as highlighted by Michele and Kristen, or those of mitigated challenges associated with bringing communities together in new ways as the narratives Brian, Niles, and Robin highlighted, their growth during a challenge was evident. As Summer shared, to be open to this type of growth, a leader must begin by understanding their own biases. While this journey is constantly evolving, educational leadership preparation programs can offer their candidates the tools they need to begin with an understanding of self and use that understanding as a first step in addressing the unique challenges related to leading schools for inclusivity.

Promising Practices for Leadership Preparation Programs

As societal challenges become increasingly interwoven with education practices, how can programs ensure they are preparing leaders for the present and the future? The steps might involve the following collaborative actions that Michele shared with her teams: affirm, reflect, (re)align. First, programs must affirm their values and their purpose. Does everyone in the organization know the core purpose of the work? Is the *purported* purpose the practiced purpose?

Once affirming the direction of the program, it is vital for leaders to reflect. There is an adage that to know what a person or organization values; you look at their checkbook. Examining where one spends the most resources (temporal or financial) reveals their true values. If a program asserts a commitment to inclusive leadership practices, yet only offers one course in diversity and inclusion, then it is time for realignment. The next step, aligning, or realigning, ensures that program providers establish a path for candidates to have a comprehensive experience that meets the program's purpose.

Educational leadership programs that prioritize inclusive practice make inclusion and diversity a priority for the potential and current school leaders they serve. For instance, Summer shared her views on what this might look like in practice:

> Every class would have a lens of inclusion and the professors would support those views with the appropriate literature from the field. Leading for all must be a running theme throughout, and it must begin with a diverse selection of cohort members. Not only should students hear from the experts, but they should also be encouraged to share and learn from each other. The unique perspectives and experiences that students/leaders bring to the table should

enrich the academic experience. Students can also benefit from professors who have had diverse professional experiences at home and abroad. Their experience and research areas of focus can provide ideas for further reflection that expand the inclusivity lens beyond what might be considered the norm.

Niles echoed Summer's sentiment by highlighting the connection to the relationship between authentic practice and research that careful program design can provide:

> A thoughtfully designed program prepares a candidate not only to be a researcher, but an action researcher, that is, one who serves in the capacity while simultaneously working with a team to implement change. Designing a program around an action research model can help both the student and the school site experience immense growth and positive change.

Expanding these ideas into the realm of theory linked to practice, Robin shared:

> Gaining additional knowledge in a program that is well-balanced in theory and practice can help a leader hone her authentic and inclusive approach to leading. Embedding real-life opportunities to engage with peers in the program and collaborating on practical scenarios are two levers which candidates can use as a reflection tool to shift their own leadership practices. When a preparation program's coursework provides candidates with opportunities to reflect on how they can remain on a continuous journey of providing inclusive leadership, it can be a conduit to improving equity in marginalized communities.

Brian suggested that university leadership preparation program models vary in their approaches to equip students for success. He recommended that programs focus on such critical levers as instructional leadership, human resources, school law, operations, and school/community relations, etc. He continued:

> By establishing a continuum of course work featuring school/community relations at its impetus, a leadership preparation program can ensure that participants learn the core value of successful school leadership. The successful school leader connects with the communities the school serves. It is imperative to establish and maintain open lines of communication across the community to identify needs beyond the walls of the school.

Kristen offered the following promising practices which tied in with the suggestions of her colleagues:

> Educational leadership preparation programs have a unique opportunity to enhance instructional delivery to build the capacity of candidates to lead

for inclusivity and equity. Candidates need protected time to network with leaders from various districts and settings to discuss challenges and solutions unique to their buildings and contexts. One way to support leaders is for preparation programs to enable students to take part in collaborative discussions with their peers. Allowing leaders to observe schools that are thriving in areas such as inclusivity, equity, and social emotional learning is a step toward building inclusive practices. Promoting engagement in a book study or virtual webinar related to inclusive practices with shared reflections and discussion of implications for the workplace could be key. Facilitating conversations about stereotypes and misconceptions and modeling how to do this effectively can help leaders better understand new ways to approach inclusivity.

RECOMMENDED STEPS FOR PREPARATION OF INCLUSIVE LEADERS

Based on analysis of the ideas generated by successful current school leaders who have had the unique experience of leading during a pandemic, the following steps are recommended as complements to high leverage strategies for the preparation of inclusive school leaders.

Encourage Self-Assessment and Reflective Practice

It is more important than ever that leaders have tools for assessing their inclusive practice capacities and reflecting on their progress. Self-assessment and reflection are foundational constructs through which preparation programs can prepare leaders for inclusive practice. Preparation programs are encouraged to develop awareness of and provide access to available resources for inclusive leadership. The Council of Chief State School Officers, the Center for Effective Educator Development, Accountability and Reform, and the National Collaborative for Inclusive Principal Leadership have developed resources that include scholarly literature, recommendations for evidence-based practices, and practical tools for assessment and development of inclusive leadership practices (Cowart Moss, Bryant, & Evans, 2020).

Summer suggested that a thoughtful leadership program with an inclusive lens should be intentionally designed to create opportunities for ideas around inclusion to be discussed. Given the current political landscape, race is at the forefront of many discussions, and inclusive leadership focuses on all marginalized groups. It is important to make sure that the conversation extends beyond race. It is also important to provide inclusive leaders with the tools to have these conversations. In some ways, having the conversation is easier to do in a diverse setting like my current school. Other colleagues come from more homogenous districts or schools and pushing back on the norm can be harder in that setting. Give faculty members the opportunity to work in or study diverse settings so that they can bring back firsthand knowledge from the field. Ground each class in what the literature says about inclusion and expose participants to different perspectives. Above all, provide ample time for self-reflection. The inclusive leader must know their heart and be willing to use their voice for those whose voices have been silenced.

Promote Inclusive Mindsets

Inclusive leaders think in terms of *each* rather than *all*. In order for all stakeholders to feel valued and that they belong in a school community, each person must belong. This nuanced perspective is responsive to unique cultural experiences and values that individuals bring to the table (Cowart Moss, 2020; DeMatthews, 2019; McLeskey, Waldron, & Redd, 2019). Inclusive leadership requires principals to contextualize their work, while remaining intentional and hypervigilant. These actions must be ongoing. They are not accomplishments, rather a way of leading and seeing the world. (Berry, Cowart Moss & Gore, 2019; Mette, 2019).

Robin suggested that programs could promote inclusive mindsets by spending more time on deepening the understanding of how school leaders can equip teachers with strategies to support students. Program providers could also consider developing networks of school leaders from other countries and create "school leader networks," whereas programmatic shifts would involve graduate students sharing ideas and innovative practices on improving inclusive school leadership practices.

Michele recommended transforming leadership preparation by beginning with future leaders in teacher preparation programs. She described an established routine for promoting inclusive mindsets in her district called "lens work." Candidates are offered a scenario and assigned a lens (e.g., teacher, parent, principal, student) through which they view the situation or challenge. Each participant records their responses to the issue through the viewpoint of their assigned lens. Finally, the question is posed: whose voice is missing? Without fail, candidates recite groups of contributing professionals and impacted communities whose voices are not represented. Candidates remind one another to ask who is missing from the conversation. Lens work is a significant first step in preparing quality educators.

One of the more surprising impacts of COVID-19 was the collaborative efforts of diverse schools, systems, and states. Michele stated that for many, this was the first time a challenge was nationwide. Although local resources and responses varied, the national conversation needed equity-focused, diverse voices. Education organizations developed opportunities to virtually connect leaders worldwide, leading to new strategies, relationships, and even policy. Can this be replicated on a more permanent basis through educational leadership preparation?

Develop Skills, Strategies, and Provide Resources for Responsive, Inclusive Leadership for Each Student

The Council of Chief State School Officers (CCSS), in collaboration with the CEEDAR Center and the Oak Foundation, developed a *Guide for States on Principal Leadership* which includes a list of high leverage strategies for inclusive principal leadership. Educational leadership preparation programs are encouraged to embed the high leverage strategies throughout course and program content and clinical practice. Strategy three calls for the transformation of principal preparation and licensure to address the knowledge, skills, and dispositions principals need to lead inclusive schools (CCSSO, 2020).

Brian noted that as program providers revisit their current state as part of the continuous improvement cycle, there is validity in aligning programs to schools' ever-changing needs. One way of ensuring a program meets the individual needs of current and future students is to create surveys and forums specifically designed to solicit input regarding the issues leaders face today. COVID has required a shift in leadership at both the school and district levels. A greater focus has been placed on ensuring basic needs are met for our students and families. Focus has also increased on the need to provide social and emotional support for students and staff members alike. While the onus of leadership preparation programs has traditionally focused on improving student academic outcomes and organizational management, COVID has reminded us that leaders must first ensure basic needs are met before learning can occur. "We must Maslow before we can Bloom" re-focuses the work of today's leader, and programs must align to that work.

During COVID-19, one of the major shifts for educational leaders was leading in a time that was completely unfamiliar, mainly because most had not taught virtually. Depending on the district, teachers taught virtually, in-person, or concurrently, which seemed to be the greatest challenge of all. Niles offered that program providers could greatly benefit students by providing ideas for leading departments and supporting teachers during a pandemic. It would also help to learn about state and local agencies that provide resources, especially those in rural and urban districts, where they can be limited.

Niles continued by describing a class focused on diversity in the field, in which students discussed disparity and inequity among race and gender, and took a privilege walk, which is an activity he will always remember.

Additionally, he shared that reading books such as *The Essential Conversation* by Sara Lawrence Lightfoot and articles by Gloria Ladson-Billings, whose quotes rang true in his mind were all extremely impactful experiences, but he emphasized that there is a next step. Leadership preparation programs can build the capacity of candidates by sharing information about the inequities among people with disabilities. Going deeper into the reality of intersectionality among this group will reveal that 18% of people with disabilities are currently employed nationwide. This will help to push past a fixed mindset, even among those who work in the field of special education.

FURTHER CONSIDERATIONS FOR LEADERSHIP PREPARATION PROGRAMS

A review of scholarly literature and voices from the field yielded considerations for continuous improvement of educational leadership preparation programs as they strive to prepare inclusive leaders. Guiding questions for collaborative consideration and continuous improvement include: 1.) What scholarly perspectives are included in your leadership preparation programs that help candidates recognize the importance of ensuring inclusive and equitable learning environments? 2.) What clinical experiences has your leadership preparation program used to provide access and opportunity for candidates to develop and practice skills relevant to leading schools for inclusivity and equity? 3.) How has your program enhanced instructional delivery to build the capacity of candidates to lead for inclusivity and equity?

Kristen encouraged leadership program providers by reminding them that they can build the capacity of candidates to lead for inclusivity and equity by remaining committed to the inclusive leadership endeavor. Program providers should challenge leaders to re-evaluate their local school and district practices, policies, school website, and social media pages. Challenge leaders to examine the resources available in the media center and vet the books that are being offered to the children. Are they inclusive? Are they meant for all, or just the majority? Challenge leaders to engage in a pulse check with their employees to validate equitable treatment of all staff members and encourage them to recognize all employees for their contributions. Teach leaders how to become more inclusive by teaching them how to create a safe space for employees to speak up and confidently express professional concerns and needs.

In closing, Michele provided a powerful reminder that change will require a commitment to courage. If change at scale is to occur, then programs must be courageous in their dedication to creating quality learning experiences that meet their learners' social, emotional, academic, and professional needs. We must affirm, reflect, and align our purported purpose with our practices, yielding a more impactful and effective preparation model for leaders.

REFERENCES

Albert Shanker Institute. (2015). *The state of teacher diversity in American education*. ERIC Clearinghouse.

Bagwell, J. (2020). Leading through a pandemic: Adaptive leadership and purposeful action. *Journal of School Administration Research and Development, 5*(S1), 30–34.

Berry, J., Cowart Moss, S., & Gore, P. (2019) Leadership in high need/high performing schools: Success stories from an urban school district. In E. Murakami, D. Gurr, & R. Notman (Eds), Leadership, culture and school success in high needs schools (pp. 131–148). Information Age Publishing.

Boser, U. (2014). *Teacher diversity revisited: A new state-by-state analysis*. Center for American Progress.

Cook-Sather, A. (2002). Authorizing students' perspectives: Toward trust, dialogue, and change in education. *Educational Researcher, 31*(4), 3–14.

Council of Chief State School Officers. (2020). *Supporting inclusive schools for the success of each child*.

Cowart Moss, S., Bryant, K., & Evans, G. (2021) *Inclusive principal leadership, self-assessment and reflection protocol* (unpublished manuscript).

DeMatthews, D. E., Kotok, S., & Serafini, A. (2019). Leadership preparation for special education and inclusive schools: Beliefs and recommendations from successful principals. *Journal of Research on Leadership Education, 15*(4), 303–329.

DeMatthews, D., Serafini, A., & Watson, T. (2020). Leading inclusive schools: Principals' perceptions, practices, and challenges to meaningful change. *Educational Administration Quarterly, 57*(1), 3–48.

Dilworth, M. E., & Coleman, M. J. (2014). *Time for a change: Diversity in teaching revisited*. National Education Association.

Fernandez, A. A., & Shaw, G. P. (2020). Academic leadership in a time of crisis: The coronavirus and COVID-19. *Journal of Leadership Studies, 14*(1), 39–45.

Finkel, E. (2011). New directions for special ed. *District Administration, 47*(6), 51–57.

Grissom, J. A., Kern, E. C., & Rodriguez, L. A. (2015). The "Representative Bureaucracy" in education: Educator workforce diversity, policy outputs, and outcomes for disadvantaged students. *Educational Researcher, 44*(3), 185–192.

Gross, J., Haines, S., Hill, C., Francis, G., Blue-Banning, M., & Turnbull, A. (2015). Strong school-community partnerships in inclusive schools are "part of the fabric of the school...we count on them." *School Community Journal, 25*(2), 9–34.

Khalifa, M. A., Gooden, M. A., & Davis, J. E. (2016). Culturally responsive school leadership: A synthesis of the literature. *Review of Educational Research, 86*(4), 1272–1311.

Kozleski, E. (2019). System-wide leadership for culturally responsive education. In J. Crockett, B. Billingsley, & M. L. Boscardin (Eds.), *Handbook of Leadership and Administration for Special Education*. Routledge.

National Council on Disability. (2018). *The segregation of students with disabilities*. National Council on Disability. https://ncd.gov/sites/default/files/NCD_Segregation-SWD_508.pdfb

Ravitch, S. (2020). Flux leadership: Leading for justice and peace in and beyond COVID-19. *Penn GSE Perspectives on Urban Education, 18*(1), 1–31.

Reyes, J. A., Elias, M. J., Parker, S. J., & Rosenblatt, J. L. (2013). *Promoting educational equity in disadvantaged youth: The role of resilience and social-emotional learning. Handbook of resilience in children*. Springer.

Rigby, J., Forman, S., Foster, L., Kazemi, E., & Clancey, S. (2020). *Promising District Leadership Practices for Transformative Change in the Context of COVID-19*. University of Washington.

Shogren, K. A., Gross, J. M. S., Forber-Pratt, A., Francis, G. L., Satter, A. L., Blue-Banning, M., & Hill, C. (2015). The perspectives of students with and without disabilities on inclusive schools. *Research & Practice for Persons with Severe Disabilities, 40*(4), 243–260.

Singh, A. A. (2019). *The racial healing handbook: Practical activities to help you challenge privilege, confront systemic racism, & engage in collective healing*. New Harbinger Publications.

Smith, L., & Riley, D. (2012). School leadership in times of crisis. *School Leadership & Management, 32*(1), 57–71, https://doi.org/ 10.1080/13632434.2011.614941

Taylor, K. R. (2011). Inclusion and the law: Two laws—IDEA and section 504—support inclusion in schools. *Education Digest, 76*(9), 48–51.

Theoharis, G., & Causton, J. (2014). Leading inclusive reform for students with disabilities: A school- and systemwide approach. *Theory Into Practice, 53*(2), 82–97.

Villa, R. A., & Thousand, J. S. (2003). Making inclusive education work. *Educational Leadership, 61*(2), 19–23.

Weiss, H. B., Bouffard, S. M., Bridglall, B. L., & Gordon, E. W. (2009). *Reframing family involvement in education: Supporting families to support educational equity*. (Research Review No. 5). Columbia University Teachers College.

U.S. Commission on Civil Rights. (2019). *Beyond suspensions: Examining school discipline policies and connections to the school-to-prison pipeline for students of color with disabilities*. https://www.usccr.gov/pubs/2019/07-23-Beyond-Suspensions.pdf

CHAPTER 12

INCLUSIVE LEADERS BUILDING BRIDGES TO LEARNING

Heather P. Williams
Boise State University

Jennifer L. Snow
Boise State University

Inclusive leaders create systems where *each* human—child and adult—feels valued, supported, and safe. Leaders leverage strengths so individuals advance their learning within the system (Cowart Moss, 2020; Ryan & Cox, 2017; Mette, 2019). Although inclusive leadership practices are grounded in special education, inclusivity is about creating equity and opportunity for all students, not just those with special needs (Theoharis et al 2008). The need for inclusive leadership is critical following a global pandemic, societal unrest, and growing political and cultural divides. School leaders are not just leading humans in school buildings. They are also explicitly leading them in their homes, their communities, and their places of shelter from life's storms. It is increasingly evident that school leaders must build inclusive bridges across divided communities and lead systems that help students navigate the sometimes-disrupted world between their places of learning.

In this chapter, we explore the leadership journeys and practices of three principals who share a common vision for a student-centered learning system and have been participants in an improvement network implementing policies towards that vision. Additionally, the participants are graduate students in the same educational leadership program; therefore, this research provides opportunities to examine continued learning as leaders, including the role of higher education in supporting inclusive leadership practices. To orient readers, we begin with an examination of the intersection of where various paths converge on individual leaders' practice. First, we examine the key features of inclusive leadership. We then explore policy decisions that provide the context for inclusive leadership practices and discuss leadership identity development within a community. After the discussion of our conceptual framework, we detail our data sources and methods before reporting findings that illustrate how leaders develop an inclusive leadership stance. We explored the following questions:

1. How did these leaders develop their inclusive practices to authentically create systems of inclusion? What experiences sustain or support their inclusive leadership practices?
2. What is the relationship, if any, between the implementation of mastery education policies and their inclusive leadership practices?

We close the chapter by discussing implications for inclusive leadership and for leadership preparation programs in preparing inclusive leaders.

CONCEPTUAL FRAMEWORK

This chapter focuses on how inclusive leadership practices are developed and create the capacity for better student outcomes. We draw on critical (Theoharis et al, 2008; Sapon-Shevin, 2003; Freire, 1990; Frattura & Capper, 2007) approaches to inclusive leadership practices that examine how leadership dispositions develop, grow, and are supported over time. We discuss each element of our conceptual framework, starting with the literature that informs our view of inclusive leadership, and how educational policies, such as mastery-education, have provided context for the shift. We also discuss relevant research related to leadership identity development and how leadership preparation programs can foster inclusive leadership.

Inclusive Leadership

Inclusive principals create strong school cultures and distribute leadership to serve all learners well and ensure all students feel safe, supported, and valued in school. In promoting equity for "all," inclusive principals respond effectively to the potential and needs of each student. Inclusive principals ensure high expectations and appropriate support so that each student—across race, gender, ethnicity, language, ability, sexual orientation, family background, and/or family income—can excel in school. Existing studies of inclusive leadership practice indicate that leaders play a critical role in creating and sustaining inclusive learning environments (DeMatthews et al 2020; Hitt and Tucker, 2016).

Dillon and Bourke (2016) identified three elements of inclusive leadership: 1) fairness and respect, 2) value and belonging, and 3) confidence and inspiration. The authors explained that fairness and respect are "foundational elements that are underpinned by ideas about equality" in both how people are treated and opportunities they receive. Further, Dillon and Bourke (2016) discussed the importance of "personalizing individuals" so they feel valued for individual contributions and unique perspectives while also feeling a sense of belonging to the group. Finally, their study highlighted the importance of leveraging diverse thinking and motivation of the group in the leaders' decision making, creating conditions for high team performance through individual confidence and motivating others to do their best work. The importance of inclusive leadership practices cannot be understated in today's educational system if we intend to address long standing social and economic gaps. Casey and Sturgis (2020) clearly state, "An equitable education system will celebrate and prioritize communities that have been historically oppressed, recognizing their health, wellness, and ability to thrive are essentially meaningful and also essential to the future of our country" (p.10).

Policies and the Context for Inclusive Leadership

Every Student Succeeds Act (ESSA) of 2015 provided U.S. leaders more flexibility in decision-making to determine how to best serve students. Subsequently, many states have enacted state laws, policies, or regulations to encourage districts and their leaders to innovate and/or move to a more student-centered system. However, many argue the path to inclusive leadership began in Spain in 1994 with a UNESCO policy statement (Abawi et al, 2018; DeMatthews, et al, 2020), and is based on access, opportunity, equity, and removal of barriers or factors that exclude or marginalize learners, such as lower expectations for students whose demographics do not fit the traditional student model or other types of educational exclusion (UNESCO, 1994).

Personalized, competency based, mastery-based, and deeper learning are all buzzwords that point towards the educational enterprise seeking ways to improve the traditional educational system and working to make it more inclusive of all learners. This push towards "systems of learning where individuals and communities can access diverse learning assets and experiences" in the "learning ecosystem" has provided context for emerging state and national policies focused on meeting the needs of each student (Hannon et al, 2019). The learning is focused on each student, rather than on the institution or system, and learning for students and adults is tied closely to "personal purpose, fulfillment, connection, and community" (Casey & Patrick, 2020). This includes allowing students voice and choice in their learning pathways, as well as learner-centered resource allocation, school/district design, and capacity building, allowing leaders of institutions to have some ownership for each student's success through the conditions they create for diverse learners. This represents a shift in thinking for many traditional leaders and learners, "...it recognizes that we cannot merely tinker with institutions and systems designed for the purpose of separating and sorting, and that we must build new and more equitable systems in their place" (Casey & Patrick, 2020, p. 13).

By 2019, all U.S. states except Wyoming had policies allowing students to earn credits based on outcomes demonstrating academic proficiency instead of acquiring traditional Carnegie units (iNACOL, 2019). These competency-based or mastery-based models build on individualized learning tailored to the uniqueness of each student. Mastery-based learning is specifically described as "a standards-based, student-directed, individualized, and data-based learning environment emphasizing increasingly real-life application" (DeLorenzo, et al, 2009, p. 76). Central to mastery-based reforms is the notion that more students will reach proficiency in a given subject if they are able to advance at their own pace and learning experiences are tailored to their interests and needs (Lewis et al., 2014; Sturgis & Patrick, 2010; Ryan & Cox, 2017).

Leadership Identity Development

Leadership preparation programs, based on state and national standards, are likely to create the conditions needed for candidates to develop the knowledge and skills of inclusive leaders. Working within a cohort structure for educational leadership candidates, we believe in cultivating and sustaining "communities of practice" (Lieberman & Miller, 2008; Wenger, 1998) where leadership candidates learn with and from each other. Wenger

(1998) identified characteristics of communities of practice including mutual engagement, shared practice, and collaborative endeavors. In a systematic review of literature on communities of practice, Vangrieken and colleagues (2017) described formative communities that improved educator practice. Seeking "unwelcome truths" (Groundwater & Mockler-Smith, 2015) and a "shift to uncertainty" (Snow-Gerono, 2005) allow vulnerability to exist in a community to further inclusive leadership and equity serving *all people* within the system.

METHODS

Employing a multiple case study design (Stake, 1995; Yin, 2018), we investigated inclusive leadership practices of three principals in different systems. Principal interviews allowed us to discover and describe, from their perspectives, what experiences helped to shape or sustain their inclusive leadership practices. We also interviewed their central office supervisors to further examine each system's context. Viewing cases individually and then across cases allowed for development of nuances within individual contexts to elaborate on inclusive leadership practice development.

Data Sources and Analysis

We drew on comparative case study elements using Bartlett & Vavrus' (2017) framework that encourages comparison across three axes: horizontal (one case compared to another); vertical (comparison of influences at different levels national to school or micro to macro); and transversal (comparison over time). Inclusive leadership practice is part of leadership preparation programs based on the National Educational Leadership Preparation (NELP) standards (NPBEA, 2018), specifically as part of standard 3: equity, inclusiveness, and cultural responsiveness. Therefore, we used stratified sampling, where participants were selected from a pool with the following criteria: a) program completers of our executive educational leadership program in the last eight years and b) employed in systems identified as working to implement mastery education. Once the population was identified, we stratified the sample across geographic regions in our state, system size/type, and school building leadership roles to get a healthy mix of perspectives.

Semi-structured interviews ensued with the principals, their supervisors, teachers, and students. Questions focused on the application of inclusive leadership practices and development of those practices. Questions were developed from program curriculum and workshops on inclusive practices at our university.

School leader and supervisor interviews helped determine links between lived experiences of the different groups and the intersection of inclusive leadership practice. Interviews were audio and video recorded to ensure accuracy and later transcribed. The interviewer kept a reflective journal to focus on learning, make adjustments in data collection, and uncover any possible bias. Field notes taken during the interviews described nonverbal cues within each bound system. Two researchers engaged in line-by-line coding of interview transcripts, noting salient themes. Next, we shared research memos and engaged in a meeting to ask probing questions of the codes and potential themes. Corroborating themes were established between bound systems (middle school principal, high school principal, charter school principal) through triangulation with field notes and artifacts. Initially, both researchers identified 36 codes. After meetings and analysis, we collapsed or merged evidence to create three integrated themes contributing to a potential framework for inclusive leadership development.

As we worked through the data from each principal's system, we developed a "sketch" of each participant's beliefs and perceptions regarding inclusive leadership and relationships, if any, to the implementation of mastery-based education. The emerging data was divided into categories related to the two research questions. Each principal's finished portrait is discussed in the findings section.

Study Context

The participating principals are all practicing secondary administrators (covering grades 6–12) in Idaho who graduated from the same leadership preparation program and have been involved in implementing mastery-based education programs. They work in different types of schools: middle school, high school, and a grades 6–12 charter school.

The middle school is located in a town NCES (National Center for Educational Statistics) defines as "town-fringe." It is inside an urban cluster that is less than or equal to 10 miles from an urbanized area. The school serves about 550 students in grades 6 through 8 within a larger district that serves just under 5500 students PK–12. It is a Title 1 school.

The high school is located in a "rural-fringe" community based on NCES data. It is a census-defined rural territory less than or equal to five miles from an urbanized area, as well as rural territory less than or equal to 2.5 miles from an urban cluster. The school serves about 1200 students in grades 9 through 12 within a larger district that serves just under 4200 students PK–12. It is also a Title 1 school.

The charter school is located in a "suburb: midsize" community based on NCES data. It is located in a territory outside a principal city and inside an urbanized area with a population less than 250,000 and greater than or equal to 100,000. The school serves 500 students in grades 6–12 within a larger charter network system that serves approximately 2500 students in grades 6–12. This charter was written to serve alternative school students, so all enrolled students must meet criteria for an "at-risk" learner. Idaho defines "at-risk" students as meeting any three (3) of the following criteria in Section A, or anyone (1) criteria in Section B.

Section A:

Has repeated at least one (1) grade.

Has absenteeism greater than ten (10%) percent during the preceding semester.

Has an overall grade point average less than 1.5 (4.0 scale) prior to enrolling in an alternative secondary program.

Has failed one (1) or more academic subjects in the past year.

Is below proficient, based on local criteria, standardized tests, or both.

Is two (2) or more credits per year behind the rate required to graduate or for grade promotion.

Has attended three (3) or more schools within the previous two (2) years, not including dual enrollment

Section B:

Has a documented pattern of substance abuse.

Is pregnant or a parent.

Is an emancipated youth.

Is a previous dropout.

Has serious personal, emotional, or medical issue(s).

Has a court or agency referral.

Demonstrates behavior detrimental to their academic progress.

The information presented in Table 12.1 is an overview of demographic data for participating principals' schools. Data is based on U.S. Census data and state accountability data. The profile contains information regarding ethnicity, socioeconomic conditions, and school-based information useful in identifying similarities and differences between the sites where the participants work.

In addition, we provide the context of each principal's journey in educational leadership. The information presented in Table 12.2 is an overview of demographic data for principal participants. The data contains information regarding ethnicity, education attainment, leadership and teaching experience.

TABLE 12.1 Overview of Sample Schools' Demographic Characteristics

	Principal M's Middle School	Principal H's High School	Principal C's Charter School
Ethnicity			
White	89%	47%	67%
Hispanic	9%	51%	30%
Other	2%	2%	3%
Males	49%	51%	53%
Females	51%	49%	47%
% of students qualifying for free or reduced lunch	47%	89%	81%
% of students qualifying for special education services on an IEP	12%	10.6%	16%
% of students qualifying as English Learners	4%	22%	15%
Student:Teacher ratio	18.8:1	20.8:1	16:1
Teacher retention rate	82.8%	83.6%	92%
Median Household Income	$71,125	$49,875	$40,949
% of households with broadband Internet	85%	71.6%	70.5%

TABLE 12.2 Overview of the Individual Principal's Demographic Characteristics

	Principal M: (Middle School principal)	Principal H: (High School principal)	Principal C: (Charter School principal)
Ethnicity	White	White	White
Gender	Male	Male	Female
# of years in current role	3 years	5 years	2 years
# of years worked in leadership roles in education	18 years	13 years	8 years
# of years worked in education overall	26 years	15 years	22 years
Taught in PK–12	Yes	Yes	Yes
Teaching experience	6–12 History	6–12 social studies and mathematics	K–6 general education
Highest education level	Educational Specialist degree	Educational Specialist degree	Educational Specialist degree

Limitations

We intentionally selected leaders who graduated from the same leadership preparation program. Additionally, participants needed to work in systems identified as implementing mastery education policies in Idaho. Mastery education in Idaho is defined specifically as policy implementation under Idaho Code 33-1632. The law (Idaho Code 33-1632) directed the Idaho State Department of Education to move Idaho towards "an education system where student progress is based on a student's demonstration of mastery of competencies and content, not seat time, or the age or grade level of the student." The law created the Idaho Mastery Education Network (IMEN), allowing Local Education Agencies (LEAs) to apply to the improvement network building support for the implementation of mastery education in their local school systems. These leaders and their contexts may not be representative of the larger population of inclusive leaders.

Findings

Findings explore each principal's beliefs about inclusive leadership practices, pathways to their development and funds of knowledge related to inclusive leadership practices. We present a "portrait" of each leader related to the research questions and examine vertical and transversal comparisons of their practices. Then we create a collage of the portraits to present a horizontal comparison of our findings about inclusive leadership. All principals and their supervisors agreed they practice inclusive leadership; however, perceptions and beliefs about inclusive leadership varied among the three principals. Across all three leaders the themes of Inquiry and Openness, Building Community through Relational Work, and Equity and Advocacy were evident in their inclusive leadership practices. These constructs were built on a foundation of people-centered frameworks (Mastery-based education that is student-centered) and building from the movements of Listen to Connect to Act.

PORTRAIT 1: PRINCIPAL C—
THE CHARTER SCHOOL PRINCIPAL

Principal C is in her second year as a charter school principal. She has served eight years as an educational leader with experience at all grade levels. She obtained her Educational Specialist degree in 2018. Principal C is a learner and loves to focus on "the learning", for adults and children,

Figure 12.1 Principal C's word cloud.

in almost every conversation you have with her. Principal C's interview had 11 codes that she used at least four different times during our interview. Her highest frequency terms when discussing inclusive leadership practices were value individuals, providing common experiences, and listening. Interestingly, the highest frequency terms used by her team describing inclusive leadership were value individuals, empowering others, and relationships. The word cloud in Figure 12.1 depicts the frequency of codes used by P and her team when describing inclusive leadership practices.

Principal C discussed the importance of learning as the leader, "...that's really one of the most important things as an inclusive leader, is just to make sure you're open to learn." Principal C talked about growing her people's abilities by caring for them and their growth. She discussed doing this through listening and expressing an openness, requiring that she must first and foremost be a learner herself:

> ...as a leader I'm also a learner and I have a responsibility to continue learning, and that means self-reflection.... I'm digging deep into problems when things come up, and I am listening, and asking myself am I empowering people? What has to lead is that person's story, and this other stuff is quieter in the background, or we get lost as humans in that space.

As a leader she values individuals in the learning process, and she attributes some of her development as an inclusive leader to her own life experiences where she felt "outside" like she did not belong.

> I've just had a lot of life experiences myself, where I have lived on the outside of society, if you will, as a teen mom that's something that I felt right away. Like, oh so you are no longer an acceptable high school student, it was like one day I was kicked to the curb you know. So, that's really tough, because when somebody is being kind of metaphorically kicked to the curb for whatever reason, maybe a behavior, maybe something that this group doesn't agree with, they're in this outside space. There's some damage that happens there so I think it's really important that we are mindful of the labels we give each other and what that means. I think when we can be reminding ourselves on a daily basis, that our work is really about people. The real purpose is helping someone get better.

She also attributes her inclusive leadership development to her leadership preparation program, especially the focus on the closed cohort and the program focus on building belongingness e within the learning community.

> Listening to my cohort's journeys that the different folks in our cohort had and what got them there you know, and then, when you listen to their stories we are refining what we had in common from our hearts. Then we did the strength-based leadership work... Listening to that with each other and finding out how we could help each other was powerful. So now, years later, I have a whole team of people that I have as support for my leadership because I know their strengths and they may have something I don't have. And I think that's just a really great way for any leader to lead, you know is, do you know each other? Who's in the space that's learning and working together, what do they have special to offer?

Principal C made several connections to her inclusive leadership practices and the implementation of mastery education. Her supervisor talked about the importance of mastery education in their system as it connects to their leadership practices, "... I think it's all directly related. I honestly think this mastery work has springboarded our leadership and everything else to a whole nother level." Both the principal and those in her system talked about the importance of being lead learners in their practice. "As we do this work with mastery, you know you need the teachers to take ownership and be leaders of their own world." Principal C talked about her role in leading that effort.

> The system needs to be responsive to every student in the classroom, so I started right away studying the kids to figure out what they need. I was finding them a resource, so that they could just keep moving in some way in their

learning. I would always have to try to find a way to help them see, no you're where you're at... that is fine, and validate where they were and help them grow. In our mastery policies, we have opened the door to instructionally meet anyone where they are. With the learning plans and portfolios, we're showing growth from where they were to where they are.

PORTRAIT 2: PRINCIPAL M—
THE MIDDLE SCHOOL PRINCIPAL

Principal M is in his third year in his current role as middle school principal. He has served 18 years as an educational leader, mostly at the secondary level. He obtained his Educational Specialist degree in 2016. His office is covered in memorabilia and pennants from his university alma mater. Principal M is an approachable leader and prides himself on "taking care of his people" , staff and students. Principal M's interview had nine codes that he used at least four different times during our interview. His highest frequency terms when discussing inclusive leadership practices were: trust and safety, consistency, and listening. The word cloud in Figure 12.2 depicts the frequency of codes used by him and his team when describing inclusive leadership practices.

Principal M discussed the importance of building trust, so the environment is safe to innovate and make mistakes, even for the leader. "People can respect you if you're willing to own it and you don't operate under this

Figure 12.2 Principal M's word cloud.

air like, I'm the principal and I don't make errors. The worst thing you can do, in my opinion, is, if you do, or you say something like that you have to own it." He also talked about what sustains his practice as an inclusive leader. Principal M gives credit to his professional network, including the cohort of peers from his leadership preparation program, as helping him to problem solve and sustain his practice as leader.

> My cohort from the program and that professional network is a huge, valuable resource. I feel fortunate that I've got people I can reach out to and ask for help.... Being able to go to the army and say hey, what do you guys do about this? How is your district doing that? What's this? We do that all the time because we have built really good trust. It's a small little group. But we trust each other to really get an honest answer.

Principal M talked about learning how to be an inclusive leader. He grew up in poverty, knowing what it is like to be an outsider, so he strives to give back and help pull others up. He also recognizes the importance of valuing individuals and their circumstances. Principal M works to break down barriers with students, parents, and staff to achieve common goals,

> Probably one of the most rewarding things I've ever done professionally is just helping to break that wall down and get the community involved back into the schools. I grew up in poverty, I can speak poverty with anybody, you know, and I think when you can tell your own story and you can relate to some groups in a way. It kind of takes them back like, 'Okay, even though this guy is the principal of our school he can talk my language and understands where I am coming from.'

He talked about how he was impacted early in his leadership career by a mentor who showed him what it meant to be an inclusive leader.

> I was blessed to work with my mentor principal for many years because he taught me that as a leader I'm not here to lead, I'm here to work with you. I'm here to build capacity in you. I learned I have to listen and empower people, and I think that's a huge piece as leaders, we have to build that culture, because it's a trust issue. You know people aren't going to open up to you and be heard, if they don't trust that it's secure for them to be heard.

Principal M also attributes his Educational Specialist program with further developing his skills. He said, "It wasn't just learning about leadership from a book. We talked about it and went and had experiences, you know, and talking about being on the balcony vs. the dance floor. You know, being able to stand back and see things and observe and, to this day, I still use that term about being on the balcony and seeing the bigger picture. I think the experiences of the program are just as valuable as the academic information if that makes sense."

Principal M discussed mastery education most often in all of our interviews. It was embedded in his leadership style and the way he talks about education in his building. Mastery is fundamental to how Principal M defines inclusive leadership practices. He stated, "Just because kids aren't on an IEP doesn't mean there doesn't need to be some sort of accommodation for them to succeed, and so that's what mastery is, in my opinion. I think that's what it's done. It took it from being just a special education conversation to an everyone conversation. Setting up systems so that everybody succeeds at their level."

PORTRAIT 3: PRINCIPAL H—
THE HIGH SCHOOL PRINCIPAL

Principal H, in his fifth year in his current role as high school principal, has served 13 years as an educational leader, mostly at the secondary level. He obtained his Educational Specialist degree in 2020. His desk is covered in sticky notes and messages, and he will be the first to say that organization is not his thing. Principal H comes from a coaching background, and he is always talking about teams, how to build his team, how to get the right people in the right places to make great things happen in his school, and making sure everyone has a team they identify with and belong to. He is still a "coach" every day, for students and adults, from his principal role.

Principal H's interview had five codes that he used at least four different times during our interview. His highest frequency terms when discussing inclusive leadership practices were: value individuals, diverse perspectives, and communication. The word cloud in Figure 12.3 depicts the frequency of codes used by him and his team when describing inclusive leadership practices.

Principal H stated, "People feel included when you come to them and ask them for their advice and their expertise; you want to know their opinion." Principal H serves a highly diverse community that is very different from his own background. He talks about enjoying learning about the culture and community of his students and families outside of school. "The cool part is I get to understand a little bit more about these kids and their families and what their values are, and in the classroom, it really wasn't much different." Principal H uses the diversity of his school community to improve his leadership.

> Most decisions we make, we make as a group and that's not always the most efficient way to do it because you do have to bring everybody in to talk about

Inclusive Leaders Building Bridges to Learning ▪ **231**

Communication
Value individuals
Listening
Strengths based leadership
Diverse perspectives

Figure 12.3 Principal H's word cloud.

> what's going on. But it does help everybody to see different perspectives and get on the same page when a decision is made. It helps everyone understand the decision. I go to the students and let them voice their opinion ... and then I always ask well, what do you think would be good in this situation? They will give me a bunch of ideas and we'll write those down and we'll go back and make a couple of changes and recognize them, but we just usually go straight to the student ideas. It makes them feel like they are being recognized in the school for their ideas. That's been fun, for me, I love it when they have these good questions too.

Principal H discussed aspects of his leadership program that helped develop his inclusive practices. Like the other participants, he appreciated the cohort aspect and explained how the diversity within the group helped him to realize the diversity that exists in education.

> It really made me start to think more about how you really have to understand the story, you have to understand the community, you have to understand the school. There's so much more that you have to understand to make a decision. It also really brought me in and made me feel like I was a part of a team trying to help somebody else out. I still get emails from the cohort every now and then and we work together to solve problems. That is really cool to be part of something bigger.

He sustains his inclusive leadership practice by reading and building a professional network that helps him see the value of individuals and diverse perspectives. Principal H is early in his adoption of mastery education and indicated he still had a lot to learn. He also thought it was important to recognize individuals learning at their own pace. The closures connected to COVID-19 have made his traditional high school start considering how to catch students up, how to really assess what they know, and what they still need to learn. He stated, "We are looking at mastery and how we can include the kids and also help the parents know what is going on and what it looks like."

Across all three leaders the most common codes related to inclusive leadership practices were: value individuals, diverse perspectives, and empower others. In the following section, we build a framework for the development of inclusive leadership practice based on an integration of these leader portraits.

BUILDING INCLUSIVE LEADERSHIP PRACTICE

Reviewing these distinct cases allowed us to also look across cases for commonalities. We identified common codes across the cases that allowed for the development of a continuum built on a foundation of people-centered practice where inclusive leaders began with an inquiry stance embracing openness to multiple perspectives. This stance led to deep relational work focused on developing and participating in communities of practice and an outcome of advocacy through empowering others and considering equity for individuals and systems. This continuum (see Figure 12.4) begins with *listening* and moves to *connecting* and then *acting* for inclusive leadership.

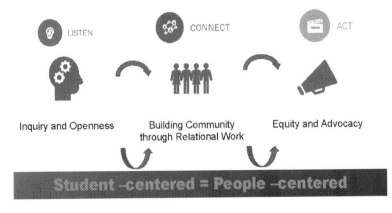

Figure 12.4 Framework for inclusive leadership development.

The framework presented in Figure 12.4 was developed based on findings from these cases as a means for considering development as an inclusive leader. Moving through a continuum of listening and connecting to action provides for a framework of inquiry, building community, equity and advocacy based in people-centered work.

Each of the leaders in this study—and their teams—described how important individuals are to their positions as leaders. This valuing of individuals was a building block to forming a community of practice where voices were heard and valued in decision-making processes. The leaders began with a *learner* perspective. Principal C repeated how important it was to "make sure you're open to learn." Principal M also said, "I learned I have to listen and empower people, and I think that's a huge piece as leaders, we have to build that culture... people aren't going to open up to you and be heard, if they don't trust that it's secure for them to be heard."

This inquiry and openness are a necessary precursor to building the community of practice inclusive leaders in this study cultivated. They all discussed the importance of the support of their cohorts from the educational specialist program. And, these cohorts cultivated trust, openness and learning from each other during their programs. Having this model supported these leaders developing communities of practice within their systems as well. Again, Principal C emphasized "who's in the space that's learning and working together" when she talked about strengths-based leadership–both from her graduate program and within her educational system. Principal M also emphasized his graduate program as key to his inclusive leadership practice: "My cohort from the program and that professional network is a huge, valuable resource." And Principal H drew from his coaching experience and ensured everyone was a part of the "team" to "get the right people in the right places to make great things happen in his school."

Once the community was strong, there was space to empower individuals, including students, such that inclusive leadership became about advocacy for all people in the community. When Principal C shares how important it is to listen, she emphasizes "asking myself am I empowering people?" Principal M also talks about empowerment. He suggests a move from special education practice to become more expansive, so it is "setting up systems so that everybody succeeds at their level." And Principal H describes a process where he would go to students for insights and perspectives to value their voices and empower them and advocate for their roles in decision-making, for example on how a simple schedule change will impact them as a collective, or even on a controversial student newspaper issue.

Each of these themes within the cases in this study are built on a foundation of people-centered practice. Mastery-based education is focused on student success by identifying their individual needs and empowering them to follow a path toward their own development. This student-centered focus in each of the cases in this study was also employed with a people-centered focus throughout the educational systems. Inclusive leaders valued individuals, listened to, and connected them so they could act together for empowered individuals and communities to become agents of change in their communities and systems. Principal C said, "I think when we can be reminding ourselves on a daily basis, that our work is really about people. The real purpose is helping someone get better... In our mastery policies, we have opened the door to instructionally meet anyone where they are. With the learning plans and portfolios, we're showing growth from where they were to where they are."

Through the moves of Listen, Connect, and Act, inclusive leaders practice inquiry and openness to build communities of practice and empower others to advocate for equity. Inclusive practice began with student-centered practice in these cases and built toward people-centered practice including faculty and staff in education systems along with the communities served.

DISCUSSION AND IMPLICATIONS

The local language of each school community provided important insights into how policy is being translated into practice and whether there were socio-cultural differences among schools in how inclusive practice was perceived, described, and valued by the system itself. Identifying language from the leaders, their students and teachers, along with their physical environments allowed for key touchstones to emerge for each inclusive leader. We sought to understand the context of each leader's lived experience as we studied the phenomena of "inclusive leadership" and what it means both to the leader and their system. The study design did not rely on a common definition of inclusive leadership because what it means to be an "inclusive" leader is highly contextualized. We discovered the word "inclusive" itself has different meanings for different individuals and groups of people, therefore tensions exist between contextualization and the lack of common vocabulary. Ensuring shared language in a context may be paramount for effective inclusive leadership practice as the shared discourse allows individuals to act in communities of practice with stated values.

Based on the findings from this study, the cultivation of inclusive leadership could benefit from modeling communities of practice where inquiry and openness help community members learn together, so more people in the community are empowered to take action for equitable practice, norms, and outcomes. Leadership development programs with a focus on inclusive leadership could focus on acting in community and developing inquiry communities so leaders could experience and then emulate those practices in their systems. Emphasizing the importance of listening and connecting before moving to action and a foundation of honoring individuals could also stimulate more inclusive leadership practice. Inclusive leaders may also need networks for their own work to be able to persevere through challenges they may face in practicing inclusive leadership.

This chapter sought to describe practical applications of inclusive leadership, including its potential relationship to the implementation of mastery education. We were interested in understanding the journey of leadership development and application of leaders affiliated with one leadership preparation program. As researchers and faculty of educational leadership programs, we were particularly interested in inclusive leadership and how we may support such development in our candidates, including preparing them to lead inclusive educational systems where acceptance, tolerance, and belongingness for each individual is the norm.

Further research could include studying the cultivation of inclusive leadership through specific program practices or outside of specific education policy, like mastery-based education. Likewise, the outcomes of inclusive leadership, particularly on the students in the cases included here, could highlight the power of specific practice or policies within education systems.

REFERENCES

Abawi, L.-A., Bauman-Buffone, C., Pineda-Báez, C., & Carter, S. (2018). The rhetoric and reality of leading the inclusive school: Socio-cultural reflections on lived experiences. *Education Sciences, 8*(2), 55. https://doi.org/10.3390/educsci8020055

Bartlett, L., & Vavrus, F. (2017). Comparative case studies: An innovative approach. *Nordic Journal of Comparative and International Education, 1*(1), 5–17.

Casey, K., & Patrick, S. (2020). *A promise for equitable futures: Enabling systems change to scale educational and economic mobility pathways.* Aurora Institute.

Cowart Moss, S. (2020). Infusing inclusive leadership into a program redesign at Georgia State University. *UCEA Review, 61*(1), 17–19. https://www.pageturnpro.com/UCEA/93982-UCEA-Review-Winter-2020/flex.html

DeLorenzo, R. A., Battino, W, Schreiber, R., & Carrio, B. (2009). *Delivering on the promise.* Solution Tree.

DeMatthews, D., Billingsley, B., McLeskey, J., & Sharma, U. (2020). Principal leadership for students with disabilities in effective inclusive schools. *Journal of Educational Administration, 58*(5), 539–554. https://doi.org/10.1108/JEA-10-2019-0177

Dillon, B., & Bourke, J. (2016). *The six signature traits of inclusive leadership: Thriving in a diverse new world.* deloitte-au-hc-six-signature-traits-inclusive-leadership-020516.pdf

Every student succeeds act (Essa) | U. S. Department of education. (2015).

Frattura, E., & Capper, C. A. (2007). *Leading for social justice: Transforming schools for all learners.* Corwin Press.

Freire, P. (1990). *Pedagogy of the oppressed.* Continuum.

Hannon, V., Thomas, L., Ward, S., & Beresford, T. (2019). *Local learning ecosystems: Emerging models.* Qatar Foundation.

Hitt, D., & Tucker, P. (2016). Systematic review of key leader practices found to influence student achievement: a unified framework. *Review of Educational Research, 86*(2), 531–569.

INACOL. (2019). *Map: A snapshot of K–12 competency education policy.* https://aurora-institute.org/blog/inacol-releases-updates-to-the-snapshot-of-k-12-competency-education-state-policy-across-the-united-states/

Lieberman, A., & Miller, L. (2008). *Teachers in professional learning communities: Improving teaching and learning.* Teachers College Press.

Lewis, M. W., Eden, R., Garber, C., Rudnick, M., Santibañez, L., & Tsai, T. (2014). *Equity in competency education: Realizing the potential, overcoming the obstacles.* Jobs for the Future.

Mette, I. M. (2019). The state of supervision discourse communities: A call for the future of supervision to shed its mask. *Journal of Educational Supervision, 2*(2). https://doi.org/10.31045/jes.2.2.1

Mockler, N., & Groundwater-Smith, S. (2015). Seeking for the unwelcome truths: beyond celebration in inquiry-based teacher professional learning. *Teachers and Teaching: Theory and Practice, 21*(5), 603–614.

NPBEA. (2018). *National educational leadership preparation (NELP) Program standards–District level.* Retrieved from: www.npbea.org

Ryan, S., & Cox, J. D. (2017). Investigating student exposure to competency-based education. *Education Policy Analysis Archives, 25*(24). http://dx.doi.org/10.14507/epaa.25.2792

Sapon-Shevin, M. (2003). Inclusion: A matter of social justice. *Educational Leadership, 61*(2), 25–28.

Snow-Gerono, J.L. (2005). Professional development in a culture of inquiry: PDS teachers identify the benefits of professional learning communities. *Teaching and Teacher Education, 21*(3), 241–256.

Sturgis, C., & Patrick, S. (2010). *When success is the only option: Designing competency-based pathways for next generation learning.* International Association for K–12 Online Learning. United States Department of Education.

Theoharis, G., & Causton-Theoharis, J. N. (2008). Oppressors or emancipators: Critical dispositions for preparing inclusive school leaders. *Equity & Excellence in Education, 41*(2), 230–246. https://doi.org/10.1080/10665680801973714

UNESCO. (1994). *Salamanca statement and framework for action on special educational needs.*

Vangrieken, K., Meredith, C., Packer, T., & Kyndt, E. (2017). Teacher communities as a context for professional development. A systematic review. *Teaching and Teacher Education, 61,* 47–59.

Wenger, E. (1998). *Communities of practice: Learning, meaning, and identity.* Cambridge University Press.

CHAPTER 13

RAFAEL'S STORY

A Portrait of a Latinx School Leader in Georgia

Taylor Barton
Fulton County Schools, Atlanta Georgia

"IT JUST TAKES ONE TO BELIEVE"

There was just a fence. On the other side of it, life would change. Months after telling his kindergarten classmates, "*My mom lives in the United States She's going to come and pick us up. She's coming for us,*" Rafael, his mother, four siblings, and other Mexican immigrants were on the threshold of a new life. The coyotes had warned the group to wear black because of U.S. Border Patrol helicopters monitoring the border. Rafael, at six years old, was in black, but the pregnant lady beside him wore a white dress. As the whir of helicopters approached, exhilaration quickly turned to panic. While he could hide under the cover of night, this lady was luminescent. Although six, Rafael knew he had to protect the woman, for her own good, and for the good of the group. "*I grabbed a bunch of grass and put it on top of her. I also gently laid on top of her because I had nothing but black clothes on. I had to think of something quickly. Solve a problem that came up.* After an eternity, the helicopter passed

Inclusive Leadership, pages 237–251
Copyright © 2024 by Information Age Publishing
www.infoagepub.com
All rights of reproduction in any form reserved.

237

over without noticing them, and they stepped through the fence and into the United States.

This study explores the lived experiences, both personal and professional, of Rafael, an inclusive Latinx school leader in the state of Georgia. This research paints a portrait of experiences and emergent themes that have shaped him into the inclusive leader that he is today. Rafael's experiences are presented to paint a picture of him as a complex and vibrant individual paving the way for others. This study tells the story of an individual who has overcome hardship and is using his leadership position to help others attain success. Furthermore, his story provides insights into the lives of an underrepresented group in Georgia's school systems. His experiences are brought to light, and his stories of courage, perseverance, and integration crystallize into a unified portrait of a practicing inclusive leader. For Raphael, inclusive leadership means someone who can not only include those around him, but also someone who pulls others up. Someone to come to the aid of others and lead the way even in the most perilous of times.

Guiding Question

What are the lived experiences of one Latinx school leader in Georgia?

Bias and Limitations

The lived experience of one individual is not generalizable. Additionally, this study does not provide an exhaustive depiction of the lived experiences of all Latinx administrators in Georgia, nor does the research examine the lived experiences of school administrators outside of Georgia. .

Validity and Data Collection

To answer the question, "What are the lived experiences of one Latinx school leader in Georgia?," I crystallized data from interviews, artifacts, document analysis, a response to text, and observation of context. Utilizing the elements of Portraiture and Phenomenology, data was crystallized from multiple sources to shape the essence of the individuals (Lawrence-Lightfoot & Hoffmann Davis, 1997; van Manen, 1997). The first step in this process was a thorough analysis of the data from all the sources in order to identify emergent themes and patterns. The data were then reviewed again to compare findings between all sources.

Data analysis was an ongoing, reflexive process. Data crystallized through the writing process, in which themes emerged after being hidden in plain sight. This came from a consideration of the sum total of the data points, and the realization of connections between data. A depth of understanding was reached not just in formal passes of the data, but in the synthesis of information through the writing process. Crystallization of multiple data points allows for validation through the confirmation of details and reliability of the individual in describing lived experiences, as well as validity of the data collection (Ellingson, 2014; Tracy, 2010). This ongoing, reflexive cycle of data analysis allowed for a natural emergence of themes, free of preconceived frameworks or conclusions.

Findings

I met Rafael after I spoke to a group of graduate students. While most attendees shuffled out after the talk, I was approached by a tall, Latinx man with hair slicked back in a short ponytail, goatee, and black rim glasses, similar to those issued at basic training. After exchanging pleasantries, I could see his desire to grow in his career, and to connect with me because of the Latinx population of my school. From our very first conversation, I could sense his passion for his community. Over the course of other conversations, I learned just how deep those passions run.

Personal History

His journey of thousands of miles brought Rafael to a coffee shop in an affluent suburb of Atlanta. As I drove to meet him, I passed a variety of landscapes, from urban to rural to the strip mall packed landscape of the suburbs. We picked a time in the early afternoon, which gave him time to make it to his second job working at a shipping company. The parking lot was full of high-end sedans and SUVs, as well as a golf cart, the preferred mode of transportation for many of the town's residents.

I entered the shop and noticed that most of the patrons were White. And there was Rafael, sitting in a reserved room waiting for me, his hair slicked back in the familiar ponytail and wearing a t-shirt from the university where we met. It struck me as an intentional move, wearing this shirt. In a sense, it was a badge of honor. Even before hearing his story, it was as if Rafael was telling me, "Look at what I accomplished, after all those miles."

We sat down at the end of a long wooden table and Rafael began to tell me his story. Throughout the hours of us sitting and talking, he rubbed his hands together, squeezing them as he thought, as if they would help him remember a few more details, a few more memories. He leaned into the table, eager to tell his story. He smiled and laughed quickly as he talked and paid no attention to his flashing cell phone. He was totally present, and totally in the past.

Rafael was born in a rural town in Mexico about an hour outside Guadalajara. He speaks almost as if his childhood began once he entered the United States. His only memory of life in Mexico was looking forward to his mother's return so he could travel to the United States with her. She had settled in Atlanta with her brothers. She was coming back to take Rafael and his siblings away from their abusive father. After crossing the border, his first American memory was eating Fruit Loops as he awoke on his first morning in the United States. *That was my first American experience.* Rafael laughs and tells me that Fruit Loops is still his favorite cereal.

After a long drive from California, Rafael settled in Georgia with his mother, siblings, and uncles. *It took us about a week and a half to get there.* His mother enrolled him in school, and Rafael began to practice his "English." *I used to think that English, when they say, 'You got to learn how to speak English,' used to mean speak proper Spanish.* So, he practiced on the playground, attempting to speak his best English by speaking proper Spanish.

Rafael, his mother, and six of her twelve children, lived with his uncles. During that time, he found a father figure in one of his uncles. *He would come home from work, six o'clock in the afternoon, in the evening, and he would say, "Hey, come on, let's go play." We'd go play soccer. "Let's go ride a bike" or whatever. That was a lasting impact because he showed me that I don't have to be sitting in the house the whole day. He got me into sports.* At the time, neither of them would have an idea of how athletics would change Rafael's life.

Rafael moved around in his first four years in Georgia, attending five different elementary schools. In these schools, the majority of the students were Latinx, and during these years Rafael encountered his first influential teacher. *My third grade ESOL teacher really helped me the most with learning and picking up the language. And that had an impact as to how I would teach my ESOL students and my regular students. She had a major impact on me understanding how to learn to read and how to teach somebody how to read.* The groundwork was being laid for Rafael to help ESOL students in the future.

When his mother purchased a house in his fourth-grade year, he and his siblings were the only Latinx students in a majority African American school. Rafael learned to assimilate, a life skill that would serve him well in his future.

> It wasn't that different finding friends but it was a difference in not having somebody to be able to speak to in my same language and talk about the same things that we liked. I kind of had to quickly assimilate, from foods to shows to sports. Up to then I was only used to playing soccer. I had to learn how to like baseball, basketball, especially basketball. We were heavy on basketball.

In middle school, Rafael started to develop a goal-oriented mentality when he saw others recognized for achievements. Considering the sacrifices his mother was making working long hours to provide for the family, he knew he could do better. He remembered a middle school awards ceremony where he made a conscious decision to excel academically to honor his mother's hard work. *All the people that were getting certificates and medals for doing good with their grades, all the other kids sat on the floor, and had to watch. And so that pushed me.* By his eighth-grade year, he got to the floor. Even though his mother couldn't make it to the ceremony when he was finally recognized, bringing home the certificate made the effort worth it. *I was able to show her, "Hey, I know you're working all the time, but look, this is what I am doing at school."*

It was clear to me that these experiences from childhood related back to Rafael's mother. In almost every experience, his mother is somehow mentioned. Her impact. Her servant nature. Rafael refers to her repeatedly, as if everything he does is a way to repay her.

As Rafael entered high school in South Atlanta, he set a goal to graduate from high school, something his older siblings failed to do. During this time, he kept to himself. *Back in high school I wasn't sure I could be a leader. I had some doubts. I was seen as a follower and a lonesome person. I kept to myself in high school.* Being a private person, he never shared his motivation to graduate with anyone, not even his mother or uncle, but he knew what he wanted to do. *My plan even as a ninth grader was to graduate from high school, work a couple of summers, and save enough money to go back to Mexico. And go back home and find the industry where I could use my English language.* However, a chance encounter on the soccer field changed the trajectory of Rafael's life.

> I remember the spring of my ninth-grade year, the football coach came out to the soccer field and asked the head coach, "Who out here can kick a ball the farthest?" And he pointed to me. He took me out to the football field, threw a couple footballs and was like, "Here, just kick the balls through the goal post." So, I did it. I had no training or anything. All three went through the field goal post. He said, "You're our kicker for the next three years."

As he learned the sport of football, Rafael became a prolific kicker for his high school team. He was recognized as the Georgia High School Athlete of the Week, and he was interviewed with his mother on a local news channel. He also received letters from college football coaches from the universities of Michigan, Alabama, and Illinois offering Rafael full scholarships to kick for their teams.

The irony is that football was an unfamiliar sport to him. Soccer was his first love. Even on the television spot about his prowess as a football player, Rafael showed off his various soccer jerseys. He admitted that before he started receiving the letters, he didn't even attempt to understand the rules.

I didn't know the rules. At what point do I kick a field goal? I didn't know about those downs or fumbles. When he first started playing in tenth grade, he'd watch the game and wait, not knowing when it was his turn to go in. *It was like, "Go kick a field goal," "Oh, it's my turn? Ok, let's go."*

A little confused how football could open up academic opportunities for him, Rafael enlisted the help of his tenth grade English teacher. *My junior year I was like, "Why are these schools writing letters to me?" Then my English teacher started telling me, "These schools want you to go play for them. You can receive scholarships for them."* Over the course of his four years, this teacher became a mentor to Rafael, and saw potential in him that others had overlooked. *She introduced me to the understanding that I can do better and go to college. I started thinking about that plan.* She guided him as he navigated the unfamiliar waters of preparing for life after high school.

During these high school years, Rafael developed an interest in teaching. He enrolled in a Teaching Insights course during his senior year, a program for high school students interested s in teaching careers. This was a natural fit for Rafael, as he regularly tutored his younger siblings after school. *I always grew up helping my little brother and sisters with homework. So, I always felt like I was ok with helping kids and teaching them.* Academically and athletically, Rafael began to carve out a new path for his life. Just as he led the way crossing the border from Mexico, he would lead his family in graduating high school and going to college.

His high school years were not without setbacks, however. From both an African American teacher at school and from the Latinx community, he experienced racism and people trying to deter him from success. *I had a Social Studies teacher tell me in the classroom that I shouldn't speak "that" language with my peers. The only thing I was trying to do in that classroom is try to help my friend understand the assignments.* The irony was not lost on him that a Social Studies teacher told him not to speak Spanish. *I was thinking, as a Social Studies teacher, how can you tell me not to speak a language when we're studying about different cultures and history of the world?*

He also battled negative attitudes from within his own community. When he began to play football in high school, he was approached by his brother-in-law's brother. He mocked Rafael for playing football and told him he wasn't going to be successful. *One of the things that my brother-in-law's brother said to me was, "Wow, look at you. If you can't even make it in soccer, what makes you think you are going to make it in football?"* But Rafael used these interactions as motivation. *I would take that as, "Thank you for saying that to me, cause that only makes me fight a little harder."* When people doubted Rafael, he kept those moments as motivation to overcome obstacles. *You telling me I'm not going to make it; I'm going to show you I'm gonna make it. And that I think really inspired me to understand football and do well.* In the face of his detractors, Rafael excelled in the classroom and in athletics.

Rafael did not just graduate from high school, he graduated with honors. He won the award for top male scholar athlete. *I was the number one student athlete for the graduating class. The highest GPA and the best overall athlete in the school.* He didn't achieve this goal for himself. He did it to pay back his mother for her sacrifices. *My only goal back then was to graduate from high school as a gift to my mom.* He admits that without the help of teachers, he would not have made it. *I think in high school the biggest difference was finding some educators that cared about me and my future.*

When deciding where to attend college and play football, Rafael followed the advice of an African American counselor at his high school and committed to play at a college in Georgia. Before he graduated, the coach of the team left that school and went to a Historically Black College and University (HBCU). Ever loyal, Rafael followed the coach to the new university, and yet again found himself to be one of a few Latinx students in a majority African American educational setting. *It wasn't that hard, or culture shock in college, it was just like me fitting in with the family.* Since elementary school, Rafael had grown accustomed to assimilating into majority African American environments.

Being the first in his family to go to college was an honor Rafael took seriously. He knew if he succeeded, it would open doors for others in his family. While he earned accolades on the football field, Rafael started to focus on a career after college. Rafael set a new goal, be the first in his family to graduate from college. He made sure he took his academics seriously.

> I think just the experience of being able to go to a college and say I played college football" was great. At the end of the day, it molded me into ensuring that I did my part as the student athlete. Because I was so afraid to lose my scholarship in college, I had to make sure I was a good student. There was parties on campus but being the first one to go to college as well set a good example for others, molded me into ensuring that not only the athlete part was being taken care of but the student part as well.

During this time, life after college began to take focus as Rafael pursued a degree in education. *I did a few practicums and stuck to it. I said, "I'ma go into education."* It's this air of certainty that I have grown accustomed to seeing in Rafael. He sets a goal, and he achieves it. It's that simple. Earning his degree and becoming a teacher was the next step on a journey that started by tutoring his siblings, and the high school teacher preparation course. It made sense.

After four years in college, Rafael graduated with an undergraduate degree in teaching. Seeing his mother on his graduation day from college is a memory he will never forget.

Seeing my mom there in the stands I told her, "You never told me, 'You need to stay in school, you need to stay in school'" like we tell a lot of our students in the school, but I wanted to show her that all the hard work that she did is paying off.

After graduation, Rafael moved back to Atlanta, and began teaching. Early on in his career he met his wife. *So, I met my wife right after college. I was at a teaching conference trying to get a job. She's a teacher, too.* His wife also has two daughters, whom Rafael refers to as his daughters. I was not surprised to learn that Rafael's wife is African American. Since elementary school, Rafael has assimilated into African American environments and connected with the culture.

I asked Rafael if there is ever a disconnect with his wife given their different backgrounds. *There's never a disconnect. We're both minorities, but we live in a majority community. Population is Caucasian, but we could come in here and have a conversation with anybody.* Choosing to live in this majority Caucasian, affluent area seemed odd to me. Of all places, why here? But as I reflected, I realized that for Rafael, assimilation is almost a way of life. *Living here, I've learned to assimilate a lot. Throughout my years growing up, I learned to understand what different cultures like and do.* From the age of six, he has been in situations where he was different, and he had to figure out how to survive.

Living in this community serves as a symbol of success for Rafael. *It's an affluent community. I was just blessed to be able to afford to live here with her. It's just a matter of working hard.* He is quick to point out, however, that he doesn't see major differences in the lifestyle in one community or another. When his siblings ask him about where he lives, he points out one main difference. *I tell them that life is not that much different whether you live here or over there. It is quieter at night.* No matter where he is, Rafael has learned to fit in.

Professional Experiences—"Take out your phones, turn on the flashlight."

Rafael began his teaching career in a suburban district south of Atlanta. He taught there for four years as a fourth and fifth grade classroom teacher. He received his ESOL endorsement because he wanted to impact students with similar backgrounds to his. After receiving his endorsement, he taught one year of middle school and realized it was not his calling.

During his first few years of teaching, the county where he worked started furloughing teachers to account for budget deficits. To supplement his income, he started working nights at a shipping company, and he has not stopped. Just as his mother worked long hours, Rafael continues to work two jobs. *And that's what I've been doing since 2010. I work not only in the school, but in the evenings from 6 to about 10, 11 o'clock sometimes.* He now works a second job to pay for his daughter's education.

At his next school he started to transition into a leadership role, laying the groundwork for his journey to inclusive leadership. In the next four years, he became a lead ESOL teacher and worked on special committees within the school. *That school and the principal there opened me up into more opportunities for leadership.*

During this time, Rafael found that many students at his school did not have the support they needed to complete homework. In between teaching and the shipping company, he set up a table in a local park and began tutoring students in the afternoon. *I would go to the apartment complex, take the kids to the park, and do homework with them.* Driven by a desire to help students with backgrounds similar to his, Rafael would spend a few hours every afternoon helping out students to complete their homework. *I started doing that for the whole year. I would go there in the Fall, in the cold, it would get dark, like around 6:00. I remember one time, I just told the parents, "Take out your phones, turn on the flashlight."* Even in the cold and dark, Rafael was willing to go the extra mile to help students.

At this new school, he became more comfortable in leadership positions. *That experience there with leadership as a lead ESOL teacher opened me up to being a leader in a school and being able to present in front of people.* As usual, Rafael assimilated and became successful in this new environment.

With the urging of his wife and colleagues, Rafael went back to school, got his master's degree, another family first, and his leadership certificate. He applied for Assistant Principal jobs, but did not find a fit, and he moved schools again. He was not without opportunities before this point, however. The county where he originally taught called him asking if he'd be interested in being an assistant principal at a dual language school. While initially interested in the job, Rafael knew he did not yet have the skills to make the jump. *I don't want to go into something new and be working on my master's as well. I like to be fully prepared for the new job.* Always measured and strategic, Rafael knew it was better to wait.

In this new school in a new county, he was again the lead ESOL teacher, and his leadership experiences grew. He was given the opportunity to lead a summer program, which made him feel like a principal. *The principal allowed me to take the role of a principal. Use this opportunity to make it your own program.* This experience gave him the confidence to start actively pursuing assistant principal jobs again.

The following Spring, Rafael applied for assistant principal jobs around metro-Atlanta and was hired out of an applicant pool of 300 people. In retrospect, Rafael is glad he waited. *I made the right decision by waiting to finish up my degree before I started the AP job. Because it was very stressful at times, but super busy.* Finishing his degree before becoming an Assistant Principal allowed Rafael to fully focus on his job.

Currently, Rafael is an assistant principal at a metro Atlanta elementary school. The school is PreK through fifth grade and serves 956 students. The student population is 96 percent Hispanic, as reported by the Georgia

Department of Education, and 90 percent of the students are English Language Learners. When I visited his school, I quickly saw that this was a perfect fit. Rafael is exactly who his students and his families need.

I visited him at school on an early October morning. Driving up, I was struck by the contrast in environments between the affluent suburban coffee shop where we first met, and the urban context of his school. A street over from the school, men sat waiting for work outside shops. I pulled up, and it was apparent Rafael's school has seen better days. The building looked as if it had not been updated since the 1960s. Trailers lined the few grassy areas the school had. A disheveled dumpster sat on cracked pavement in a parking lot that seemed too small to fit the cars of a full faculty.

As I walked into the school, the vibrancy of Latinx culture came alive. I didn't realize it, but Rafael invited me to the school's Hispanic Heritage Month performance. Two ladies at the front desk were wearing colorful dresses with flowers in their hair. Rafael greeted me, wearing a black suit with a green shirt and red tie and socks, a subtle display of the colors of the Mexican flag.

He took me on a quick tour of the school and introduced me to staff members and a special guest visitor for the day's performance, a Latinx business leader from the state power company. One of the first things I noticed was how much the students here looked like the students at my school. I realized why Rafael and I connected so much during that first encounter; we both share a passion for serving the same types of students.

After the tour, he escorted me to the cafeteria, where final preparations for the performance were being made. I took a seat at the back of the cafeteria, trying to take the most unobtrusive perch so I could observe Rafael within the greater context of the school. Immediately, it was clear that Rafael was running the show. Third, fourth, and fifth grade classes arrived in lines and sat down on the cafeteria floor. The single row of chairs surrounding the area where students sat were filled with teachers and a few Latina mothers with small children. Most of the teachers appeared to be female African Americans. Besides the music teacher conducting the student chorus, I was the only white male in the large room.

Rafael opened the show by greeting everyone, "Good morning. Buenos Dias." He introduced the first act, the chorus of students. As they sang, he took pictures from the back of the cafeteria. He then introduced the next act, a pair of dancers from Vera Cruz, Mexico, and after they performed, he introduced the next speaker, a local Latinx police officer. Then, a teacher read from a PowerPoint about the history of Hispanic Heritage Month, and what it means to be Hispanic. The show was capped off with the special guest I met earlier. She spoke of her own experiences growing up, which were strikingly similar to Rafael's. She spoke of following your dreams and highlighted inspirational Latinx figures. She told students, "Never be ashamed of who you are."

At some point during the first show, the principal entered the cafeteria, dressed in traditional Latin clothing. While Rafael was fully engaged in the show, the principal seemed to float—not engaged with staff nor students and was consistently on his phone during the performance. It made me sad to see the disconnection, but as I glanced towards Rafael, he didn't seem to notice. Perhaps this is how it usually is.

At the end of the performance, the students were dismissed from the cafeteria by the principal, and then the stage was reset for the lower grades. As students entered the cafeteria, they hugged Rafael. This second time around, Rafael seemed to grow more confident in his role as coordinator of the show. He danced with students as the chorus sang. His positive presence filled the cafeteria. The principal did not attend the second show.

Between the two shows, I talked with the guest speaker, and I suggested to her that she include Rafael in her examples of inspirational Latin figures. She told me that she intended to celebrate him in the first presentation but ran out of time. However, when she presented the second time to the lower grades, she talked about Rafael to his students. She explained how Rafael's heroism in caring for his students is an inspiration to her. Rafael's reaction to the surprise was one of humility. I have come to know Rafael well enough to know that on the outside he was humbly stoic, on the inside he was glowing.

After the second show, Rafael led the guest speaker and me back to his office. Along the way Rafael explained that the classroom doors were decorated by parents for Hispanic Heritage Month. Rafael's office door was marked with a portrait of him on his door. I assumed that the painting was made by a student. In the portrait, he has the familiar glasses, goatee, and is wearing a bright blue shirt and red striped tie. The doors symbolized the influence of Rafael's inclusive leadership in the school—celebrating Latinx culture and displaying a portrait of a Latinx leader.

Rafael's office is a long, rectangular, windowless room with his desk in the middle, set off against the wall to the left. At the front of the room, to the left as you enter the door, were boxes of refreshments and permission slips. Farther back, testing bins were stacked up and behind his desk sat filing cabinets and a banner of his alma mater. On the wall, Rafael has his diplomas displayed. On his desk, he has a daily devotional, *La Biblia a Mano*, and a photo of two chihuahuas. It looks like a combination between a PTA storage room and a typical assistant principal's office.

The three of us sat and chatted about school, and Rafael's newest idea of starting a computer class for his parents. It is apparent that on top of his assistant principal duties, he also serves as a liaison to the students' families. I wondered what the parents' involvement in his school was like before he got here. It's clear his presence has made an impact. Rafael also talked with the special guest about plans for an upcoming ceremony. In the same place where Rafael tutored students at the folding table until dark, there will now be a pergola constructed in his honor where students can meet and learn. The ceremony would take place the following month. It will be called "The Learning Nook." This space serves as a symbol of Rafael's impact. What began as a simple table, illuminated by the cell phones of parents, is now a wheelchair accessible learning space that can comfortably fit up to fifteen students.

Emergent Themes

Leadership

When asked about his leadership style, Rafael is quick to reference his mother, and how she was always concerned with taking care of others. *At the end of the school year, we do a big lunch before our teachers go home. Everybody kept asking me, "When are you getting something to eat? When are you getting something to eat?" But I told them I'd rather have everyone eat first then I'll go by, There's plenty of food.* Rafael sees his role as school leader is to serve others.

> I told everybody, I come from a hard-working family. I don't mind picking up the broom and sweeping if y'all need assistance. And there were some times where we would have to pick up the broom, the principal and I, and just sweep the hallways just to make sure that the school looked good for the community.

Rafael also sees the importance of being a Latinx leader in a school for Latinx students and parents. *A few kids tell me, "I never saw somebody dressed up like you."* When he was growing up, Rafael never saw any Latinx males dressed in suits. Moreover, all of the Latinx males he knew had day labor jobs. Serving as an inclusive leader for his school community is important for Rafael, in the same way that being a role model for his siblings drove him to succeed.

Helping parents is central to his inclusive leadership. *Being a first-generation immigrant helps me be able to make that connection with some parents.* He can connect with them in a way that many school leaders cannot.

> Even though you're not from the same place, you are still able to connect with them, and the parents see that. Because a lot of the parents are from Guatemala or from Honduras, and we have different cultures from Mexico, and it's different from my upbringing. But they see me as a person that they can approach.

Influential Figures

When Rafael thinks of the influential figures in his life, he lists three people: his mother, his uncle, and his high school English teacher. In a methodical manner he worked through why he felt that these three people made an impact on his life.

Mother—Rafael spoke about his mother throughout our time together. She seemed to provide the motivation and strength that Rafael needed in order to achieve what he has accomplished in his life. Her inspiration and impact didn't come from words as much as it did with her actions. *With her it was more of seeing what she did on a day-to-day basis.* She taught Rafael work ethic and how to care for others. She also helped Rafael's family transition from life in Mexico to life in the United States, laying the groundwork for Rafael's ability to assimilate into a new environment. *We blended in from our traditions to American traditions, Santa Claus and presents.* Through her working long hours, she provided for her children. Despite these long hours, she still made time for her family. These lessons shine through in everything Rafael does, from serving students at his school to working an extra job to pay for his daughter's education.

Uncle—Although he moved back to Mexico years ago, Rafael feels that his uncle served as the father figure he needed during his youth. Not only did his uncle get him involved in sports, but he also provided life lessons about hard work. Rafael recounted a time when he sat with his uncle after Rafael received a paycheck for a part time job. *He was like, "If you ever doubt that you did something to earn that check, that means you didn't earn it. The next week, I need you to work harder to make sure you feel like you earned that check at the end of the week."* From his uncle, Rafael learned that you need to go above and beyond in your work, and success is earned.

Teacher—It wasn't until tenth grade that Rafael had a mentor in school who truly believed in him. *I never had a teacher who told me, "You have the potential to do a little better." Once I started working with her in high school, she really made that impact on me, and I always knew I could do better.* This teacher helped Rafael see his potential, and also served as a guide to graduating high school and attending college. Without her, Rafael contends, he wouldn't have seen the path to college that was provided to him through football and academics.

Poetry Reflection

Below is Rafael's response to the poem *América* by Richard Blanco (1998). I have included his personal reflections to allow his voice to be heard.

América reminds me mostly of the gatherings that my family had when I was a child. All major holidays, Thanksgiving, Christmas, New Year's, etc. were the same in our household. My family that lived nearby would visit my mother's house for the food and dancing. Although we would celebrate with traditional American foods, my mother would always cook something to remind us of our heritage: Pozole, camarones a la diabla, tamales, etc. Our first Christmas here in the states, I remembered my mother cooking a turkey for the first time; the turkey was donated by a local church. We also had dressing and cranberry sauce, but to please my uncles and cousins she cooked a large pot of chicken pozole.

My mother was quick to adapt to American culture and explained to us that we should celebrate the national holidays like everyone in the states since we're now living in the United States. On the Fourth of July, we ate hot dogs and burgers with tacos de carne azada on the side. For New Year's we would have some greens, cornbread, and chicken, with carnitas or tamales on the side. Like Blanco's parents, grabbing items for our traditional dishes required going to the nearest Mexican food store since neither Kroger, nor Quality Foods carried the items that my mother needed. Everyone loved coming to the house and enjoyed the food, music, and laughter that our family events had.

My uncles and cousins would talk about returning home, building their own houses, and buying land during our gatherings. They would talk about all that they missed from home: the Sunday soccer games they would play and watch on tv, weekends going to el palenque (arena for bull riding), listening to live mariachis, and of course the cantinas. Over the years some of my uncles and cousins would actually go back home and realize their dream... sending money back home on a weekly basis to their spouses or parents allowed them to build their own homes and save enough money to go back home to create a living. Others, including my brothers and sisters, would stay here in the states and find themselves someone to build their own family here.

Still to this day, this poem reminds me of my childhood life with my family. Unfortunately, now that all of us are married and we all have families, this tradition only comes around during the Christmas holiday. Nonetheless, all of my family gathering around, having both American and Mexican food and enjoying our time together is a wonderful experience. Those uncles and cousins who are no longer here with us are missed, but calling our sisters and family makes it possible for us to see each other so they get to tell us everything that they are doing and enjoying back home.

Rafael is the embodiment of an inclusive leader. Because of his background, he recognizes inequities and draws upon personal and professional experiences to open doors for others to create equitable learning environments, especially those who experience the same types of challenges that he has faced. However, an inclusive leader like Rafael, not only opens the door for others, but walks alongside them, saying, "Here's where I've been, and here's where you can go."

Inclusive leaders see the unique story in each individual and relate their own past with others' stories. They take the cultural capital they have obtained through heritage, relationships, and experience, and project it into their leadership. Though inclusive leaders have a keen awareness of their own lived experiences, they also regularly practice reflection and consider the perspectives of others. For this reason, they view leadership as a "coming to the table" of variant thoughts, opinions, emotions, and experiences, all for the goal of a positive future for students and staff. Rafael's story is an important one, and it continues to welcome more and more students and staff to the table.

REFERENCES

Blanco, R. (1998). *América: City of a hundred fires.* University of Pittsburgh Press.

Ellingson, L. L. (2014). "The truth must dazzle gradually": Enriching relationship research using a crystallization framework. *Journal of Social and Personal Relationships, 31*(4), 442–450.

Lawrence-Lightfoot, S., & Davis, J. H. (1997). *The art and science of portraiture.* Jossey-Bass.

Tracy, S. J. (2010). Qualitative quality: Eight "big-tent" criteria for excellent qualitative research. *Qualitative Inquiry, 16*(10), 837–851. https://doi.org/10.1177/1077800410383121

CONCLUSION

Sheryl Cowart Moss
Georgia State University

Rolandria Justice Emenuga
Justice Consulting Group

This book has been a labor of love and a dream deferred. We sent out our initial call for chapters as the COVID 19 death toll surpassed one million worldwide. There was fear and confusion all around. We had gone through lengthy quarantine periods, travel was almost non-existent, and remote learning was the norm. Racial tensions reached a boiling point. The work of doing school changed in ways we could never have imagined.

As we were able to start venturing out in our masks, clutching our hand sanitizer bottles, we hoped the worst was over. We soon learned that new and daunting trials awaited us. Many things would never be the same. Most of us would agree that we were looking forward to getting back into our school buildings, but new and greater challenges awaited us. More than thirty years ago COPIS member Ed Pajak suggested relationship, or human relations effectiveness, was the most important dimension and the common thread among all his dimensions of supervision (1990). During the depths of the pandemic, we had to find creative ways to sustain relationships, because we suddenly realized how quickly and profoundly we suffer from isolation.

As we returned to our schools, younger children who should have been in school for a couple of years entered for the first time, with no idea of what school could or should be. Older students seemed to have completely forgotten how to be in school settings. School districts felt intense pressure to make up for lost learning time, but soon realized that social and emotional learning would have to take priority.

Our writing community suffered unexpected challenges and delays as we, too, navigated the new normal. The silver lining is that the extra time gave us space to process all that we had experienced. We had space to gain a bit of perspective from somewhere other than the middle of it all. This time of extreme challenges also illuminated the very reasons we need inclusive leadership in our schools

The findings and stories in this book take on renewed importance with this extra time and perspective. Our authors have been very forthright about how they, and those who participated in their studies, have been changed. We believe in inclusive leadership... seeing each child and each teacher and each other... valuing the social capital in our organizations... holding each other accountable in supportive ways... intentionally searching for goodness.... these principles are the only ways to thrive in the midst of chaos. Relationships. Seeing and being seen. How fundamentally important. How inclusive...

REFERENCE

Pajak, E. (1990). Dimensions of Supervision. *Educational Leadership, 48*(1), 78–80.

ABOUT THE CONTRIBUTORS

Taylor Barton, EdD is a K–12 school leader in Fulton County Schools, Atlanta Georgia. He specializes in inclusive and transformational leadership practices, digital learning, and leadership development. Under his leadership, his high poverty, high English Language Learner school attained national recognition as a model school. He currently leads a Title 1 digital school serving grades 3–12. Dr. Barton holds a doctorate in Educational Leadership from Georgia State University, a Master of Arts in Teaching from the University of Maine, and a Bachelor of Arts in English from Furman University.

Toni Barton, JD, M.Ed., is the Founder and President of Spelligent, an organization focused on supporting leaders with designing schools that are inclusive-by-design, meaning learner variability is at the core. She is an experienced practitioner who has served in roles such as Director of Student Support, school principal, and special education teacher in both district and charter schools. She has presented on inclusive practices at various conferences, including SXSW EDU, EdSummit, and the National Charter School Conference.

Jami Berry is a clinical associate professor at the University of Georgia. She has served as a dissertation chairperson or committee member for over one hundred doctoral students, and her graduates include local school leaders, system level leaders, superintendents, and university faculty members throughout Georgia and the United States. Her work in high needs schools

Inclusive Leadership, pages 255–261
Copyright © 2024 by Information Age Publishing
www.infoagepub.com
All rights of reproduction in any form reserved.

and leadership preparation has been guided by a desire to understand educational structures through a broader lens and use that knowledge to drive the continuous improvement of UGA's programs, the systems and leaders they serve, and above all each student.

Karen Bryant serves as the director of the University of Georgia Gwinnett Campus. Prior to joining the graduate faculty at UGA, she worked for 30 years in K–12 education; serving as a classroom teacher, assistant principal, principal, district director of curriculum, district director of federal programs, and district leadership development mentor. Her research interests include collaborative partnerships between school districts and educator preparation programs, action research as a tool to prepare effective scholar-practitioner leaders, and inclusive school leadership.

Jennifer Bubrig is a clinical assistant professor of Elementary Education at the University of Memphis. Currently, Jennifer teaches teacher preparation courses and supervises clinical practice for teacher candidates in partnership with Memphis Shelby County Schools located in Memphis, TN. One of the most fulfilling parts of her work is to see her former teacher candidates thriving in the field while serving as mentors for her current teacher candidates. Jennifer has presented nationally on her work, including the 2017 annual meeting for the American Association of Colleges for Teacher Education (AACTE).

Logan Caldwell is an assistant professor at the University of Memphis. She is a National Board Educator as a Middle Child Generalist. She has published in STEM, science education, and assessment for all learners. She double majored in Curriculum and Leadership Instruction with a concentration of Instructional Design and Technology by earning her master's and Doctorate in this field. Her research and professional interests include educational technology, STEAM/STEM, and increasing science self-efficacy in elementary preservice teacher candidates.

Robin Christian is the proud principal of Barack and Michelle Obama Elementary School in the Atlanta Public School District. Firmly committed to the work of improving student achievement, Robin loves working with school communities and partners to make a difference for all children.

Sheryl Cowart Moss, PhD recently retired from Georgia State University where she directed the EdD in Educational Leadership, one of the first programs in the United States to infuse principles of inclusive leadership throughout the curriculum. She is passionate about the work of inclusive leadership and is most proud of her leadership graduates who serve in building, district, and state leadership roles. A former high school principal, she has received numerous awards for her service to the field. Dr. Cowart Moss has led initiatives in inclusive leadership for the CCSSO and serves as a Content Specialist for the CEEDAR Center. She has presented and provided technical assistance on inclusive leadership nationally and internationally. As the Editor for this book series, she looks forward to Volume 3!

Amie Cieminski, EdD is an associate professor of educational leadership and policy studies at the University of Northern Colorado (UNC) in Greeley, Colorado. Dr. Cieminski began her career as a secondary Spanish teacher and served in many K–12 leadership roles including elementary principal and director of professional learning before joining the faculty at UNC. Her research interests include leadership development and inclusive leadership.

Emily Crews, EdS, holds degrees in elementary education, special education, and educational leadership. She has published and presented on teacher development and interventions for Multi-Tiered Systems of Support. Emily is currently an Instructional Intervention Coach in Florida.

Niles Davis is an assistant principal at Loganville High School in Walton County, Georgia. A dedicated and experienced special educator, his dissertation topic was improving postsecondary outcomes for students with developmental disabilities.

Zachary Dominello is a school principal and special education director in the Denver-Metro Area of Colorado. As a doctoral candidate at the University of Northern Colorado, he is committed to the study and practice of community empowerment, social justice, and equitable practices in all facets of education.

Michele Dugan is the coordinator of resource development in the Department of Human Resources for the Forsyth County School District in Georgia. Her research focuses on the effectiveness of alternative certification programs for educators and how the programs are impacted by instructional leadership.

Georgia Evans is a clinical assistant professor in the Leadership, Research, and School Improvement Department at the University of West Georgia. She has been an educator for 46 years and is passionate about ensuring all students receive the best teachers and leaders possible. Dr. Evans developed and delivered the Equity Labs for the State of Georgia in 2018 and 2019.

Vanessa L. Giddings has 22 years of experience in the field of education and is a doctoral candidate at the University of Northern Colorado. She

258 • About the Contributors

is dedicated to creating inclusive school communities where all students belong and thrive.

Steve Haberlin is an assistant professor of education at the University of Central Florida. His scholarship examines the intersection of mindfulness and meditation practices in educational settings. He is the author of *Meditation in the College Classroom: A Pedagogical Tool to Help Students De-Stress, Focus, and Connect*.

Sheri C. Hardee is the dean and a professor in the College of Education at the University of North Georgia, where she began working in 2009. She has a PhD in Social Foundations in Education and an M.A. in English from the University of South Carolina, Columbia. Her research explores equity, equality, and inclusion in regard to access to and support in institutions of higher education, utilizing postcolonial and feminist theories.

Alexandria Harvey, PhD is a senior program associate at WestEd. Her areas of expertise include topics around equity, race, and disability. Additionally, Alexandria has experience providing technical assistance and professional development by building the capacity of state education agencies, institutes of higher education, local education agencies, and other partners to improve equitable outcomes for students with disabilities.

Will Hunter is a professor of special education at the University of Memphis. He serves as the Principal Investigator (PI) of the West Region Tennessee Tiered Supports Center at University of Memphis. Dr. Hunter's background includes working as a special education teacher, administrator, and mental health intervention specialist. Through instructional coaching, Dr. Hunter has supported teachers in the Western Tennessee region with the implementation of Tier 1 (MTSS) interventions within the classroom. Dr. Hunter is the lead editor for the book: The Mixtape Volume 1: Culturally Sustaining Practices within MTSS featuring the Everlasting Mission of Student Engagement.

Maya Israel, PhD is an Associate Professor of Educational Technology and Computer Science Education at the University of Florida. She is also the research director of the Creative Technology Research Lab. Her research focuses on strategies for supporting academically diverse learners' meaningful engagement in science, technology, engineering, and mathematics (STEM) with emphases on computer science education and Universal Design for Learning (UDL).

Rolandria Justice-Emenuga brings 20 years of experience as a teacher, school leader, and consultant. Her company, Justice Consulting Group, helps leaders feel supported, empowered and pushed to be their best, authentic selves. She holds degrees from Duke University, Seton Hall University, and Georgia State University.

Margaret Kamman, PhD is a co-director at the Collaboration for Effective Educator Development Accountability and Reform (CEEDAR) Center and an Associate Professor of Special Education at UF. She has experience and expertise in beginning teacher quality, induction, secondary reading instruction, district, and principal leadership.

Brian Keefer is the principal of Sharon Elementary School in Forsyth County, Georgia. His research focuses on equitable professional development opportunities for educational leaders in Georgia.

Erica D. McCray, PhD is professor of special education and associate dean for personnel affairs, inclusive excellence, and external engagement at the University of Florida. Additionally, she is director for the Collaboration for Effective Educator Development, Accountability, and Reform (CEEDAR) Center. Dr. McCray has been recognized on multiple levels for her teaching and research, which focus on the influence of diversity on educational practice and policy.

Marla W. McGhee, PhD is a retired professor of educational leadership. Before joining the ranks of higher education, she served the public schools of Texas as a teacher, curriculum area director, and campus principal at the secondary and elementary levels.

Kristen McRae serves as the principal of Timber Ridge Elementary in Henry County, Georgia. Her dissertation explored the implementation of innovative leadership practices to promote creative learning opportunities.

Kris Melloy has served as an educational professional for 46 years. Her work includes being a classroom teacher, university professor and leader, high school principal, and district-level personnel. Dr. Melloy is a student success coach in a school district in Colorado.

Ian M. Mette is an associate professor of educational leadership and the director of the School of Educational Leadership, Higher Education, and Human Development at the University of Buffalo. His research interests focus on the development of culturally responsive instructional supervision frameworks and developing equity-oriented school leaders in predominantly White rural spaces. Specifically, his work targets bridging the gap between theory and practice to inform and support equitable school improvement efforts for all students.

Sylvia Robertson is director of the University of Otago Centre for Educational Leadership and Administration (CELA) in Dunedin, New Zealand, and co-director, UCEA Centre for The International Study of School Leadership. She lectures in Education Studies at the University of Otago College of Education. Sylvia has research interests in school leadership and principal preparation and has published on leadership in high-needs settings, leading through change, and transformation of leadership identity.

Catherine Rosa was a school leader in P–12 education for 19 years working in high-poverty schools with language learners providing bilingual immersion with a focus on arts integration. She holds an EdD in Educational Leadership from the University of Georgia, an MBA from Brenau University, and a BA in Art with minors in Psychology and English from Mercer University. She has worked in higher education since 2002 teaching Educational Leadership, Curriculum and Instruction, and Arts Integration.

Wesam M. Salem is an assistant professor of elementary education at the University of Memphis. Her research focuses on social justice and equity practices in education particularly pertaining to Muslim American students at the intersectionality of identity, culture, religion, and learning. Also, her work focuses on mathematics teacher educator's practices in methods courses that promote implementation of high-leverage practices (e.g., Number Talks, Notice and Wonder) and lesson plans that promote conceptual understanding. Her work has been published in journals such as Peabody Journal of Education, Reconceptualizing Educational Research Methodology, and Multicultural Perspectives.

Jennifer Snow serves as professor in curriculum, instruction, and foundational studies at Boise State University. Recent scholarship has focused on the development of teacher educators and innovative clinical field experience structures for liaisons (university faculty supporting school partnerships and teacher candidates). She serves on the editorial board for the *Journal of Teacher Education*.

Heather Williams serves as chair and associate professor in curriculum, instruction, and foundational studies, she also serves as program coordinator for executive educational leadership at Boise State University. Recent scholarship has focused on the development of systems leaders and policy implementation to improve complex systems, especially in rural communities. She serves on the editorial board for *Perspectives: The Journal of Educational Administration Leadership*.

James A. Zoll is an associate professor of educational leadership at the University of North Georgia, College of Education. He received his PhD in Educational Leadership from Mercer University. He came to UNG with years of successful experience as a K–12 teacher and principal. His passion and research surround preparing educational leaders for the exciting work of school leadership, with a focus on embedding the principles of inclusive leadership across coursework and within EPP programs.